'A glorious celebration of Jane Austen, and a glorious celebration of friendship too. You'll want one copy for yourself and another for your own BFF'.

Lucy Worsley, historian, television presenter and author of
Jane Austen at Home

'At last – a delightful book about the often overlooked relationship between Jane Austen and her live-in best friend, Martha Lloyd. Zöe Wheddon cleverly knits fact, fragments from letters and diaries and family lore to paint a fun-loving pair who, with the other Austen ladies, combined their resources to promote each other's comfort, creative endeavours and well-being. If you wish to know and experience Austen in a whole new way – through the eyes of an intimate friend – then read this book'.

Rose Servitova, author of *The Longbourn Letters* and *The Watsons*

'We'd all love to be Jane Austen's best friend. Zöe Wheddon's brilliant new book shows with authority and insight how the position was firmly taken. Martha Lloyd truly comes to life in this excellent biography of Jane Austen's best friend'.

Prof. Paula Byrne, author of *The Real Jane Austen: A Life in Small Things*

'Wheddon's debut provides a fascinating glimpse into a rarely-explored but key relationship in Jane Austen's life, that of her lifelong friendship with Martha Lloyd. The author brings almost forensic energy to examining the small but pivotal moments, mutual humour and sensibility, and essential candour that define friendship as a whole, and that were critical to the happiness and satisfaction of Austen in particular. Heartfelt, thought-provoking and wise, *Jane Austen's Best Friend: The Life and Influence of Martha Lloyd* is a powerful testament to female friendship, its effect on genius, and the confidance and confidence it can inspire. We might not know of Martha Lloyd today without Jane Austen, but Wheddon makes a very strong case that we wouldn't have the literary genius we know and love without Martha Lloyd'.

Natalie Jenner, international bestselling author of
The Jane Austen Society

For Matt, my best friend and my very own 'Mr. W.'

Jane Austen's Best Friend

The Life and Influence of Martha Lloyd

Zöe Wheddon

PEN & SWORD
HISTORY

First published in Great Britain in 2021 by
Pen & Sword History
An imprint of
Pen & Sword Books Ltd
Yorkshire – Philadelphia

ISBN 978 1 52676 381 5

Typeset by Mac Style
Printed and bound in the UK by TJ Books Ltd,
Padstow, Cornwall.

Pen & Sword Books Limited incorporates the imprints of Atlas,
Archaeology, Aviation, Discovery, Family History, Fiction, History,
Maritime, Military, Military Classics, Politics, Select, Transport,
True Crime, Air World, Frontline Publishing, Leo Cooper,
Remember When, Seaforth Publishing, The Praetorian Press,
Wharncliffe
Local History, Wharncliffe Transport, Wharncliffe True Crime
and White Owl.

For a complete list of Pen & Sword titles please contact

PEN & SWORD BOOKS LIMITED
47 Church Street, Barnsley, South Yorkshire, S70 2AS, England
E-mail: enquiries@pen-and-sword.co.uk
Website: www.pen-and-sword.co.uk

Or

PEN AND SWORD BOOKS
1950 Lawrence Rd, Havertown, PA 19083, USA
E-mail: Uspen-and-sword@casematepublishers.com
Website: www.penandswordbooks.com

Contents

Foreword

As a child growing up at Chawton House (once owned by Jane's rich older brother and my fourth great-grandfather, Edward Austen Knight), I was always fascinated by the visitors who came to see Jane's cottage and my family's ancestral home. With so few clues surviving, a certain mystery surrounds Jane Austen's personality, her views, the loves of her life and the choices she made. One thing is for sure, Austen devotees are forever keen to know more, to be closer to Jane, and who better to look to for clues than Martha Lloyd?

Other than Cassandra, no one knew Jane Austen as well as Martha Lloyd. She was a companion to Jane, a confidante and a supporter. Martha knew Jane's secrets, including perhaps her greatest secret of all – her writing.

The close friendship that started in childhood continued for the rest of their lives and Jane thought of Martha as a second sister. 'With what true sympathy our feelings are shared by Martha, you need not be told; – she is the friend & Sister under every circumstance,' Jane wrote to Cassandra in October 1808, the year before the ladies moved to Chawton.

Jane was an unpublished author when she arrived in Chawton. Two years later *Sense & Sensibility* was published and I can only imagine how the ladies would have rejoiced together.

Today, Martha Lloyd is perhaps best known for her cookbook, her handwritten record of the recipes cooked at Chawton Cottage (Martha's cheesecakes have always been a favourite of mine), but her contribution to Jane's life and works cannot be ignored. By getting to know Martha and the intimate friendship she shared with Jane, we get a step closer to understanding Jane Austen.

This beautifully written book gives us all a fresh insight into the friendship shared by Martha and Jane and a delightful glimpse into the inner world of Miss Jane Austen.

Caroline Jane Knight
Jane Austen's fifth great-niece
Founder & Chair, Jane Austen Literacy Foundation

Acknowledgements

I am so grateful to so many people without whom I would never have been able to pursue the dream of finally answering all those questions in my mind about Martha and publishing this book.

Firstly, I want to thank Catherine Curzon for contacting me on a mission to 'pay it forward'; her belief and encouragement are the reason you are holding this book in your hands today.

I am so grateful to Jon, Aileen and Michelle, and all the team at Pen and Sword, who offered me this opportunity and were always on hand to answer my many questions and with whom I could check in, confident in the knowledge that their support was always there. I owe Aileen cake. I have not forgotten.

All the people at Jane Austen's House, past and present: Mary Guyat for her support, Janet for a lovely cup of tea and chat at Chawton about Martha, and especially to Sophie Reynolds, who has supported me in the most friendly way.

Thank you to Jane Austen's relations who continue to show all her best qualities. I am so grateful for their confidence in me and their support for my project. Rebecca Smith, a relative on Sir Francis Austen's side, is such an inspiring writer and her kind words encouraged me onward. Caroline Knight, related to Jane via her brother Edward, is someone I greatly admire, and I feel so honoured to have her write the foreword for this book.

Thank you to the team of church wardens and volunteers who made me so welcome on a sunny spring day at Wymering church.

Thank you to David Rymill and the team at Hampshire Archives for all the work that they do and the kind interest they took in this project.

My special thanks to Karrie Brown for her beautiful illustration; she has truly captured the essence of Jane and Martha's friendship.

Thank you to all the individuals who helped with permissions to use photographs and for all the interesting conversations that we had along the way.

Thank you to the world of Janeites on Twitter and Instagram for their encouraging enthusiasm.

Thank you to my colleagues who asked me about what I was doing and didn't wane in their interest despite me talking about it – a lot.

Thank you, too, to the most important ones in my life: to my loving husband, Matt, who supported me unfailingly and with much love; my creative and encouraging Mum, Elizabeth; and my amazing grown-up kids, Josh, Becca and Tom, who gave me the benefit of their academic and technological expertise, held my hand and messaged me with words of kindness when my self-belief wavered.

I wanted to tell Martha's story so much and all these people and more helped me over the finishing line. I will be eternally grateful.

Introduction

It is *also* a truth universally acknowledged that a woman in possession of a great talent must be in want of a brilliant best friend and Jane Austen was no exception. She may even have appreciated that friend more than we will ever know. That is to say she enjoyed the delights of having someone in her life who would become one of her closest and dearest, nay even beloved people, but was not bound to her by the calls of family duty or a father's will. By Jane's own definition, Martha Lloyd was that friend, 'the friend and sister under every circumstance.'[1]

Much is known, guessed at and imagined in relation to her strongest and most precious female bond, that with her older sister Cassandra. When Jane was born, her own father, delighted in his new daughter, instantly connected her with the notion of friendship when he declared her 'a plaything for Cassy and a future companion.'[2] We know that Jane also had other female friends of whom she was sincerely and deeply fond, such as Madam Anne Lefroy, who lived in the rectory at the nearby village of Ashe. She was a most cultured and revered person of high-standing in the local community, who herself introduced the smallpox vaccine to local children and who loved to encourage the intelligence and interests of the young Jane. When Madam Lefroy was killed by a fall from her horse on Jane's birthday in 1804, Jane still recalled this precious woman four years later in a poignant poem that demonstrated just how deeply her loss was felt.

Anne Sharp, one-time governess to her brother Edward's children, was also someone that Jane just clicked with, perhaps partly as they sought refuge together from the oppressive atmosphere that found them both at the lower end of the pecking order at the Godmersham estate, but also due to their shared love of theatre and literature.

The Bigg sisters, who lived at the nearby Manydown Estate, remained consistently within Jane's friendship circle despite marriage and miles getting in their way in later years. Her cousin Eliza de Feuillide was perhaps her most exotic 'plaything', an inspirational free spirit to whom Jane felt a true connection that was mutually expressed and enjoyed long before Eliza married her brother Henry. It is true also, to a certain extent, that Martha's own sister Mary was, in her own way, a friend of Jane's.

Friendship has many levels and is defined in many different ways by the individuals involved. So, what makes a friend a best friend? What is it that venerates a person into a category all of their own? It's a bold claim to make, calling someone out as your own best friend, let alone to make that attachment in the name of a world-famous and much-beloved authoress. To be clear that I was seeking the correct evidence and uncovering a friendship that was truly special and unique, I made sure that I took advice on how to qualify the meaning of best friend. I posed this question to a modern audience and found in the responses a happy continuation of a tradition of age-old terms used to explain the mysteries of the closest of friendships. The values that surfaced were as clear as a bell and had by no means been lost in translation through the mists of time. The answers that came back were as relevant in Jane and Martha's day as they are today. Matters of the heart are as timeless as they are human.

To be classified as a best friend, one must be a kaleidoscope-like constellation of a set of fundamentals, of foundational pillars arranged in as unique a pattern as a fingerprint, particular and peculiar to the two individuals involved yet universal enough to be recognised as constants, as patterns, as key elements, that if missing or watered down would downgrade a relationship from best friend to just friend or maybe even that dreaded word, acquaintance.

First and foremost, for many people it is non-negotiable that a best friend be dependable, reliable, always there when you need them and someone you can count on to never let you down (well, almost never). This sentiment comes closely coupled with a sense of loyalty to one another; a best friend will stand by you and have your back. Then, of course, into this recipe we must add someone who is kind and caring, who gives you the best hugs and the strongest love, who shows you empathy and just 'gets' you. They make you feel safe and comforted, they give proofs of love. A common denominator in the most special of friendships is also the huge dollop of fun found therein. There is a shared sense of humour, and best friends can have the stupidest of conversations and will burst into laughter at the strangest of things. They may be found laughing until their sides ache and their eyes water, and yet onlookers might well be standing by in bewildered silence.

A best friendship can also mix the light with the shade; it's not all silliness and giggling, although there is a lot of that. A best friend is marked by their honesty and at the same time, their utter acceptance of you with no judgement. In this type of friendship both parties anchor one another. They can give honest feedback, tell the bare truth, the whole truth and nothing but the truth and as one anonymous respondent put it, 'let you know when you are a hot mess.' But they do it in love, and you know that they have your best interests at heart. You can disagree and still work things back to that special place, you can be an idiot and they will still be as easy-going as they always have been, in the end. A best friend is like a cave of wonders because you can wander in and share your secrets and know that they can know everything and yet will still honour their word and be trustworthy. You can definitely take shelter from the storm in that cave.

Best of all about female BFFs is they are soul sisters. They are someone that you click with and connect with on a different level to everyone else. When there is an experience to be shared, you think to tell them first and in return, you come to mind first for them also. There is basically no situation that you could ever ask for or imagine that would not be better with them there. You miss them when you are away yet as soon as you are back together, even if a significant amount of time has passed, it is as if you have never been apart. Finally, it is not the words that they say, the gifts they give you, the things they do for you or even their hugs, but there is a special quality to the way a best friend makes you feel. They leave you feeling better than before they walked in, and they make you feel valued and respected and plain old good about yourself. They lift you up when you are troubled and consider your wellbeing as much as their own. They encourage and inspire you to be the best version of yourself that you can be. They seem to instinctively know how to treat you, the way you want to be treated, perhaps even better than you treat yourself.

Martha Lloyd occupied a sure and steady place centre stage in Jane Austen's heart from a young age, and Jane held on tightly to her friendship throughout her journey towards a literary career and beyond, even to the very end of her life. Although heartbreakingly they would become sisters, in the legal sense, only posthumously, Jane often referred to Martha in the most familial of terms and felt as though she had been blessed with a treasure, another who occupied the same precious place in her heart and mind as her blood family.

In this book I shall seek to shape and outline the special nature of the friendship between Jane and Martha, to examine the intersections and crossovers of their day-to-day encounters with everyday life that prove that Martha's status as Jane's BFF can be borne out time and time again. In other words, we shall be able to view Martha and Jane just like one of the '3 or 4 families in a country village' that Jane so loved to observe and dally with in her own written works.[3] Often when we talk about best friendships, we quite rightly idealise them, but it is also important here to look at the mechanics of how Jane and Martha wove themselves together and expressed their friendship. We will examine their actions towards each other and one another's interpretations of them. We will go behind the scenes of their mysterious bond and in so doing discover their heart-warming recipe for friendship. We will be totally assured that Martha Lloyd was more, so much more than just the housekeeper or nursing companion to Jane's mother as she is so often depicted.

Through an examination of Jane and Martha's personal histories; Jane's letters to Martha, her sister Cassandra and others, as well as references to family documents and memorabilia, I hope to demonstrate in the most interesting and compelling of ways the factors that defined this special relationship. I want to examine the characteristics and distinguishing features of their friendship – the 'telepathy, honesty, humour, empathy, generosity, encouragement, steadfastness and trust' that Martha and Jane Austen shared.[4] These are the qualities upon which the status of best friend is founded and the evidence upon which this special relationship can be conferred and confirmed. It will be as if we are sat with them now huddled around the fire, with a warm drink each and a good book on our knee – chatting about life, the universe and everything, as viewed through the lens of a very special and unique pairing.

Who amongst us has not once wished that they had been a companion to Jane Austen? Is there a Janeite in the world today who does not count themselves Jane's friend in their own imaginations, who wishes time and time again to have the miraculous joy of being entertained and shocked in equal measure by the sprack wit of the famously enigmatic and private authoress? Who is not wistfully wishing and longing to bear witness to her generous nature and literary talent first-hand? This is an examination of the life and times of Jane Austen through 'some aspect… that traditions do not emphasise' – through a unique key and close relationship thus far neglected and unfathomed.[5] This is not the biography of a marriage or a romantic connection, but it is something arguably just as special, maybe for many of her readers even more personal – it is the account of a best friendship.

Through tracing the tale of Martha and Jane, we will get to see the human side of our heroine author and really feel like we can get to know her better. In looking back somewhat longingly at Martha and Jane's friendship we can examine all their shared interests, including the hits and misses of their romantic love lives, their passion for shopping and fashion, their connection to their community and the female biography of the period, their family histories, their lucky breaks, their epic fails and their girly chats. In this way, it is my aim for us to 'recover a personal Jane Austen', to allow us the opportunity to spend time in a 'plausible emotional and psychological hinterland', to create something like our own time-travelling coffee shop, wherein Jane Austen is revealed to us in a different context, in a different light, through the prism of the magical link of friendship.[6] By studying her via her life-long friend of nearly thirty years, we can get to know her through a different narrative and interpret the facts that we do have in a new and pleasingly revealing way.

Through spending time with her best friend, we will gain an insight into the life-changing force of their friendship and we too will feel closer to her inner circle, a place that the enigmatic and private authoress Jane herself, and latterly her family, sought to protect and contain away from the interested and the prying. Through this exploration of a portrait of a friendship, we can open up a portal into the world of Jane Austen and enter in via a different path. We can sneak a peek at a side of Jane that was previously prohibited to us and protected from view. Through an examination of the type of woman that Martha was and the nature of her friendship with Jane Austen, we can learn more about the type of person Jane was. Through turning back the clock to her youth, we can subtly reveal less of the older maiden aunt and her submissive middle-aged reputation, and more of the refreshingly spirited woman that Jane undoubtedly was.

In highlighting the life and link of an important woman in Jane Austen's life, we are revealing what Kathryn Sutherland called 'the hidden lives'.[7] In re-looking at the evidence of Martha and Jane's friendship we can reveal the importance to her of the female society that she kept. I believe that as the most important female friend in Jane's life, the family that Jane chose for herself – Martha Lloyd is the perfect unbiased and unfettered, untainted and untethered test for our hypothesis about Jane, the friend. Set apart from but also importantly embedded within the family context, there is no other person better placed for us to stand next to in order to help us get up close and personal with Jane. In scientific terms Martha Lloyd is our perfect experimental model for finding a new way to get to know Jane, for unearthing and perhaps even excavating a different version to any other we have known before. This is an opportunity not to be missed.

Through this, our Martha Project, we will mark the defining moments of their shared lives together and capture an image of Jane Austen's friend. Indeed, there once was a time when we thought we had a true likeness of Martha, where she was sat in full bonnet with a sweet little dog upon her lap and wearing what looked remarkably like a topaz cross. But alas, the specific techniques used to produce this daguerreotype photograph were developed long after Martha's death. So, the insight of which we speak will be a picture painted with words, not just mine but Jane's, her family's and Martha's family's too. Little by little we will piece together what it would have been like to hang out with Jane Austen and to sit back and relax in her company. We will find out what qualities she possessed as a friend and which she sought out in a life beyond her family. In so doing, it is my hope that this will help us to look behind Jane's eyes the way old friends do, to see a little deeper into her heart and mind, and perhaps even into the very nature of Jane Austen herself.

As we go on this journey together, we may find ourselves rekindling our own friendship with Jane, as we learn to identify with her in new ways and re-read her works in the context of our newly acquired knowledge and our wider understanding of her strongest social bonds and friendships. We may learn more about her values and what mattered to her and we may learn to cherish her individuality and uniqueness as only a friend can. My hope is that through applying our own understanding and experiences of friendship to what we discover about Martha and her relationship with her friend, we will enjoy a 'persuasive and more satisfying interpretation of the puzzle which is Jane Austen' and feel her to be more real to us than ever before.[8] What an honour, delight and thrill the prospect of that is. Other than discovering further letters and memorabilia, we can only hope to sort once again through the currently available treasures, to reflect once more upon the sources that we have and hope that we can wash away a little more silt and gain a better glimpse of, and a little more insight into, the woman who entrances us still. For Jane Austen fans around the world, it is so emotionally fulfilling to visit places that Jane Austen frequented and to walk where she walked; it is better still to have her take us by the hand on a stroll across the Hampshire fields with her and her best friend, and for us to share an afternoon with kindred spirits. That, I hope, is what this book offers.

Chapter One

In the Beginning

Martha Lloyd was born in November 1765 in Bishopstone, Wiltshire, a county in the south-west of England. Her father, the Reverend Nowes or Noyes Lloyd, presumed of Welsh origin, was also the son of a vicar, the Reverend John Lloyd of Epping in Essex, although their extended family had been rooted in Norfolk for many generations. Martha's mother was the aristocratically connected yet emotionally scarred Martha Craven. Proud of their Welsh heritage, it was she who tried to change everyone's pronunciation of Lloyd to Floyd, believing that this was the true Welsh way.

Martha had a little brother, Charles, born in 1769 in between her two sisters, Eliza, born in 1768 and Mary, born in 1771, the year that their father would become rector at Enborne, Berkshire. Just like her rather famous namesake from the biblical family of Lazarus, Martha – whose name means 'mistress' – was to become a very capable leader of her household; she would often be the one running the kitchen and overseeing the hospitality. It would not be in her nature, however, to complain or nag for others to help; no, far from being a martyr to her duties, Martha knew how to have fun too. Another translation of the meaning of her name, 'Lady' – was a somewhat prophetic nomenclature that we shall return to later. Mary, whose name alternately meant 'wished for child' (which might leave the child in question feeling quite spoilt, presumptuous and a little entitled), and 'bitterness', which would also be viewed by some, perhaps even Jane in particular, as having totally lived up to her name.

Martha's family knew the strong bonds of a tight family circle. The move from Wiltshire to Enborne brought them into close proximity with Martha's cousins as her mother's sister Jane had married Thomas Fowle – also a Reverend, based in nearby Kintbury.

Martha, Elizabeth, Charles and Mary began to grow up in the bosom of their extended family, spending all their time together with their four male cousins. Yet just as in Jane's childhood, where her own brother George suffered from developmental difficulties which led him to be cared for outside of their home, a tragedy was to strike at Martha's siblings too.

In 1775, just four short years after their move, smallpox broke out in the vicinity of their neighbourhood and the surrounding area of Newbury. Martha's family were all struck down with the disease. Unfortunately, it was the confluent sort, a severe and rare strain, with much worse symptoms than more common forms of the condition. In the Lloyd family's case, the lesions or pustules ran into one another, forming large pus-filled abscesses that pulled the skin really tight and filled every available space with horrifying sores. It is believed that the smallpox was 'brought into the house by the coachman, who concealed the fact that it was in his own cottage.'[1] Elizabeth escaped lightly and recovered fully; sadly though, Martha and Mary had it very badly and were left with the blight of permanent scarring, 'the marks of its virulence' remaining on their faces.[2] Worse still, in a devastating blow, on 11 April 1775 their young 7-year-old brother Charles Lloyd died of the epidemic. The memory of him as a gentle and mild child lived on within the heartbroken family. The children, for some unknown reason, had never been inoculated.

Martha, Eliza and Mary had no formal schooling and about 'the average allowance bestowed at that time.'[3] Their mother taught them to read and write, and their learning would have related to the natural rhythms of the parsonage and the church calendar. Just like the Austen family, there would have been a tradition of reading a daily portion of Psalms and lessons. The young Lloyd girls were given needlework, lacework and knitting work daily, with a little history, writing and arithmetic from a local master at home thrown in. There was no foreign language or music tuition but according to family memory, the sisters did sing well. However, with a nod to the influence of their mother and perhaps hers, they were brought up in keeping with the highest of social expectations of behaviour. Mrs Lloyd thought it important to have gracious deportment and to be good at dancing. The sisters were given dancing lessons once a week for a while in Newbury. Unusually for parsonage daughters, they were also considered good horsewomen, as they had access to the horses of their well-connected family in the neighbourhood and rode them regularly.

However, this on the whole happy lifestyle was due to come to an end in dramatic fashion. Over a period of months, the Reverend Mr Lloyd had gained the reputation in the family as a 'nervous hypochondriac'.[4] Feeling increasingly unwell he had retreated to his own room, with only enough energy and reserves to be entertained by games of cards with his daughters. This, indeed, was a sad decline in a truly religious and respected man, known for writing exceptional sermons that others were only too happy to preach from themselves.[5] When his end came on 28 January 1789, the hope of his reputation was all that he could offer the young Lloyd women as an inheritance.

An interesting twist of family and fate followed, that just goes to prove that we can never tell when something is truly bad news for us or actually a positive part of our path in good disguise. In this very same year Eliza married their cousin Fulwar-Craven Fowle. He and his brother Tom had studied as pupils under Reverend George Austen at his boarding school at the Austen family's Steventon Home, and so James Austen was present at their wedding. It is even believed that on visits to the Fowles's home, the Austen family – particularly James and Henry but possibly the girls too – would have met and mixed, as the Lloyds were practically permanent fixtures at their nearby cousins' home. So, it was that links between the two families, families with so much in common already, began to grow and a ripple of relationship pulsed out amongst the younger generation.

With all the merriment of the theatricals in the barn at Steventon around this time, there is conjecture that Martha and Mary may have been part of the group who marvelled in the audience at the Austen family's creativity and intellect, and at their sheer exuberance and taste for the dramatic and comic culture. Some believe that Mary may have begun to become beguiled and entranced by James, even if he only had eyes at that time for his exotic French cousin, Eliza de

Feuillide. If the Fowleses were invited along, as they had long been considered part of the family, then it is no leap of faith to envisage the Lloyd women in attendance too. Certainly the Austen family trace the origins of these friendships way back into the 1780s. Martha, with her love of music and dance coupled with her famous good humour, would have been quickly educated in the artistic mother tongue of the Austen family, and witnessed their liberal and open appreciation of all manner of satire, drama and comedy.

When Reverend Lloyd died and the three Lloyd women found themselves duly homeless and in need, it is therefore not so very unexpected nor so much of a surprise for us to learn that the Reverend George Austen, known for his practical and generous nature, suggested that they rent the newly-available Deane Parsonage from him. He, who was so quick to notice and praise the provision of Jane as good company for her sister Cassandra, could not have known that with this offer he was creating a way for another happy friendship to flourish.

Martha was a full ten years older than Jane Austen and as such, perhaps it was more expected by Mrs Austen that Mary, aged 18 and described variously as sensible, good-humoured, unaffected and pleasant, would become more of a friend and mentor for 13-year-old Jane than 23-year-old Martha. Indeed, Mary would continue to become a firm favourite, not only of Mrs Austen but also within the local Hampshire circle of the great and the good. Yet it was Martha with whom Jane immediately formed a bond, for 'firm friends' they very quickly and surely became.[6]

This was not the first time that Jane had shown a preference for having a friend of a more mature age, as her significant friend, Madam Lefroy, was twenty-six years older than Jane. Locally infamous as a passionate and intelligent society hostess, wife of the rector of Ashe, she often welcomed Jane into her home. She was a nurturing and sensitive woman with a strong heart for pastoral care. In reading her letters to her family, even considering that she was caring for a sick husband and sometimes fighting illness herself when writing them, it is clear that she sensed in her purpose a natural empathy as a protector of the young. The day-to-day business of her own children's lives was high on her radar; even as what we would call 'an empty nester', she was acutely aware of their every possible need, strongly identifying herself with, and basing her own happiness upon, her role as a mother. She had a longing for family life to be returned to normal whenever her sons were away and it is easy to imagine the intellectual and kindly fuss she may have made of Jane, and the interesting and stimulating conversations that they may have had, that she too may have been hungry for. A possible home from home for Jane, the Ashe rectory's mistress had a 'personality anchored in religion and her family' just like Martha did.[7]

At Deane parsonage, spring had sprung for Martha. Living with her mother and sister Mary they now shared the latterly much-maligned, yet not it has to be said, unimproved dwelling of downstairs drawing room and dining parlours, four bedrooms, ample sturdy storerooms, servants' chambers, a coach house with stabling, and best of all perhaps, a large meadow for a garden.[8] Family folklore later recorded moans and groans about the place as members recalled the Lloyds' home as a 'low damp place with inconvenient rooms and scarcely two on the same level,' but from this humble house, seeds were sown that would grow into an affinity between Martha and her beloved Jane Austen.[9] A rich and lifelong tapestry of kinship had started to weave itself together.

Martha, it seemed, had a head start on a pattern of life so familiar to Jane Austen; she was cut from the same cloth, which gave them a blueprint for their friendship of an almost made-to-measure design. With Martha single and now living only a mile and a half away at Deane, a firm friendship sprung up between the families, encouraged and spurred on by a positive response from Mrs Austen, who by all accounts wholeheartedly gave her full approval of the family. This gave Jane all the permission and encouragement she could wish for in order to foster friendship with Martha – in the very house where three of her siblings were born. Time, too, had intervened on Jane's behalf as the Austen house was now less in use as a school and no boarders remained; Jane and Cassandra had all their own formal teaching and learning behind them and were both firmly back at home. Excitingly, a second room had been made available to the

Austen daughters – a sort of dressing room space with a pianoforte in place and a door they could close on the world. The stage had been cleared. A new chapter had begun in all their lives.

It was in this privacy that their new friendship was practised and vice versa, in time away from chores and obligations – time when Jane's friend could come over and listen to all her latest secret thoughts and wild musings. Martha's friendship intertwined with Jane at a particular moment in time, in an era of great shaping of her personal and emotional life and at a stage when she was searching for, and beginning to assert, her own identity. From the very beginning, Martha was a key part of the nurturing of Jane's talents and ambitions. Martha began to enable her friend to explore and to experiment. Like any good friend, she created an atmosphere of safety that became an atmosphere of growth for Jane's courage in regard to trialling and trying out her writing ideas.

'When we search into their personal lives…we glean nothing but a little chopped dull chaff of details in which all trace of the sacred germ is lacking,' wrote Reginald Farrer. But on the contrary, I believe that in the huddle of this friendship bubble we can see the confidence and vulnerability of a writer beginning to emerge, and in Martha's fanning of the flame we can glimpse more truly the flame itself; the 'suggestion of the genuine Jane Austen' which Farrer seeks.[10] Without key people to encourage her, Jane may never have forged on with her work at this time. Her family were most certainly the closest to her, but for a young person emerging from childhood and aiming to stamp her own personality on the world about her, so too was her trusted companion. The very act of these kernels of genius being shared with someone not part of the family, as they were 'read aloud for the benefit of her chosen circle in the younger generation,' signals the intimacy of that friendship and the importance of it to Jane at that time in her life, as her fledgling ideas were just beginning to take flight.[11] This friendship is breathtaking in its intimacy and truly valuable to us, worthy of further investigation and sombre consideration. Some assert that the family were extremely introverted in the sense that they had all they needed in one another and did not have wide circles of friends outside of each other, nor were they 'in urgent need of friends beyond their doors'.[12] Jane's inclusion of Martha to such a degree is therefore all the more poignant and worthy of our gaze; it evokes more than a little envy in us and bears further scrutiny. Through looking into the friendship of Martha and Jane we see something of Jane Austen herself, perhaps even more clearly than ever before.

It may have been that Martha's temperament, coupled with her being older than Jane, helped cement their friendship at this time. Jane, aged 12, had been described by various relations and family acquaintances who knew her as being 'set apart', 'prim, whimsical and affected', 'an odd fish', a little more difficult to get on with than Cassandra.[13] She may have found it easier to relate to someone a little older than herself, rather than someone the same age whom she tended to find too fanciful and full of triviality. Jane, by all accounts, was actually very shy at this age. She was also, since her early childhood, totally devoted to and bound together intimately with her sister Cassandra, even to the point of becoming anxious on separation. So much so that she had wandered out for many a mile as a tiny tot to meet her sister coming home in the carriage and later had followed her to school, moving away from her home and separating herself from her mother, years in advance of her needing to go herself.

Jane was not one for making friends in childhood outside of the rectory gate. She was considered 'mute and uncertain with her peers, a timid observer' and some even believe that her shyness at times 'divided her from James and Henry.'[14] Years later, when looking after a child of a friend, Jane was shocked by the remarkable confidence, easy way of speaking, and the special ability to converse and socialise that the said child possessed. It caused her to ponder and reflect upon how totally different she was at that age and to acknowledge how her own shyness had hampered her ability to communicate. 'What is become of all the Shyness in the World?' 'She is a nice, natural, openhearted, affectionate girl, with all the ready civility... so unlike anything that I was myself at her age, that I am often all astonishment and shame.'[15]

It was in this context and at this moment in time that Martha moved into her life. The fact that Jane coupled herself closely with her speaks volumes of Martha's temperament and also the power of their mutual friendship. Martha was a strange mix of being both amusing and highly sensible, experienced yet not educated into a forced air of formality. Martha was rooted in her Christian faith and religious observance; she was in Jane's eyes so 'secure in herself' yet 'so quick to appreciate a mood or take part in foolery.'[16] Biographers agree, Martha must have been a true boon to Jane. They believe in addition to her dependency, her shyness and anxiety at the prospect of being separated from Cassandra, that Jane was a girl 'too full of Oxford and fancy French ideas', the influence of the Austen family upon her rendering her too unusual when set in the context of the rural Hampshire life of her counterparts.[17] Either way, this period represents the foundation stone in the friendship between Jane and Martha, and paved the way for future mutual support, trust and jolly good fun. Martha had become a vital tool in enabling Jane to both set and keep her creative spirit free.

Chapter Two

Early Writings

It was at this time that Jane was embarking on her earliest experiences of life as an author. Her *Juvenilia*, 'Early writings or works written in one's youth,' 'not simply immature or apprentice writings' were being crafted, honed and tried out upon her nearest and dearest.[1] This circle is known now as having been notoriously, even famously, tight. Biographer Park Honan believes that in being shut away upstairs in their recently acquired little room, Jane was able to flex her literary muscles, sense of humour and burlesque fun. It was here that 'She could laugh at anything she liked or say outrageous things aloud,' and that 'she gained confidence to do so in privacy.'[2]

Martha was one of the very few individuals and perhaps the only non-family member invited up into that space. If it was here that the most lewd and bawdy ideas could be read aloud, tried out and tested, then Martha was part of that sacred yet impudent audience; she was the trusted ear. Their shared sense of humour and inclination to giggle meant that Jane's ability to set Martha off into fits of laughter with her words quickly closed the age gap and any other besides.

These early entries in the literary career of Jane Austen are widely regarded in their own right as more than just childish scribblings and ways of dawdling away time. They are increasingly considered by scholars as important 'literary and historical documents' – 'records of a youthful writer's response to her times' and Martha was there to witness them, a huge part of the 'teenage' Jane's life at the time of this early developmental stage of the young authoress.[3] She was part of the small group who listened to and enjoyed the 'effusions of fancy' as Jane's father famously called them, and was present as Jane ironed out the wrinkles in her words and tried on various ideas and styles for size.[4] Martha was a key element of providing Jane with what became nostalgically known within the family as 'a sufficiently settled and sympathetic' environment in which to evolve.[5] As one of Jane Austen's closest and most frequent companions in this period, she had an influence on creating the atmosphere so conducive to experimentation and practice in which a very young Jane thrived.

The fact that these works are now praised for showing Jane Austen's 'consistency and continuity' in her writing proves just how vital and influential that ambience was on Jane's creative mind.[6] It is said that the juvenile stories 'seem predictive of the author's brilliance.'[7] It could be argued that this 'highly conscious experiment' by Jane Austen would not have been carried out to the same degree or in the same free-spirited way if she had not had Martha within the ranks of her audience, amongst the small group of her treasured and invested, encouraging and eager entourage.[8] Martha and Jane found the same things funny and enjoyed having fun together; they were able to be broad-minded, suspend reality and just be plain old silly together. The burlesque jokes and sheer 'naughtiness' had them rolling about with laughter on the floor of that upstairs room. The 'keen sense of fun' reflected in the stories found a ready and willing listener in Martha and alongside Jane's family, she helped provide the perfect conditions to encourage Jane's creative urges.[9]

Brian Southam believes that this motivation for pleasing her own special treasured audience stayed with Jane as she continued to write her novels in the future. He maintains that her chief concern was to 'entertain her closest audience, whose encouragement was the *spur of her wit* and whose presence was felt.'[10] The family later described the *Juvenilia* as reflecting life at home during this time and the ambience of 'conversation rich in shrewd remarks, bright with playfulness and humour.'[11] Jane grew up in the Steventon rectory with banter and her mother's famous 'sprack wit' at the table, filling every day, yet one can imagine that it was altogether easier for Jane to let rip with the original drafts and ideas and play around with these to her heart's fullest content with her friend and her sister first. Here she could learn how 'to engage with readers' by 'slipping private jokes into her stories' without fear of humiliation, correction or serious censorship.[12] What young person doesn't love to secretly poke fun at the adults around them, with the emphasis being on the secrecy of it all. The sense of playfulness conjured between the two young friends set just the right tone for Jane's imagination to run riot and created a safe place for mucking about with words out of earshot of potentially disapproving adults.

It is this playing with the reader, this 'awareness' of her audience and the power of her narrative voice as an author to be in constant contact, counting upon their collusion in her meaning, that are pointed to as part of the DNA even of Jane's later novels. Many draw links between the early written stories with their exaggerated plots and unruly truth-telling characters and what Jane went on to produce decades later, claiming that it was through what Jane Austen was grappling with at this young age (the ideas that she was trying out, as it happens, on Cassandra and Martha in that cloistered room), that she 'learned to write her mature, self-aware, ironic fictions.'[13] Martha's influence in those early days was to have a far-reaching impact in helping Jane to find, tap into and later develop her own writing style.

This is all the more remarkable because Martha was not a friend who had received the same sort of formal schooling as Jane, nor indeed had she read so widely, deeply or so voraciously. She is often defined as someone of less literary and scholarly worth to the young authoress. Jane did possess in her, however, a friend whose extra ten years of age had afforded her valuable life experience with which many of the quite adult jokes, the irony and the satire would have chimed. Martha could not be so easily shocked, nor was she as emotionally immature as someone Jane's own age might have been, and their mutual humour made for a winning combination. G.K Chesterton asserted that Jane Austen's *Juvenilia* were totally motivated by 'the gigantic inspiration of laughter' and there can be no doubt from Jane's letters as to how much she valued and shared Martha's love of laughing and their own particular brand of teasing.[14] Jane adored it that she could induce Martha to succumb to the giddiness of silliness. As a point of fact 'Jane Austen's childhood oeuvre has been asserted as definitely 'not child-like' and a more mature friend would have been just the right sort of person to appreciate the wider themes being explored.[15]

Having Martha as part of her everyday inner circle, with their shared love of mirth and making each other laugh, may well have fuelled Jane Austen on in the *Juvenilia* towards the 'directions in which their author was later not permitted to go.'[16] The themes of the works such as the blatant breaking of social rules and norms, the use of language and behaviour considered totally unbecoming of ladies or people of a particular social standing in the eighteenth century, a new reality where moral comeuppance and rules did not exist, would have had Martha in hoots. They spent so much time together and Jane would read passages out aloud with Martha always an interested and willing listener. She got so good about it that in years to come, Jane joked about not leaving Martha alone with a manuscript for fear she would write it herself from memory. Martha was privy to private readings of this ruthless and no-holds-barred comedy at the earliest stages of its creation and formed part of the audience of Jane Austen's consciousness. Martha was one of a very small circle who heard and was present at the inception of the unfiltered versions of Jane Austen's writing, her writing in its purest of forms, saying exactly what she wanted to say, about whom she wanted to say it and using the exact language that she wanted to use.

When you read Jane's surviving letters you can feel the same irreverent and hilariously cutting tone coming through the page. The mockery is sharp but done in jest, with the spiteful comments not held in a harsh heart, just a clever and observant mind's eye, able to pinpoint areas ripe for comment and spotlight the true thoughts lingering in hearts and minds. There are some who think Jane later had to change her style to be publishable, and Cassandra definitely decided to censor many of the letters, to keep the pointed yet oh, so funny remarks private. In those early days, however, Jane did not have to hide her true thoughts or curtail the parameters of her writing when with her family or Martha. These works, and the humour in them, seem to point to a true facet of Jane's personality and authorial voice. The question remains, what if she had been able to follow this arrow beyond the trusted audience of her family and Martha? The works written at this time and in this bubble, to which Martha was one of the most frequent visitors, point 'to the alternative Austen who might have been a different writer.'[17]

What they do is to shine a mirror into the eyes and heart of Jane Austen at the time when her friendship with Martha was at its earliest, and we get to see her inner thoughts and ideas as they were coming to her then. We can see into the past and become part of the moment; we can share their presence and imagine what it was like to be Jane's friend at this time. Perhaps, in this early fiction, we are seeing a truer Jane and through this likeness, the intimacy of the two friends is revealed. When sharing her work with Martha and her close family, Jane 'felt no need to hide her sparkle under a bushel.'[18] To make oneself that vulnerable is the real mark of closeness and a strong social bond. It is further proof of the importance of Martha as a friend to the real Jane – in the sharing of this brazen wit and the inclusion of such forbidden and anarchic thoughts, we can understand just how well the two got along and just how comfortable they were in each other's company. The freedom that Jane felt alongside Martha and Cassandra, up in the little secret room, sparked an atmosphere fit for her wit and creativity, for her 'uninhibited gusto' for her muse, for her writing, for Jane Austen to explore her dream of being published.[19]

Jane alludes to her favourite novels, plays and works of literature in the *Juvenilia*, making it not inconceivable at all that she should include the influences of conversations with her friend, even if most of those conversations were a matter of Jane bouncing ideas off of a bemused and beaming Martha. Martha's friendship may or may not be quoted or used directly in Jane's work – the secrets may well be woven quite subtly into a storyline or a dialogue, but Jane did not write for 'dull elves, as have not a great deal of ingenuity themselves.'[20] We can be sure that Martha understood the inferred meanings meant for her. Many study the *Juvenilia* to better understand Jane's development as a writer and I believe that we can also read them and discover what friendship felt like for Jane. Southam believes that it is truly important to consider the influence of Jane Austen's family and her childhood reading upon her as a writer. I agree and I believe in the same sense that it is important to consider the impact of the friend that Jane chose to become part of her life – the family that she chose for herself, the appreciator of her talent and a partner in her 'belly-laughing' crime.

The family certainly regarded these early writings as something personal, intimate and special, to be treasured and passed only amongst themselves. For many years, no one outside of this group even knew of the *Juvenilia* and it was published only little by little for the first time from 1922 until as late as 1951. For Martha to have been privy to these writings and to have been Jane Austen's primary free-time friend at the time of their writing shows just how inside the 'intimate and sympathetic' circle of Jane's relationships she was.[21] The *Juvenilia* were dedicated by Jane Austen to this special, bespoke audience, her group of trusted family and close friends. This small detail prompts many scholars to pause and reflect. It shows that the stories and writings really did mean something to Jane herself. She cared enough to copy them out into special notebooks provided by her father, she had someone to share them with and she could revel in the simulation of a bona fide dedication, just as real authors wrote.

At a later date from when she first wrote it in *Volume the First*, yet literally within only the first few months of their friendship, Jane added a fulsome dedication to Martha at the beginning of her short story *Frederic and Elfrida*. Scholars have noted the later addition of the dedication, it being in a different stage of Jane Austen's handwriting. For us as students of their friendship, this just adds importance to Jane's attachment of this story and of her heart to Martha. Including Martha in a dedication of a story, as only a handful of friends and family were, raises our interest in the story itself and piques our intrigue and imagination as to why she chose so purposefully this particular tale for her. She probably copied it out and gave her a copy too. She writes: 'My dear Martha as a small testimony of the gratitude I feel for your late generosity to me in finishing my muslin cloak.'[22]

The dedication is written in an exaggerated form of the accepted formal tone of the type of dedication that authors of the time used. It almost reads like a joke between the two, a mimicking mickey-take of the formal and long-winded dedications in some of the books that Jane would have read in her father's library. However, it does, as others have pointed out, denote a 'half-serious embrace of the convention' and that the wording, layout and style of the sumptuous dedication was thoughtfully conceived with quite a degree of due diligence.[23] The observation of this literary formality and then the mindful inclusion of the dedication at all was an indication of the aspiration that Jane held in her heart to become published. Juliet McMaster has attested to the validity of the *Juvenilia* and importance as 'accomplished works, fragments that represent carefully crafted letters for public consumption'.[24] She believes them to be a fundamental indicator of Jane Austen's development as a writer at this time, and for us, knowing that Martha was included and part of her inner circle, we cannot help but get excited for Jane that she had a caring and encouraging friend as a sounding board and recipient of her grace and muse. Someone who Jane felt would understand and welcome her experiments, and support her ambitions.

Southam believes that there may even have been 'a secret between Jane Austen and the relation or friend to whom the work was dedicated.'[25] Already the two friends had spent many an hour together, sharing confidences and enjoying exploring life. It is highly probable that secrets and hopes were passed between the two. Knowing this makes reading this story a treat. A tale already told, there must have been something of a shared message or a hint of a link with Jane's new friend, quite probably some sort of meaningful hidden and obscured message only obvious and de-codable to Martha, in order for Jane to choose to dedicate this, one of her very first entries, to her friend.

There is a comment made in the story about the different excellencies of Indian and English Muslins and it is believed that in adding that word 'Muslin' to the dedication, 'a link between Martha and the characters in her story' is both conferred and confirmed.[26] Some believe that 'here she feminises and domesticates the official letter of dedication', but I believe Jane meant that story to mean more to Martha than simply a reference to household work; she did not limit Martha, as many have since, to the domesticated roles in life.[27] This may be a direct link with wordplay on a familiar chore to them both, but the twisted and fanciful, highly romantic plot, rooted in comedy, is probably a greater reason for the dedication and why Martha came to mind. Maybe even the true reason is too hidden, as the friendship between the two was warm, intimate and personal, so perhaps there is an in-joke or a shared experience that none but they were conscious of. The pair loved to be highly entertained and amused and so this in itself may have been the trigger for Jane; 'the individual relationship implied', the humour alone may have been enough to have jogged her memory of this story and for it to have reminded her of something sparked by her budding and blossoming friendship with Martha.[28]

Certainly, one biographer is convinced that Jane dedicated this story to Martha due to the capacities of her personality, that Jane witnessed in Martha her 'keen, warm, uncritical laughing friend.'[29] Thus, revealing to us the importance of her value to Jane. To have this particular story dedicated to her then does contain an implied meaning, a worthiness, the viewpoint from which Jane decided upon Martha having it, as she was simply the most deserving of it.

The topics and themes touched on in the story are reminiscent of many conversations between close friends. Amongst other things the story considers 'destiny, love, friendship, marriage, beauty and fashion' but scholars agree that this, the very first story transcribed into her 'carefully assembled' Volume, is all about creating and providing 'a good family laugh.'[30] They say that the strength of a friendship is being able to laugh at oneself and each other without offence being caused or taken. Jane's intelligence and wit could scorch the page, and the lines in the story in reference to 'the new neighbour' do not only include a complimentary view of said neighbour's appreciation of a good quality of muslin, but also comment on 'the horror of her new friend's appearance' including references to her 'forbidding squint, greasy tresses and swelling back.'[31] All this physical mickey-taking of the new acquaintance, dedicated in the full knowledge that Martha bore the terrible scars of the smallpox, proves that both parties enjoyed what in the modern world we might call banter, but was certainly strong and blatantly undisguised teasing. There is a fearlessness, a daring and a boldness here, yet also a strong message that her friendship with Martha was way more than just skin-deep.

This was not going to be a friendship based on outward appearances or vanity. This friendship was going to be worth so much more to both and there must have already been a mutual and, perhaps as yet unspoken, shared understanding of this.

But what about the content of these bawdy stories that painted adult life in all its shameless excesses and truths and held up a mirror to the expected conduct, reflecting back the very different reality of many people's worst behaviours and morals? Could it be that Jane did indeed take some inspiration from the tales Martha must have told her too, particularly those concerning her own grandmother, the cruel Mrs Craven? If Martha knew the truest version of Jane, then Jane came to know the truth about Martha's scandalous family history too and yet how emotionally grounded and strong her friend had managed to remain. Martha was now descended from a decent, honourable, respected and upright branch of her family, but things could have turned out completely differently for her.

Martha's mother was born with the sort of aristocratic connections that Jane's own mother could boast of, which was most likely some of the reason why she was so keen and open to welcoming the Lloyds into her society. Born Martha Craven, Martha's mother was the daughter of the Honourable Charles Craven, Governor of South Carolina, who would later settle in Gloucestershire and then Brimpton, Newbury. He had married Elizabeth Staples, a woman who behaved so politely, was so perfectly poised in society, so kind, so well-mannered, so cultured and well-regarded. Behind closed doors though, she was the stuff of legend, of terrible nightmares, a leading lady straight from a Grimm Brothers' fairy-tale. Tyrannical and cruel with a terrible temper, her behaviour towards her children was unkind to say the least and verged on the neglect and abuse of her offspring. Things with her went from bad to worse for Martha and her six siblings as their mother sidled up to another wealthy businessman nearby whilst still married to their father. Working away at Mr Jemmet Raymond of Barton Court, Kintbury with her wiles and her ambition, she married him as soon as her poor husband expired.

Having persuaded her son John to marry her new husband's kin, the young daughters became fearful for their own futures and could not tolerate her behaviour towards them any further. The push of their mother's unpredictable and limitless disregard for them, alongside the pull and lure of freedom and escape, proved too much of a temptation. As soon as the opportunity arose, Martha's mother and some of her sisters ran away, living at different times at a boarding school, their brother's home and with an aunt in Wiltshire. The sisters all bolted as one, with little planning or security for their hopes. Like jumping from a burning building or abandoning a sinking ship, one by one they ran for what felt like their lives, in fear of their mother returning and blocking their escape. One sister, Jane, married well – to a Reverend Thomas Fowle, a vicar at Kintbury; Margaret married a yeoman farmer named Hinxman; but another, alas, chose a local horse dealer with little financial stability to offer her. Martha's mother thankfully landed safely, marrying not only a 'beneficed clergyman', but one 'of respectable character and good position.'[32] She found her Noyes Lloyd and the course of her life and that of her descendants then ran a lot more smoothly.

The recounting of this history must have fuelled Jane's already rich and alert imagination and intellect. We can just imagine her eyes out on stilts and as wide as saucers, perhaps her quill noting down points of interest, the shaking of her head as she alternately questioned Martha for clarification or stopped to exclaim at what she was hearing before urging her to continue. For Jane Austen, behind her ideas for her stories lay the 'seriousness of the intelligent young writer'.[33] It is true that she loved to laugh and joke, to make fun and to play around with words that she would never get to use in polite society or her everyday life. However, the many emotional layers, the unbelievable twists and turns of the life lived by the notorious Mrs Craven would have been serious and irresistible food for thought. Reflected in this gripping and terrible tale there would have been so much of the character of Martha's cruel grandmother for Jane to observe and to mimic. Not to mention a whole new layer of sympathy and concern for her friend.

Chapter Three

Moving Away

In March 1792, James Austen, Jane's elder brother, married Anne Mathew. As we all know, with the provision of a position within the church, in James's case the curacy of Overton and supporting his father's work at Steventon, the new recipient of the post is entitled to accommodation within the area and never is this more pressing than when that said incumbent has just wed. Unfortunately for Martha, her mother and sister, this meant that they had to vacate Deane parsonage. They had to move out lock, stock and barrel and find somewhere else for their lives and their worldly goods to reside.

Quite shockingly for them all, their enforced eviction meant a move out of the locality and the life they had built for themselves since their father's death, to a house some sixteen miles away at Ibthorpe, on the outskirts of Hurstbourne Tarrant, near Andover. Mrs Lloyd was not the only one growing older, with Martha now 26 and Mary 21. The family would need to become part of yet another new social network, settling themselves and their reputations into the area in the process. What hope there was ever to be of her daughters marrying and settling down must have plagued Mrs Lloyd constantly just as it would have the inimitable Mrs Bennet. The ramifications of this 'hard blow' were huge; not only did they result in a total life upheaval for Martha, they also had huge implications for Jane Austen, her personal happiness and her life as a budding creative and writer.[1]

There is no doubt that this turn of events brought home to both Martha and Jane just how much they both valued their friendship and how in just three short years they had come to mean so much to each other. It was not the absence of the things that they had done once in a while, the high days, the holy days, but more the small practices and homelife routines of what they had done together every day that caused them to miss each other so sorely. The distance now between them, the disruption and frustration of their daily intimacies and plans, meant their loss of the other was felt in every waking moment.

We have no evidence of what Jane gifted to Martha on this occasion, but we do still have a little poem that Jane wrote for Mary at this time. She also made her a gift of a cotton 'housewife', a little needlework bag that contained practical essentials for mending and sewing. The most poignant lines of the poem, to Mary, who was not as close to her as Martha was, really are touching:

And as we are about to part, 'Twill serve another end:
For, when you look upon the bag, You'll recollect your friend.[2]

However, interestingly, in an intriguing contradiction to the beautiful story dedicated to Martha, hot on the heels of their move out of Deane, Jane dedicated one of her stories from *Volume the Third*, called *Evelyn*, to Mary. The house move for the Lloyd ladies was ultimately understood and accepted as a fact of life, but it does certainly appear to be a burst of 'youthful tactlessness' and near needling to dedicate this particular story to Mary.[3] *Evelyn* tells the tale of a young man who simply walks into a village and into the home of a very settled and well-organised family, to be showered with all manner of good gifts and treats, wonderful food and the very purse and savings from the couple who live there. They stop at nothing in their 'generosity' to their visitor. We witness their limitless self-sacrificing servitude to their guest, to the point of them even giving their daughter in marriage and the very roof over their heads to him. In the end we find that the 'hero' of the story did not even enter the village with any intent of staying or doing it good. Instead he was en route to avenge the moral pride and romantic reputation of his sister, whose plight he actually immediately forgets about. The story tails off, with him returning to find his new wife dead and his servants living it up in his home. Indeed, to give this story as a gift, right when circumstances were as they were for Mary, seems too charmingly cheeky for words. That is until we remember that the story is written by a high-spirited, rule-breaking, laugh-in-the-face of all the nonsense in the world

16-year-old. Mary was not known herself for loving reading – or particularly for having a sense of humour. She was Martha's calmer, more officious and practical sister, so goodness knows what she made of this romp of an unfinished tale. Ironically, years later, it is her own son who takes up his pen to attempt to finish the story.

This was not the only time that Mary was included in, or rather became, the butt of Jane's comic, acerbic, sometimes biting wit and the object of her satire. In her *History of England*, we find a rare and revealing portrait of Mary, depicted in one of Cassandra's beautiful and accomplished sketches, in the role of a namesake Mary Tudor, Mary I.[4] She is cast thus on the opposing side of history to Jane's preferred Mary, Queen of Scots. It is Cassandra's hand-drawn image of Mary, complete with pockmarked skin, that becomes the personification of the disliked Bloody Mary. Mary would later sit for her portrait by a travelling artist and reportedly did not enjoy the experience at all. Perhaps she was thinking back to these little images. This Queen, short in stature and of a sickly complexion, seems another fairly cruel and pointed swipe of a comparison towards Martha's sister. Known for being well-organised and practical, there could be a kinder link between the two; Mary I was associated with putting into place the structures for laying down the 'poor laws', the government-mandated poor relief that Elizabeth I would reap the benefit of. However, the raging Protestant Queen, happy to put to the stake hundreds of people in a country already racked with famine and ruin, was not an agreeable role model in Jane's eyes, and so more likely not used here to put Mary Lloyd in a good light.

The crack of Jane's wit can be heard in the linking of Mary to the follow-up monarch, Elizabeth I, who Jane compares to her mother, in the way only a young, independently minded, opinionated and imaginative daughter can as 'the destroyer of all comfort, the deceitful Betrayer of trust.'[5] Cassandra and Martha were famously excellent at keeping private thoughts and secrets under wraps, but could it be that Mrs Austen and Mary were not so well-trusted by the young Jane in this regard?

Jane had a history at this time of making these double-edged presents and was probably somewhat notorious for it in the family.

The previous winter she had also dedicated 'a distinctly brutal story about mercenary matchmaking' to her brother Edward as a gift to congratulate him on his high society wedding.[6] We can just imagine them all rolling their eyes and Martha rocking around with mirth, clutching her aching sides. Martha seems to escape scot-free from this particular guise of her gift, as does Jane's beloved Cassandra. This then is another sign of the friendly companionship Jane was enjoying with Martha and the intimacy and connectedness they felt – Martha was firmly one of the 'us' whilst Mary and alas poor Mrs Austen remained one of 'them' at this time.

The two friends, Martha and Jane, were determined not to let go of one another and Jane began to visit and stay over with Martha at Ibthorpe House. This was a beautiful house, of a handsome size and outlook. Their mindful scheduling of visits to each other meant that happily 'the move did not end their friendship,' and instead, the distance just changed the nature of their meet-ups and orchestrating their friendship simply required a little more nurture, forethought and forward planning.[7] At age 16, gaining a little independence and stepping out to spend overnight and residential stays with her friend must have seemed quite exciting and grown up to Jane.

There was no way that Jane was about to give up on someone whom she treasured so and who was 'as intimate, merry and in tune with her' as Martha was.[8] If anything, this enforced new way of life only strengthened and deepened their friendship. It gave it new ways for it to grow and flourish, which is a healthy part of any relationship. In the early days of their friendship, Jane had rolled down the banks of grass outside the back of her house at Steventon and the pair had walked back and forth up the lane to the church in their pattens, trodden and worn shortcuts across the gently undulating hills back and forth to their homes. Now they continued to explore the beautiful countryside around Ibthorpe, walking along wooded paths and into countryside reminiscent of the beautiful pastoral scenes that Martha had been used to at Kintbury and Enborne. In this way they could share what was in their hearts and on their minds with ease and the room afforded to them at Ibthorpe meant that there was plenty of time for them to confide privately in one another. Martha's 'sympathetic presence' did not have to be grieved, although it would be so missed back at Steventon; it was not to die out but rather seeds were sown that would go on to flourish in an as yet unseen future.[9] Even if it was unbeknownst to the pair themselves, the attachment between the two young women was becoming thicker and stronger than ever. Theirs was a friendship that could be relied upon and planned for, hoped for and anticipated. Time together was high on both of their agendas. If the Austen family thought that the friendship would take a natural turn and gently fade away, they could not have been more wrong. For instead of days and hours passed in each other's company with their respective family routines calling them back to their duty, the pair now had weeks at a time to spend with one another, sharing a room, sharing confidences and with nothing else to focus on but their hearts' delight. Nothing, it seems, could ever be a substitute for Martha.

Jane was still quite as reliant as ever on her family for dictating when, where and how she might set off on other business, including that of her personal life. However, in this atmosphere of prevailing routine with settled friendships and periods of prolonged peace and quiet, this was a highly creative period for Jane. We know from Cassandra's records that Jane was in a happy place and spent the first part of the 1790s in a spurt of writing, leading on from the *Juvenilia* into her first experimentations with, and her own attempts at, various guises of the full-length novel form. Drafts that would be reworked, revised and carefully reconstructed in the future began to appear in their earliest forms. *Lady Susan* was written in the years 1793–4. *First Impressions*, which would later become *Pride and Prejudice*, was begun in October 1796 and finished in its earliest manuscript state by the end of August 1797. *Elinor and Marianne*, later to be titled *Sense and Sensibility*, was begun in November of that year and *Northanger Abbey* is believed to have been written in 1798 through 1799.

It seems no coincidence then that Jane should turn her pen to compose some thoughts on friendship at this time and it is altogether too lovely not to reflect and reminisce upon her words. In the short story *Lesley-Castle* written at the beginning of 1792, there are references to friendships between young women. Jane writes with her trademark tongue-in-cheek wit and there are hilarious cutting remarks made in a farce-like circle of friendships, relationships and points of view. Hidden amongst the barbs are some touching references to being parted from those 'so closely linked together by the ties of sympathy and friendship.'[10] A 16-year-old girl at this time needed her parents' permission and transportation to travel. Jane might well be writing with such longing about friendship because of her own forced exile in Steventon from her friend at Ibthorpe. We cannot ignore then when she has a character reflect thus:

> I once thought that to have what is in general called a Freind [sic] (I mean one of my own Sex to whom I might speak with less reserve than to any other person) independent of my Sister would never be an object of my wishes, but how much was I mistaken![11]

How lovely it is for us to imagine Jane confiding in and speaking to Martha, and to think of her so devoted to their friendship. How wonderful it is that this source of escape and respite, thankfully, was not to be cut off for good.

As Martha settled into her new home, Jane and Martha continued their friendship, keeping in contact, blending the rhythms of their own family lives and mucking in with each other's as they began to stay over, running errands together, and becoming even more of a part of each other's family scenes. When they met, their conversations were as intimate and rewarding as ever, almost as if they had never been apart and covering a range of themes common to young women of any era. Moving back and forth between Steventon and Ibthorpe, they continued to share their most pressing and intimate concerns. The exact details may change and differ over time, but the overarching longings of the heart do not. Slowly, life began a new chapter but no letters of Jane's survive from September 1796–April 1798; being so close to her family and friends for longer periods of time, perhaps there was not as much need for writing and receiving letters. This is not to say, however, that this was a time of quiet insignificance. Oh no, quite to the contrary.

James Austen's wife Anne Mathew died on 3 May 1795. This was a devastating and unexpected turn of events. There was some confusion as to whom he would choose for his second wife and he spent some time deliberating – but time was of the essence and his needs were pressing. Little baby Anna, his daughter, was now an orphan and in need of a mother, and James was busy with his work in the church, not to mention his need for someone to organise his life and run a household for him. James may have been a favourite of his mother's, famed for his intellect and creative poetry, his love of nature and exploring excursions but he, unlike his brother Frank, did not have a reputation for being practical in any way. He was a man, who if not in possession of a great fortune, was most definitely in need of a wife. Would Jane at last have her Miss Lloyd as a true sister?

Chapter Four

Love Lives

In Martha and Jane's personal lives, things became turbulent as the winds of change swept through their families once again. Jane's beloved Cassandra was in love with Tom Fowle, Martha's cousin. Known to the family from his school days under their roof, everyone was excited about the future and Cassandra's assured happiness. It is reckoned that they became engaged at the end of 1792, the year ending for Martha and Jane on a high note.

Perhaps oblivious to the depth of the pain suffered by James, her elder brother, or simply spurred to act upon the jaunty feelings of a young girl of 21 and to make the most of opportunities for fun and love as they came along, Jane had been swept up in the midst of her very own crush at the start of 1796. At a local ball the nephew of her passionate and inspiring friend, Madam Lefroy, caught her eye; another Tom, he was over from Ireland visiting his family before he returned to study Law there. She became caught in a flight of fantasy, letting her imagination have its way. Jane enjoyed experiencing the thrill of the chase and revelled in teasing her sister with her gently naughty and rebellious ways, and proving to her that she was a free spirit who just didn't care. Jane Austen, that freedom-seeking, lark and laughter lover, with her impetuous side, so evident in her youthful writings of this time, spilling out into the real world, couldn't help herself from putting down some of her thoughts on the matter in provoking and merry little messages to Cassandra. 'Imagine to yourself,' she writes, 'everything most profligate and shocking in the way of dancing and sitting down together.' She is keen to both examine and exhort him as 'very gentlemanlike, good-looking and pleasant' and to play about hinting at their involvement – 'as to our having ever met, except at the three last balls, I cannot say much.'[1] A rather blunt assessment of Jane by a neighbour at the time (later quoted by her daughter Mary Russell Mitford) as a 'husband hunting butterfly' seems rather cruel, but may capture something of her naivety and youth.[2] Jane is revelling in the happy-go-lucky nature of it all.

Her romantic escapism is brought back to earth with a bump though by the confirmation that no promises have been made or feelings exchanged and that his family and friends have found the whole thing laughable and he perhaps humiliating. Madam Lefroy certainly did not see the funny side at all and impressed upon Tom, who was destined for university and a great patronage, not to lead Jane on or to be seen to be deceiving Jane in any way. She intervened and sent him quickly back to Dublin with a flea in his ear. Years later in his old age, after a long and successful career in law and public life, Tom did admit to having some sincere youthful feelings for Jane at this time – but they did not and perhaps could not be allowed to grow by the circumstances of his own mapped-out path.

With all of this hullabaloo dying down, by the end of the year James had settled on his choice of a second wife and proposed to her … Mary Lloyd, in November 1796. Many believe that Mary had admired James since their early meetings at Kintbury and theirs was certainly a sensible match in terms of Mary's talents, if not her own wealth. If Jane had hoped that Martha might be considered, this option was off the cards from the beginning with Mary only rivalled in love by one other, also a Mary. General Mathew would continue to send an allowance for his granddaughter Anna, and Mary and James would go and visit him at Clanville, his estate. They had need of his benevolence. To say Mrs Austen was delighted is an understatement. Lashings of love and enthusiasm were handed down from her; perhaps she was remembering that Mrs Lloyd senior had aristocratic connections not dissimilar to her own. She wrote a letter to Mary, one that the family treasured ever after:

Had the Election been mine, you, my dear Mary, are the person I should have chosen for James' Wife, Anna's Mother, and my Daughter, being as certain, as I can be of anything in this uncertain world, that you will greatly increase and promote the happiness of each of the three.[3]

Mrs Austen noted Mary's reputation as a well-organised and sensible woman brought up and trained to run a house with care and efficiency. She had one eye on her own future and saw in her future daughter-in-law someone of great value and supporting benefit to herself: 'I look forward to you as a real comfort to me in my old age, when Cassandra is gone into Shropshire [with Tom Fowle] and Jane – the Lord knows where.'[4]

This witty and somewhat sarcastic remark is a rueful side glance at Jane. That look which only a mother can give. Mrs Austen was after all the 'Elizabeth' to Jane's 'Mary Queen of Scots' who in her 'teenage' ranting and letting off steam in her earlier *History of England* had scorned her as 'the destroyer of all comfort' (writing was Jane's happy place, her dreams for it and her time spent at it, her comfort zone), and the 'deceitful betrayer of trust reposed in her' (perhaps the whisperings of Jane's dreams and hopes for her writing interest to her mother had been dismissed).[5] Mrs Austen wasn't sure where Jane was going to land. Now aged 21, Jane herself had arrived at that prime time for getting married. With her head full of stories and independent ambitions, this comment is a tell-tale sign, perhaps of tacit disapproval from Mrs Austen, of concern for Jane's wellbeing and future and perhaps a recognition of the unstoppable yet temperamental drive of the need to write and express oneself creatively. Perhaps her mother was actually resigned to this uncertain future and her comments represent a yielding shake of the head, an acceptance of the inevitable, of Jane's writing career as a matter of wonderful if inconvenient and uncertain prospects.

In the next instant, following on from thoughts of Jane's future, tellingly Mrs Austen's mind immediately falls to Martha. And we are left with our mouth agape. Mrs Austen 'puts her foot in it' in an unsubtle and hilarious way. Through her remarks we have a window into the world of Martha and the intimacy she shared with the family. It seems that she had no secrets, hinting again at how involved the two families were in each other's business, due to the frequency of their comings and goings with one another. Mrs Austen makes pains, in the midst of her oblivious gaff, to show that Martha's confidence had not been betrayed by Jane or Cassandra. On the contrary, she is proud of working things out for *herself* and putting what she thinks of as two-and-two together. We are left wondering initially if she has stumbled upon a truth or if she has got the wrong end of the stick:

Tell Martha, she too shall be my Daughter, she does me honour in the request, and Mr W: shall be my Son if he pleases, don't be alarmed my dear Martha, I have kept and will keep your secret as close if I had been entrusted with it: which I do assure you, I never was, but found it out by my own sprack wit.[6]

There is no further mention of exactly who 'Mr W' is and Martha's connection to him or promises from him. Neither do we know for sure Martha's reaction to this comment, being included as it was, in such a significant family letter at a highly charged moment.

On 17 January 1797, Mary was married from Ibthorpe at nearby Hurstbourne Tarrant by the family friend, Reverend Peter Debary Senior. James himself composed verses for Mary on her wedding day, as he would go on to do at different points in their married life. In a strange reversal of fate, Mary now returned to the parsonage at Deane, where she had spent three happy years before her eviction. Now she was the mistress of the house. Mary's reputation was mostly very positive, and Jane's cousin Eliza de Feuillide had described her as 'not either rich or handsome, but very sensible and good humoured.'[7] Upon her marriage, James had taken Mary to the Vyne estate nearby to meet the wealthy and influential Mr and Mrs Chute, who he enjoyed spending time with very much and with whom he dined frequently. Mrs Chute noted that Mary was 'Perfectly unaffected and very pleasant.' Luckily for Mary and an impressive achievement on her part, the matriarch of the area liked her and pronounced her approbation upon this meeting. Sadly 'the small pox which … scarred and seamed her face dreadfully' was still a hindrance to the appearance of both Mary and Martha all these years into their adult lives, still noticeable and a mar on their marriage opportunities, but 'was it not' for this noted Mrs Chute, 'her countenance would be pleasing.'[8]

On the other hand, the differences between Mary and Martha's personalities became more and more defined following Mary's marriage to James. Jane most definitely preferred Martha's warmth and humour which she saw combined most favourably with sense and elegance. Jane noticed the 'practical, emphatic and brusque' side of Mary's personality more and more, and worse still in Jane's opinion, she could see that little Anna did not warm to Mary, and Mary did not appear to be that kindly or motherly towards Anna.[9] Although thought of initially as a seal of happiness for James as being 'simple and practical enough to delight him', Jane did not seem to share the warmth for Mary that her mother had expressed.[10] Some say that her treatment of her beloved niece Anna sealed the deal for Jane, but she made many acid remarks and shrewd observations on the goings on between Mary and James too. Jane believed him to be escaping to Steventon against his heavily pregnant wife's will and her strength of negative feeling towards Mary and her relationship with her brother results in scathing words, verging on contempt in her letters. The difference between Mary and Martha became starker and clearer and, in the contrast, she warmed even more to Martha and drew her closer as she pushed Mary further to the edges of her good will.

Having read Mary's pocket diaries it is true that they are clipped and clinical in the way that they note details and facts relating to the running of a very well-organised household. They record regular meals and dinner dates with many local dignitaries and all and only the well-connected families of note. But interestingly they are very formally written. Mary mentions her husband's comings and goings and appointments with noticeable regularity and refers to him always as 'Mr Austen'. Her sister, too, she notes consistently as Miss Lloyd. Her daughter, in reading them as an adult, noted, as I thought, that 'she scarcely ever added any remark to the fact she wrote down' yet, they are updated on a perfectly regular basis.[11] It could have been this coolness, this efficiency that carried forward into Mary's tightness of expression of emotions.

In any case for the time being, thoughts of her new sister Mary and her brother James were eclipsed by the devastating news received by her sister Cassandra in May. News had travelled slowly from the West Indies where her fiancé Tom had been serving his benefactor and family member, Lord Craven in the role of domestic chaplain. He had set sail in 1795 with the sole aim of earning some more money so that he and Cassandra might be married as soon as possible on his return. Tom Fowle died of fever on 13 February. All of Cassandra's hopes of living in Shropshire and enjoying a happy future with her love were destroyed by this cruel act of fate. Lord Craven lamented Tom's death and the fact that he had not known of the engagement when he had appointed dear Tom. He assured them all that he would never have agreed to take him otherwise. His sorrowful remorse was no salve to poor Cassandra's broken heart. The news of their brother Henry's marriage to their exotic cousin, Eliza de Feuillide, in December may have brought some cheer, but perhaps also rubbed some salt into the wound for the still-grieving Cassandra.

All had not gone well for Martha in the intervening period either. By Autumn 1798 when Jane was 23 and Martha 33, marriage, and whether they themselves would find a lifelong mate, was starting to weigh heavier on both their own and other people's minds. Jane was really worried about her friend. In letters from this period, we feel the depth of her care and concern. These two, now sisters by marriage, needed the firm foundations of their established and valued friendship more than ever.

Reading between the lines of the family records, it seems that Martha had entertained high hopes of becoming engaged to and marrying the enigmatic and as yet still unidentified 'Mr W'. Although for some it seems this was never a serious match, in the light of her sister's wedded security, Martha took a long time to recover from what we learn was to be a doomed relationship. Whether it is from the loss of this particular individual or rather just a dawning sense of pervasive despair that the rebuff brought with it, Martha was affected physically, emotionally and mentally.

Like any best friend, Jane extended tender patience and gentle concern over this period and she could not contain her joy in hearing that Martha was out and about again and planning a visit to her sister and James at Deane. To see her friend hiding away at home, not even venturing out on family visits, something so out of her character, would have shocked Jane. Moreover, if Martha hadn't felt up to doing even this for a long time, then that would have been a huge worry for her friend. Sometimes the best thing that you can do as a friend is to give that person all the time and space they need. We can sense the mix of sadness and relief when there is finally better news of her friend, that 'Martha is in better looks and spirits than she has enjoyed for a long time.'[12]

The kindness in Jane's tone and the total absence of her banter and joking around is an abrupt change in the type of repartee we are used to amongst the two friends, and leaves us with a sense of the gravitas and sombre emotions, indeed, how seriously Jane felt for her friend at this time. Jane knew her friend so well that on hearing this news, she became convinced that Martha would be bouncing back to her full natural nature within a very short time, 'I flatter myself she will now be able to jest openly about Mr W,' she wrote to Cassandra.[13] She knows that Martha is strong and that this will not weigh her down for much longer. Jane is so confident of this in fact that she completely changes tack at this point and turns immediately in her letter to mention some mundane item of lost property. In her mind, this incident has now been consigned to the past and they can both move on.

Martha did recover quite quickly after this and returned to her love of studying herbs and plants and their useful qualities. In a letter written the following month, Jane was back to teasing her for Cassandra's benefit and perhaps to console them both – that 'Martha sends me word that she is too busy to write to me now' – Jane had thought that Martha would be studying her 'medicine', gently teasing the occupations and obsessions of her friend whilst simultaneously breathing a palpable sigh of relief. 'All well', ends the letter, a happy sounding of the all-clear from Jane.[14]

Jane still kept Martha close to her heart though, and her beady eye upon her; a week later she is wishing if only 'could Lord Spencer give happiness to Martha... what a joyful heart he would make of yours', reflecting on how happy this would make Cassandra and herself.[15] The enigmatic point here is a signal that Jane might have been meddling again. Lord Spencer had just written to Rev George Austen about his sailor sons, hinting that Frank was imminently to be given a new commission – read in this light, it could be that Cassandra was angling for Frank's good news to be carried over to Martha, linking them together in happiness, and the remark that 'your chief wish is now ready to be accomplished' might refer to Cassandra and Jane's plotting and hoping that perhaps Frank could be a romantic replacement for the longed-for Mr W.[16] Certainly other biographers have thought as much. Jane, it seems, just wanted her friend to be happy and was prepared to do all that she could to make it so.

This teasing of Martha would be a source of endless fun for Jane and she was often relentless at it. In finding the funny side of a situation and endlessly prodding and pressing her friend in this area, the funny bone that was the foundation of their friendship is revealed. Jane was always fanning the flame of Martha's friendships and exaggerating any match-making opportunities, for example, with the younger Reverend Peter Debary. The Debary family lived near to Ibthorpe and were very friendly with Martha and her sister. Peter's father officiated at Mary's wedding. Jane called the Debary sisters 'the endless Debaries' and thought them truly awful, even 'odious'.[17] There were in fact four sisters and two brothers, and they often visited Martha at home. Jane found their over-talkative nature and the frivolous subjects that they chattered on about to be more than tiresome and completely wearing. Yet she tolerated talk and inclusion of the group in deference and respect to Martha. Jane believed that Martha was ripe for jesting with about Peter. He registered high up on the list of people that Martha talked fondly of and would defend – which, of course, made him a prime target for her jovial conjectures. It was simply too good an opportunity to miss. On one occasion when Martha was visiting her sister in Kintbury and was mightily delayed, in Jane's view, in returning to Jane's company, Jane fretted and dared to guess that Martha would be yet further delayed as she had gone to visit Peter and two of his sisters at Eversley where he was rector. She worked herself up into a right state anticipating her return, half-fearing and half-hoping that Martha would be away for even longer and if needs be would 'marry Peter Debary.'[18] When Martha wrote back a few days later, Jane could not resist remarking to Cassandra that Martha had reassured her she would not be leaving for there again any time soon, that she thankfully did not 'own herself in any danger of being tempted back.' Hilariously, Jane confirms with glee in her words and perhaps a big dollop of relief that Martha 'signs by her maiden name we are at least to suppose her not married yet.'[19] It is hard to figure out the tone of her voice completely; perhaps she was not convinced that Martha wasn't somehow attracted to Peter, after all they were so very close in age, shared a deep conviction of their faith and had got to know each other's families – and he could provide a reliable source of financial security. Jane seems to have been crossing her fingers both in love and charity for her friend, but also in the hope of keeping her for herself.

Jane was always to be suspicious of Martha and her penchant for men of the church. Martha was founded on her faith and Christian principles. Jane knew this. Of course, like Jane, Martha too had grown up 'in the church'; her hearth and home had always been at the centre of each Christian community that she had lived in. How natural it would be to see her settled in this way. As a result, Jane could never resist the urge to gently scold or mock-scorn Martha – teasing her for 'immoral love affairs' with clergymen.[20] When the Reverend Dr Richard Mant (master of King Edward's Free Grammar School and Rector of All Saints Church, Southampton) once showed an interest – albeit a friendly one, in Martha, a regular and most devoted attendee of the church and a practical and dedicated parishioner – Jane was thrilled to get one over on Martha and wrote with gossipy glee about it to Cassandra:

> Martha and Dr Mant are as bad as ever; he runs after her in the street to apologise for having spoken to a Gentleman while she was near him the day before. Poor Mrs Mant can stand it no longer; she is retired to one of her married Daughters.[21]

Martha is shocked but not surprised that Jane makes such a big deal of this to Cassandra and in her droll manner plays down the whole event, amiably blaming Jane for stirring up sentiments and seeing things that were not there. Martha believes that it would all have been rather a nothing, a quiet affair, if Jane had not let the cat out of the bag. 'Moi', poses Jane in response, little old me! being the inference in her jolly indignation commenting to Cassandra and relaying Martha's shake of the head 'as if the very slight manner in which I mentioned it could have been all on which you found your judgement.'[22] In her continued response, Jane takes the 'I believe you though thousands wouldn't' approach and makes out that due to her role as protector of Martha's happiness and in light of all of Martha's kindness to them both, she will forgive and overlook all – in her typical ironic tone – full of warmth and mirth. Poor Martha, when your friend knows you inside and out, the slightest whiff or a mere hint of feeling for someone else, always gets pounced upon and leads to merciless teasing – a real sign in itself of the intensity and intimacy of the rapport and bond between the joker and their victim.

Indeed, Jane was no respecter of persons in this matter and would happily make comments on whomsoever was likely to be attached to whom in their shared circle of acquaintances and neighbours. Rumours of weddings and notices of unions was something that she never missed an opportunity to make comment on. She always had an opinion on the relationship and was happy to hold forth on her thoughts on the pair, and especially to report if, in her view, they deserved each other or their happiness. 'It is reported that Sir T. Williams is going to be married,' she relays to Martha following news from her brother Charles in Portsmouth, 'it has been reported indeed twenty times before' but now 'he looks very much like a lover', she jokes.[23]

When Lady Sondes married for the second time, having been widowed and left with seven children, Jane was totally prepared to wish her happy for marrying for love. She discussed it end to end with her friend declaring 'I have laid Lady Sondes' case before Martha – who does not make the least objection to it.' This part of life was an area the two were always apt to seek each other's views on and they always had something to say, some comment to pass together. They never ran out of ideas or views. Martha 'is particularly pleased with the name,' Jane reports back to Cassandra. 'I do not agree with her there, but I like his rank very much' and here we have a hint at their private conversation. Jane lets herself get wrapped up in the wistful notions on a 'General' and a 'Sir' who was want in her mind to be full of 'strong sense', and 'highly elegant manners.'[24]

Who could yet guess where love would lead them, but it was always a topic that lit a flame inside them both. Jane believed Martha to be elegant and charming, funny and sensible. The smallpox had ravaged poor Martha and left its ugly tell-tale signs upon her body, yet Jane could not but have high hopes of her friend being a wonderful match. She was trying to match-make for others, including her friend Anne Sharp – so what hope did poor Martha have of being let off the hook. This was a subject matter that was never going to grow old or cold for Jane when it came to her best friend or perhaps, even herself.

As Christmas beckoned and winter approached in 1802, Jane was enjoying a few days away at her friends' the Biggs' Manydown estate, on the outskirts of Oakley, not so far away from Steventon, in the north of her beloved Hampshire homeland. In the evening on 2 December, when Jane was just a few days away from her twenty-seventh birthday, her friend, brother to Alethea, Catherine and Elizabeth, Harris Bigg-Wither, heir to the estate, proposed marriage to Jane. Initially she accepted, although there had been no mention in any letter, correspondence or conversation to date that she had any feelings for him or felt any attraction to him. At her age she was considered a little past her prime and a marriage proposal would have meant assured financial security for herself and, as she would have been so very aware of, her family. She must have been mindful of what practical and brusque Mary or even her connection-conscious, duty-minded mother would have thought of the proposal. Perhaps she even imagined their joy and entertained ideas of their praise of their 'clever' Jane, netting such a catch, and in an area where friends abounded, and their family roots had been firmly planted in her childhood. She may have been willing initially to suspend her own hopes and dreams in the fulfilment of the wishes and desires of others. After all, she would become mistress of a sizeable estate slap-bang in the midst of her community of well-known acquaintances from her youth. She must have felt secure in the knowledge that an acceptance from her would have been understood and supported, even by her sister Cassandra and Martha, as a practical and entirely sensible match. Love could come later. After all, in the midst of all this, Jane was hoping to secure a life for herself, for Cassandra and for Martha. She hoped that Martha would marry Frank and her fortune would also benefit her sister, and in due course, if her father died, her mother too. She felt the pull of the reassurance of such a wonderful future; a home and a life that she could make for her friend and her sister nearby – what a happy group of three they could be there together.

In her hasty consent, she was letting the material blessings on offer blind her – dizzying her into thinking that she would be able to control for the better the fortunes of her beloved friend and sister and herself. As she stayed up further into the night and thought back over the tumultuous decision she had made, her mind began to wander down the halls of her imagination and as the hours passed she came to realise that she was perhaps assuming too much, and negating the choices and feelings of others, including her own more honest beliefs. There was no evidence in her conversations of either Martha or Frank's attachment to one another, only perhaps that of the desires of her and Cassandra's hearts and she didn't really even like the stuttering, much younger Harris. And wait, this new reality would actually mean Jane being separated from her sister and most probably from her romps and visits with her friend Martha. That would all have to be curtailed, and life as she knew it would have to end. She would be expected to join forces with her husband and his needs, and the needs of his estate would have to become her reason for being. The prospect of losing the precious silence, spaces in time to rule over as her own and do with what she wanted, most notably her writing and imagining, her observing and her stories, hovered over her; all her dreams would be seriously and most definitely thwarted. Her darlings would most likely in all reality cease to be her novels and books and would become flesh and blood babies – heirs to the Bigg-Wither inheritance. Her whole way of life would be under threat and would be changed forever. She was selling all their souls.

Apparently, Jane stayed awake all night, reflecting on her 'Yes' and experiencing such a heightened sense of panic and regret that the

emotions of the night were remembered as a type of folklore by the
younger generation of female Austens. She could not go ahead with
this plan that she had set in motion. It had been made in a moment
of madness and too much in haste. In the morning, she spoke face to
face with Harris and reneged on her earlier acceptance, explaining
that she was turning down his proposal. She fled her kindly friends,
perhaps not yet able or willing to look them in the eye, with Cassandra
in tow, hurrying all the way back to Steventon, where she was met at
the rectory door by Mary. We can only imagine the negative reaction
from her at Jane's decision – her radar of suitability would have been
sounding an alarm positively off the scale at a match so desirable
and pleasant and palatable. As she leaned in to listen more closely
and heard that Jane had permitted this fortune to slip through the
family's fingers, her face must have fallen as the ramifications pierced
her mind and heart. Perhaps they would even have angered her; she
would have felt Jane's shame and the sorrow of it all almost as acutely
as Jane, perhaps, considering her own currying of favour with her
neighbourly connections and her dining partners, even more so. Jane
would have been hurrying her up, stood there as she was, loading her
belongings into the house, speaking through her sadness and in the
midst of her pain, asking her brother James to take her by carriage
back to her mother in Bath. Both this demanding of transportation
and the revelation to Mary of the events of the night before were so
out of Jane's natural way and natural order of things, a turn of events
so unexpected, and so personal and so public – we can just see how
upset she would have felt and how so utterly jolted out of herself she
must have been.

Martha was there to stand by her, their friendship itself was deepening
into more than just that of useful playmates. They were there for
each other, and in a young woman's life a broken engagement was a
momentous occasion. Sometimes the love of a friend is as strong as
the love of a family member. Martha had been the shelter in the storm
for Jane quite literally when one Sunday morning in early November
1800, a startled and scared Jane had run to the dining room window
and witnessed the felling by the wind of five of their beautiful elm
trees behind the house. She had seen the devastation around their

home with many of the other trees torn apart or destroyed leaving the elm walk, the maypole and the meadow nearby unrecognisable. In the wake of the storm and the clearing up and in the absence of her beloved sister, Jane had made plans to remove to Ibthorpe to the comfort of Martha, her dear friend in both times of joy and times of trouble. When the storms of life hit, it was just the same. In January 1799, Jane herself declared 'I love Martha better than ever' and this thought remained with her in whatever portion of the day or within whichever parcel of her life she was consumed.[25] In moments like these she felt it even more strongly.

Her young female relatives seem to agree that in the aftermath, the family came to believe that Jane rushed into her acceptance. Jane was embarrassed and left reeling, but the younger women saw courage in her emphatic confirmation of her decision to turn down the proposal. Although in years to come, some in the family would wish to bury the bad news of 'the Manydown Story' and either never to refer to it publicly or to write so ambiguously and indistinctly about it that the names of the people involved could never be traced or pored over.[26] The whole incident left a nasty taste in the family's mouth and a dent in their pride in the Austen reputation that they sought so heavily to protect in their living memories and in their communities. They had more than one eye on what revealing the whole truth could do to their current quality of life. They saw in writing of it only the opportunity for muck-raking by others. Thus, hinting that Jane and the family were at the mercy of local gossip for some time after the event.

However, in time, the Bigg family would get over the situation and the friendships with the sisters were remedied, if not totally rectified and restored. By all accounts it did take the Bigg family a while to believe that Jane had indeed really changed her mind, and that it was only 'eventually' that they fully and unequivocally accepted her decision and refusal; perhaps 'a la Mr Collins' they believed at first that she was simply being demure, charming or even plain shy.[27]

By the turn of the next year though, Harris had moved on and was on the hunt for another suitor. Eventually he was married, to the delight, approbation, and perhaps the relief of the local community and settled well away from the family home at Manydown, removing to Wymering near Portsmouth and eventually having ten children. Years later Jane was once again relaxed and happy in the Bigg sisters' company and was talking of visiting with Catherine and Alethea Bigg, and being sure of spending time with them and Martha. Cassandra would return for stays at Manydown and Jane encouraged Martha to receive and accept invitations to stay with them too. After the fire of 'the engagement' was over and the ashes had cooled, it could be said that Jane's courage paid off; she would not have stood a chance of holding on to the happy routines of her life nor the closeness of the friendships of her heart had she chosen this former fate. Her resolve to draw Martha closer only grew from this point. Now Jane knew what she really wanted. Her sister and her friend, and to write – they were the air that she needed to breathe.

Only years later did Jane's descendants hint at other more substantially founded possibilities of a match; there were mere mentions really late in Cassandra's life and once long after her death, of perhaps an attachment to a Dr Blackall, whom Jane reportedly 'admired extremely and perhaps regretted parting' from, someone whom Cassandra met again years and years later and found 'very different from their youthful hero.'[28] There are also the mysterious musings of an elderly Cassandra one day to Caroline Austen, Jane and Martha's shared niece, of a man that Jane once met whilst holidaying in Devonshire or perhaps in Lyme. Caroline was intrigued; she had 'never heard her speak of anyone else with such admiration' and the 'charming man' it seems was undoubtedly well received by Jane and set on getting in touch again to pursue their 'mutual attachment', yet sadly he then died and all was lost.[29] Later memories being what they were, apt to be confusing, only partially recalled and lost in the mists of time, we can be sure that any elements of truth would have been gleefully examined and picked over by both Jane and Martha at the time.

No letters exist for this period but we know that Cassandra burned many, either on receipt or in later life, as other family members were also want to do and it was common practice for letter writers to ask their recipients to burn correspondence on reading it, so that it was not shared even with family or visiting neighbours. Who knows what tasty titbits were batted about between Jane and Martha whilst Jane was on holiday and they were separated? The younger generations of Jane and Martha's family certainly founded their memories of events on letters on the subject. Yet, their confidences remained safe with one another just as Jane's family were certain of one thing even between Cassandra and Jane – 'that a secret of their respective friends was never betrayed to each other.'[30] Jane did not hide from her lovely friend Martha who she held so closely in her plans for her life and in whose own love life she sought to meddle with such glee and longing. The matters of their romantic lives would have been shared with confidence in the full expectation and hope of consolation and good will from one heart to the other.

Chapter Five

Fashion Fun

When the two friends were not obsessing over the local gossip about who was to marry whom in their local community, they were very much concerned with all things fashion. Just like friends today they knew what suited the other, and what didn't. They loved to talk about the latest designs for hats, for sleeves and for dresses, and they knew what materials made the best-looking outfit. Jane discussed her apparel regularly with Martha and Cassandra, and they were always swapping patterns, ideas, materials and even clothes.

Right back in the dedication in *Frederic and Elfrida* we see Jane and Martha highly aware of the subtle qualities of and the particular type of elegance created by using the right type of muslin cloth. That Martha also finished off bits of sewing for Jane is a tribute to Martha's sewing abilities as Jane was known as a fine seamstress with particular skill at making neat work.

In November 1798, Jane was all in a stew and a bother about her latest gown. No matter how much she wished that 'such things were to be bought ready-made', this was not the case, and a great deal of thought and preparation was needed.[1] In the midst of daily life, she had still not made up her mind as to what she was going to wear exactly. With the upcoming christening for Mary and James's first son, James Edward, imminent, Jane relaxed in the thought of being able to talk to Martha about it there. She knew that her friend's skill was likely to get her out of a bind and she visibly lets out a sigh of relief, 'I shall see what she can do for me.'[2] It was not just the making up of the gown, she enjoyed and relied upon Martha's design suggestions too. She could be sure that Martha would know what to do, and she trusted her judgement completely. 'I want to have something suggested which will give me no trouble of thought or direction.'[3] She had high hopes and could rest her mind, assured by Martha's expertise and that she would surely know what to do for the best.

Jane admired Martha's taste and style and considered her friend not 'blowsey' as some have described her, but graceful (we know that she received all of that regular instruction in walking and dancing), slim and above all, elegant.[4] She enjoyed styling her hair similar to Martha's all fastened up in a particular way, stating that it made her 'very happy' to do so.[5] Her clothes, too, she fashioned after Martha's, which we know is the highest compliment between friends.[6] To copy and imitate someone's style and design of dress, coat or hat is a wonderful form of flattery. It shows an understanding of the distinct flavour of, and a correlation with, that person's taste. To adopt the same trend of a close pal is one of the core signs of friendship. Even in the modern era, you can often identify groups of friends by the way they dress, with each new 'look' seemingly a type of shared uniform.

The girls regularly relied upon one another for shopping when one or other of them was going to 'Town', be that London or even Alton, Basingstoke or Newbury. As neither of them really knew for sure when they would get the chance for shopping trips, they made certain that they kept one another abreast of opportunities to shop when the occasion arose. No mail order existed, of course, so they sort of made that happen for one another. It was just not possible to get some items in a regular hometown and some shops and businesses in the city grew a particular reputation for the range or quality of the items they supplied. We can just imagine the excitement and industry ahead of one of these trips, and how news like this would have been pounced upon by Jane and Martha – two young adult women with maybe not much money but certainly a strong desire to be wearing the right version of clothes, hats and stockings.

Martha was all modesty and would not have ordered her friends about on any account. She was one who would rather be leaned on herself than to oblige others to help her. However, she loved to make the most of the chance to have nice things from time to time and to get supplies of items that she could otherwise make herself, but that would not quite be the same as a treat made by the best quality manufacturers. She had a particular penchant for Steele's Lavender Water, although in typical Martha-style this was not simply something for her own personal use or benefit. Lavender water was known for its natural antiseptic qualities and for cleaning and caring for scratches, grazes and wounds. 'Trusting to my memory rather than her own, she [Martha] has nevertheless desired me to ask you to purchase for her two bottles of Steele's Lavender Water when you are in Town, provided you should go to the Shop on your own account; otherwise you may be sure that she would not have you recollect the request.'[7] It's so lovely to see Jane take this role of needed friend, of the one with the best memory and just the most helpful go-between. Jane obviously delighted in being the altogether 'sensible' one in this situation and we do actually believe that she is not joking when she takes pains to say that Martha does not want to put Cassandra to any trouble.

When Martha was away caring for her friends, elderly acquaintances or indeed their family's children, Jane would never hesitate to help her acquire things that she was needful of and was always eager to communicate on Martha's behalf or carry out one of Martha's good deeds in her stead. One cold and dark November she did just that, going shopping for a 'ready-made' cloak at Alton on her behalf. The very act of looking for something that she could buy off the shelf, which was very much the exception rather than the norm, was a sign of the immediacy of the need. Jane is anxious to reassure Martha that although there was nothing available 'Coleby has undertaken to supply one in a few days.'[8] Jane reassures her friend as to the quality of the material (woollen), the colour (grey) and the cost, and she takes care to even hope that her friend will like the appearance and the design that she has chosen. The materials and the time of year suggest this was needed very much for practical reasons. Martha was at Barton Court in Kintbury caring for a very sick old friend and thus she didn't have the time to attend to her own shopping needs. Luckily Jane did and she was the one supporting Martha; she had her back and her wellbeing in mind. When you are in need, a practical one who is willing to help you out is the best type of friend indeed.

Even so, Jane loved to exaggerate the importance of her shopping sprees on behalf of her family and friends, and teased Martha and Cassandra again and again on the 'imposition' that their requests put upon her 'very important' time. 'Martha and you were just in time with your commissions,' she writes in her jesting manner, knowing that this will raise a smile with Martha and a raise of her eyebrows, as well as a sense of gratitude and owing her friend one, 'for two o'clock on Monday was the last hour of my receiving them;–the office is now closed.'[9] This puts me in mind of the mother who says 'the kitchen is now closed,' stressing in a light-hearted way that the family or friend will now have to fend for themselves, that they have used up all available goodwill. It is certain that Jane knew that Martha would not take this in the wrong way but would understand and laugh at the tone. She would know to be straight there with her commendations and fulsome praise for Jane – to assign to her the allotted allocation of 'brownie points' or their equivalent in Martha and Jane's day.

On one such trip Jane jokes that she will probably not be able to 'execute Martha's commission' for basically she does not really like or enjoy shopping for shoes.[10] This open and honest semi-stubbornness makes us laugh. Perhaps Jane does not really trust her own power to make the right choice or perhaps she does not particularly savour the prospect of having to go and buy such an item. 'At any rate they shall all have flat heels,' she says with a touch of stamp-of-the-foot finality – possibly this is because she normally chose this sort of shoe, that they were the sort to match her taste as she only cared for something comfortable and practical, and that she had no confidence buying any other type – which might have been to the dismay of Martha.[11] Or it could be that Martha would only wear flat heels and Jane did not have the interest for such a purchase. Either way the practical dilemma and the teasing makes us laugh. The expectation and trust placed in Jane by Martha is one that anyone who has ever shopped for a friend can relate to.

Later in this letter, we learn that Jane relented and did put herself out to buy some shoes. But she has the last laugh, as she explains that sadly the shoes will be demoted as she cannot carry them home, for even though she had left lots of room in her bags and trunks for shopping, they have many other things to take back home that are more important and more of a priority. In other words, Jane amuses her reader, 'I must allow besides for my packing.'[12] We can just imagine Cassandra, her most sympathetic audience, laughing and rolling her eyes, 'Oh Jane!' as she then relays the news to an unsurprised Martha. I suspect that the shoes will have made it home – even if they were squashed up in the trunk somewhere – but the way that Jane makes her point to her friend, driving it home just how much she has gone out of her way for such an 'unreasonable' request makes us all laugh even today.

The shopping lists are truly quite revealing and we learn so much about Martha from them, and we also get an inside track into Jane's understanding of her friend's wishes. Jane would shop for all sorts of things for Martha; she made such a range of purchases, which she often brought back with her, either as we have seen in her own trunk or posted back home included alongside items for her family. As well as clothing and accessories, she also found foods or ingredients for Martha's recipes and household requirements. She also purchased sewing materials and lambswool. This is knowledge of a wide range of her friend's tastes and not to mention that Martha trusted her to purchase the 'exact' thing that she had in mind, an expectation only entrusted to the most reliable and effective shopper friend.

Moreover, Jane was also able to go 'offlist', something only ventured by the most confident of purchasers. On a visit to see her brother Henry in London with her niece Fanny, the daughter of her wealthy and highly favoured adopted brother Edward, the pair stopped by Birchall's music shop on Martha's behalf. They had popped in to enquire after a very specific book of sheet music by James Hook, *Guida di Musica, instruction for the Harpsichord or Pianoforte.*[13] Fanny is the one who very kindly entreats Birchall to supply her request and she attempts to acquire a second volume of the work for Martha, but is sadly informed to their surprise that there is none such in print. Jane steps in with confidence; secure in the knowledge of her friend she advises Fanny to choose a different composer's work of a similar type. 'I thought that she [Martha] would rather have something than not.'[14] As a pianoforte player herself she would have known what stage of difficulty and which genre of music Martha was apt to want to play. What is evident here is that she wants to spare her friend the disappointment of having no new music to play, when she knew that Martha was probably building her hopes up in anticipation of the purchase. After all, Birchall was a London city publisher and music seller, with a much wider range of sheet music available than in her locality – so to come back empty-handed would have felt like a loss and the well-judged replacement by a friend that knew both her skill and her tastes would have felt much more like a gain. Who knows, Jane may well have had her own eye on the pieces and been thinking that in a worst-case scenario, she would enjoy playing them herself.

In every shopping expedition Jane would always send back news of each purchase and an itemised estimation or confirmation of the bill to be paid back to her. She was so sweet and so open about this, it would seem that the two obviously had an agreement on price and that they would each be happily and independently footing their own bills. The hint is always there in these remarks that the price was considered the best available in the moment and also constituted value for money. In the purchases made in Martha's absence, Jane reveals that she knew what would be seen as an acceptable price to Martha, perhaps even within a budget that they had agreed together beforehand. When Jane once goes out on a limb and buys a pair of gloves for herself that even she thinks are cheap at 'four shillings,' she knows that this will seem an unreliable purchase in everybody else's eyes and can just imagine Martha and Cassandra 'hoping and predicting that they cannot be good for anything.'[15]

Jane was what we would think of now as a particularly savvy shopper. She was not one to rush a purchase, carefully perusing all the options available. She was aware of this herself and was grateful when others indulged her as her remarks reveal, 'We must have been 3 qtrs. of an hour at Grafton House, Edward sitting by all the time with wonderful patience.'[16] She would regularly talk about where she could buy the best gauzes at the best prices on her visits to 'Town' or to Bath and whose advice she had been able to plumb the depths of in hunting out her bargains or in copying their fashion choices. She was terribly clear if something was well-priced or not and she loved a bargain: 'the edging there is very cheap,' and 'I had no difficulty in getting a muslin veil for half a guinea.' She felt on top of the world when she got value for money and bottom of the heap when she didn't: 'the muslin was thick, dirty and ragged.'[17] The shops in Basingstoke, for example, did not always live up to her standards and she despaired that she could not obtain the quality that she was looking for.

Jane had her finger on the fashion pulse and noticed even the slightest changes in trends, realising with clinical precision what type of black gauze cloaks 'are' worn and what the most attractive and worthy bonnets were being made of. The winds of fashion change were foremost in her young mind. She would not buy or wear things that would be deemed unflattering or viewed in an unfavourable way, and she was highly conscious of the messages that wearing a certain something, a certain way would send. Jane had an eye for observing the details and nuances of the latest in what to wear and what not to wear, and she readily kept Martha updated on her opinions. She knew what was decidedly out of fashion and noticed the subtle twists and turns of what was on the cusp of coming into fashion amongst women of their age and class. She commented regularly and astutely and sometimes acerbically about petticoats being short or long and how often they were flounced, or whether sleeves were now to be worn full or long. She could be all caught up in her knowledge of the style of hat to be worn and the advantages of adornments and attachments, including ribbon as an accessory and whether fruit was still a much better choice than flowers as ornamentation on hats.

All the while, she was quick to report back to Martha on her reactions to these fashions she was witness to. 'I am amused by the present style of female dress,' she once wrote from London. She spotted trends that appeared universal, 'It seems to me a more marked change than one has lately seen,' and she had a bank of knowledge that she collected and referenced in order to share this information with her friend.[18] With Martha, as with her letters to her sister, Jane loved to share her opinions on people's dress sense and she did not hold back in mocking any ghastly choices or in letting Martha know what she really thought, and how she had scoffed at what she had seen: 'The coloured petticoats with braces over the white spencer and enormous bonnets upon the full stretch, are quite entertaining.'[19] She and Martha would also observe individual people and pick over their choice of outfits together. If they found themselves caught at a rather boring or dreary social occasion, they would amuse themselves by analysing their hostess's dress and 'estimating her Lace and her Muslin,' not always unkindly but being frank with each other about what they liked and didn't like.[20] A fashion faux pas would not have escaped their notice.

Fashion was a great tool for teasing her friend too. Jane once wrote to Martha that the cost of opening and reading her letter might be more than she had bargained for, as given that the 3d she had spent on the receipt of it (for postage was paid by the addressee and not the sender of the letter), she would now have less to spend on the making up of her gown. We can almost hear Jane's cheeky squeals of delight at causing Martha's new dress, for the Hurstbourne Ball no less, to be not quite as good as it might have been. We can imagine the sucking in of air and the slight shake of the head that Martha may have given as the realisation dawned of Jane's naughty little comment. As she wrote Jane squirmed in amusement at the reckoning that she was 'lessening the elegance' of Martha's outfit – what a shameless friend she was. What a joke![21] In reality it may not have made any difference to Martha, who may have sought to save money elsewhere, or who may have already had everything she needed for her outfit. Such a prominent and witty remark at the start of the correspondence raises a smile. Jane was straight in there with a prod and a poke – their friendship easy and light, and remarks made in their habitual tone. In reality the letter was a bit of light relief for Jane, having just had the horror of the gale destroying the woodland that surrounded her Steventon home.

When it came to choosing the design of their own outfits, Jane loved to tease Martha about when she was willing 'to share or not to share' her ideas with her – hinting that a sense of one-upmanship was all the better for her. Jane would draw and sketch the patterns of the lace she was buying in her letters. When Cassandra had dared to share the pattern of their caps with Martha, Jane gently chastised her, tutting loudly and dramatically in her letter, 'Some prevailing wish is necessary to the animation of everybody's mind.' She had clearly wanted to leave Martha hankering and in the dark over how to get the same sought-after look that she so admired. Jane was laughing that Martha would now come up with some other wish for news and insider information 'which will not probably be half so innocent.'[22] When Martha borrows one of Jane's caps, as Jane herself did on occasion from her sister, Jane cannot help herself. 'I am glad she likes my cap so well,' she gently jokes, teasing Martha for perhaps using it without prior permission. She then gives the classic 'I never really liked it anyway' response, that is absolutely hilarious in the light of her being at the very well-to-do Godmersham estate at the time: 'I assure you my old one looked so smart yesterday that I was asked two or three times… whether it was not my new one.'[23] All this leaves us highly amused that the pair did so like to have the other note the impact of their new fashion ideas, and that they were always trying to steal fashion secrets from each other and spark a slight note of envy in the other as friends are prone to do. After all, we all want to be noticed and we all want to look our best.

For all her teasing, the opinions of her nearest and dearest mattered to Jane, who was always collecting and reporting back on what different members of the family thought of her gowns. Jane loved to evoke opinions about her own style choices and she always awaited the reaction of her audience – her mother's disapproval of her 'ugly' gown was greeted with private joy and she revelled in Martha and Cassandra's comments on her lace choice quite sparking and preening herself in the light of their interest. 'I am very glad you liked my lace, & so are you & so is Martha–& we are all glad together'; it's the lazy joy of it all – the freedom Jane is enjoying in talking about such frivolous and fun matters which lighten the load and make them all giggle.[24]

However, it was Martha's views on what suited Jane or not that truly held sway with Jane, and she felt assured that her sister could also be persuaded to fall into step with them too. She took it that if Martha liked something then this would be enough evidence for Cassandra to like it. 'She is pleased with my gown, and particularly bids me say that if you could see me in it for five minutes, she is sure you would be eager to make up your own.'[25] It is difficult to believe if Martha really did say these words, or if it is Jane putting them into her mouth in order to persuade and lever Cassandra into believing how lovely her gown is, and persuading her to accept it as beautiful and to be admired, perhaps even to be envied. But it's clear that they both had an understanding that Martha's judgement was not something to be played with – if she hadn't liked it, she would have said so – and it was not worth challenging Martha's opinion because it would stand tall. Perhaps Jane is also seeking to justify an extravagance to herself, in a sort of 'she made me get it' way. Almost in the same breath, Jane seems most blatantly to be fishing for a cheeky compliment and approbation. 'I have been obliged to mention this but have not failed to blush the whole time of my writing it'; here Jane paints herself as a totally modest, purely passive bystander, a passer-on of the comments, purely in the name of friendly communication. The humour implied by the tone is so charming that Jane uses Martha and the reputation she enjoyed between the three friends, and is a testimony to the high esteem in which they held her sensible and good opinion and how much Jane actually relied on her.

In all of her relating about clothes and fashion we get to know an entirely different view of Jane. We have a window into her world, a portal back in time to a stage of her life that generations of relations, looking back and describing her, like her brother Henry simply did not and could not have. Martha's conversation with Jane and the fragmentary scraps and traces we have of them, when pieced together, stand in contrast to Henry or her nephew James Edward's recollections. These were clouded and shrouded in the family view of her reputation as a 'domesticated middle-aged maiden aunt' and by the blinkers placed on their relationships with Jane as a brother, or a young child relative and not as a female best friend.[26] Martha was very much in the mix with Jane in her 'younger days' and her conversations reflect and refract her back to us. Stood alongside Martha looking into the dressing room mirror at this image of a young, forthright and happily opinionated woman, we see an entirely different Jane Austen to the one that they did.

Chapter Six

Fun and Frolics – Out and About

In line with many of the ladies of their Hampshire circle, both young and old, Jane and Martha loved nothing better than getting dressed up and heading on out to a ball. As we have learnt, they planned their outfits in meticulous detail, nearly boring themselves and everyone else to death in the process. It would never do to be seen out in the wrong thing! But the going out and the being seen? Where did that all take place? The assemblies that they enjoyed dressing up for were held in a number of different venues. Martha and Mary frequented the Newbury balls when they were living at Enborne and Ibthorpe, their network of associations stretching out into that neck of the woods. Jane never really ventured that way, and besides if they were populated by the likes of the Debaries we will understand her unwillingness to go there.

But trotting out with Martha to attend balls at Basingstoke assembly rooms or privately at their friends' houses was a highlight of Jane's youth. With Martha ten years older, it is possible that Mrs Austen saw Martha in some sort of chaperone role, a protector of the virtues of the young Jane, but she often went in this capacity herself. Mrs Austen was a shrewd observer of who was attending and with whom – so much so that Jane often left it to her to describe the list of attendees and the details of the dances. Often Cassandra was away caring for her young nieces and nephews at Godmersham in Kent and if there were any balls to be had there, she would attend those. It would often be Martha and Jane against the world, with Jane relaying their fun back to her sister. Jane saw herself and Martha as going out as equals, dead set on enjoying fun and japes together. She really enjoyed dancing and Martha was so good at it that she was proud to be seen with her, knowing that she would keep her card of dances full for the entirety of the evening.

These nights were long affairs, often not ending until the early hours of the morning and Jane and Martha stayed right until the end. One night they tumbled back from a ball at Kempshott Park, on the outskirts of Basingstoke, to the little parsonage at Deane. Jane savoured relaying the audacious news of her not returning home that night or the next. Instead she writes that 'Martha kindly made room for me in her bed.'[1] You can almost feel Jane wriggling with excitement at the rebelliousness of it all. No decorous staying over in a properly made up guest room, but huddled up with her best friend, sharing all the girly gossip of the night and poring over the details of all they had seen and observed, complete with all their very own opinions on each and every person subjected to their steely eyes. Worse, they were not even in Martha's formal bed, but a 'shut-up one', a sort of put-me-up, temporary bed – and not just in a room of their own either, but in the 'New nursery'; baby James Edward was only 8 weeks old. And what other news is to come! The poor nurse and the child were, it seems, ousted, first for Martha, and then for them both – to the floor! 'There we all were in some confusion and great comfort,' Jane daringly informs her sister.[2] We can once again see Cassandra staring in some horror at the letters on the page, and shaking her head in disbelief at Jane and Martha's cheeky purloining of the poor nurse and baby's one chance at some precious sleep. Jane's frothing and bubbling joy continues to spill out and the tale spins further – for we learn 'the bed did exceedingly well for us, both to lie awake in and talk till two o'clock, and to sleep in the rest of the night.'[3] These two giddy friends had a wonderful sleep-over, it seems – all that was missing was the midnight feast. Jane was full of happiness and evenings like these filled her with love for her friend. As they reflected on a decade of friendship together, Jane loved Martha more than she ever had before and their attachment to one another was growing with each passing year. Evenings out together like this gave Jane the space to escape and to live a little, to push back the boundaries of her life at home, to enjoy a sense of freedom and hope, to dance and be merry, and to truly act her age. Once again it was Martha that helped her to reach out and to truly be herself.

Martha's fondness for balls drew Jane into them more and more; her enthusiasm for them was well-known and if not infectious, certainly a reason for Jane to keep abreast of the balls available and to chat with Martha about them. On one occasion, just before Martha's thirty-fifth birthday, she accepted her sister Mary's invitation to Lord Portsmouth's Ball. He held a ball annually at Hurstbourne Park on the anniversary of the Earl of Portsmouth's marriage with his first wife.[4] He had once briefly been a pupil at Jane's father's boarding school, but a sickly and unsettled pupil whose unusual needs required perhaps more specialist teaching and support; he had been withdrawn. The family link with the Austens was therefore long-established and thus the verbal invitation handed to Mrs James Austen – a socialite in the area herself by now, who both dined out and hosted dinner parties on a very regular basis – is no surprise. He had not yet sent out the official invitation card, but Jane knew this to be nothing of importance to Martha, for any sniff of a ball and she would be there, it seems. Jane also jokes that conversely the ball would now be forced to go ahead with or without formal invitations. 'That does not signify,' she says adamantly and decidedly, 'Martha comes, and a Ball there must be.'[5] The certainty and laughter in her tone speaks of the sheer joy Jane held in her heart and that she saw in the light of her friend's enjoyment.

In lovingly mocking her friend's reputation and penchant for a ball, we catch the satisfaction it gives Jane to know that her friend shall be so happy again, dancing the night away. In fact, when the invitations did arrive Jane was quick to pass on the news to Martha, though intriguingly she says that 'very curiously are they worded'.[6] How we wish that we could see them now and know what Jane meant. There must have been some aspect of their joint knowledge of the Earl and his family that would have got their antennae going. The only tinge of sadness, the slight sound of disappointment in the whole affair, is the faint feeling of a stamping of a foot in her passing comment: 'I think it will be too early in her Mother's absence for me to return with her.'[7] How Jane would have loved the chance to have linked up after the ball for another girls' night in.

The prospect of a ball therefore was always a happy subject to discuss, and it pleased Jane and Martha so much, just to have them to look forward to. 'I wish you a very pleasant ball on Thursday, and myself another, and Mary and Martha a third, but they will not have theirs till Friday,' she relays to Cassandra gleefully.[8] It seems to us as readers now as if she is almost clapping her hands and hinting at a little mischief in their plans. Jane would ensure that if she or Martha were not attending, then her 'Myrmidons', her spies, either friends, her sister or her mother would be in position to report back *all* the details.[9] Thanking Cassandra for news, she was in full examination and interrogation mode: 'It gives us great pleasure to know that the Chilham Ball was so agreeable. Why did you dance four dances with so stupid a man?' Jane cannot help but enquire but rounds off the conversation with, 'Martha left you her best love,' confirming to us that they had both enjoyed the communication most thoroughly.[10]

Whatever age or stage of life they were to be in, both women remained devoted to the idea of dancing and though the invitations dwindled in time and they were no longer perhaps the belle of the ball, or were not bent on finding a beau – they still retained their enthusiasm and enjoyment of this magnificent social event. Years later when Jane was in her early thirties, the opportunity arose to revive this passion and partake in a round of balls. Jane was certainly up for the challenge and relished the thought of taking in a series of events, adding them to her diary and getting her fill, making the most of the unexpected season of opportunities. The prospect of a whole evening partying like they used to stirred up a whiff of nostalgia for Jane and her misspent youth with Martha at balls. She wrote back to her sister about one of the dates she had lined up, a ball at the Dolphin Hotel in Southampton on 6 December 1808. The ball was 'rather more amusing than I expected, Martha [who was now 43] liked it very much,' she writes in an understated but totally emphatic way.[11] Sometimes less is more. She knew that Cassandra would interpret the 'enough said' moment, and that her short but sweet absence of effusion of words would conjure up all the happy news she had had of Jane and Martha's ball experiences in the past. She could rely on Cassandra's bank of memories of the pair. They had managed not to even go out until quite late: 'It was past nine before we were sent for,' she says of the carriage that would take them to the event, 'Not twelve when we returned.'[12] The hint here being that they lasted the night, getting home quite late enough for their age, and at a suitably late hour, just like they had in the good old days when they had danced in the very same room, fifteen years earlier for Jane's eighteenth birthday. Jane was impressed with their resilience and stamina, celebrating and boasting happily about the fact that she 'did not gape until the last quarter of an hour.'[13]

Jane had enjoyed reminiscing and remembering back to the happy days of yore when she and Martha used to step out all the time. 'I thought it all over,' she said. In that pause there would have been a wonderful heart-warming moment for Jane, where her and Martha's friendship welled up in her mind filling it with memories and images from the past. It had felt a little odd doing things at her current age that she associated with her younger self, but yet she 'felt with thankfulness that she was quite as happy now as then.'[14] How wonderful then that friendship and fun had encapsulated a moment of gratitude; through the lens of her dancing friendship with Martha, Jane was able to view the arc of her life so far, to feel in touch with her authentic self and to return from a moment of reflection with happy feelings of gratitude and stability.

In a nod to their present age, however, Jane's next piece of information related to the evening is very precious, giving us a little insight into what they enjoyed doing together in their third decade of friendship. Quite sweetly and in the spirit of relaxation, giving all due regard to the requirement for getting their breath back, Jane and Martha had paid 'an additional shilling for tea, which we took as we chose in an adjoining, and very comfortable room.'[15] Don't we just love this. Jane and Martha ended their evening putting their feet up in a quieter, calmer room next door – with the strains of music and dancing in their ears, they could sit down, kick off their little shoes under their dresses and perhaps give them a welcome rub whilst taking a cup of restorative tea. At other balls around this time, Jane jokes that she could have kept going all night if only she had wanted to. There is a time for dancing and a time for stopping, and a joy in both of similar proportions it would seem.

The nights were not solely spent in each other's own company though. They may not have been among the young eligible set, but even years later they were not wallflowers or at the 'aunts by the fire sipping wine' stage just yet. Jane was asked to dance that night by a gentleman that she (and Cass) had once met. She had been drawn to this acquaintance with whom she was not on any first-name terms and whom she knew only by sight, on account of his 'black eyes'.[16] He was not a native Englishman, with those eyes perhaps Hispanic, though we don't learn which nationality he was. Sadly, although Jane enjoyed the frisson of being asked to dance, all other flirtations stopped right there. Martha, it seems, had no such invitation or we can be certain that Jane would have teased her mercilessly and would have 'revealed all' of any occurrence or interest to Cassandra. Jane always hoped to pique Cassandra's interest with news of her and Martha's shenanigans at balls.

The pair found many other activities to help while away the time. Going to the theatre remained a much more important pastime to Jane than to Martha. Jane had a detailed knowledge of plays dating back to the extensive reading she was able to undertake as a child in her father, Rev George Austen's library. Her love of the theatre as an adult extended to detailed knowledge of the actors, both those who were up-and-coming and the glorified and celebrated few. Martha, however, did not have the same level of interest, perhaps due to the more practical and religious-based format of her early education. Jane tried to drag her off to the theatre, plotting to get Henry to take them both when he was on a visit. 'Martha ought to see the inside of the Theatre...& I think she will hardly wish to take a second view.'[17] Perhaps Martha really was reluctant to go and Jane believed that she was not going to be lucky to be able to whet her appetite enough to go once, let alone twice, or it could have been that the theatre itself or the play that was currently being shown was not one that Jane believed really came up to scratch. She had very high personal standards as to what made a successful evening of dramatic entertainment, and we can be sure that she had her own views on the quality of the actors, their rendition of the script and even down to such details as the staging and scenery being offered up.

What Martha and Jane loved to do more than anything together was to get out of the house and go walking. They were insatiable and their stamina knew no end, both in their younger years, when they were their sprightly selves and later in their adult life together. We know that the happy event of living so near each other at Deane and Steventon meant the pair walked out almost daily to see each other, beating a short cut path that they left well-trodden over the three years over the brow of the hill and across the fields to each other's homes. Fast-forward a few years and on a visit to Martha at Ibthorpe House, Jane gives the game away as to the extent of their passion for walking. 'It is too dirty even for such desperate walkers as Martha and I.'[18] It had to be extreme weather conditions to put these too off from putting their boots on and getting out in the fresh air. It is difficult and perhaps too dangerous to draw lines from Jane and Martha's friendship into Jane's novels, but the image of Marianne Dashwood tramping out in the terrible weather in a lament to her lost love Willoughby, leading to her rescue from a near-death experience by the hasty and timely actions of Colonel Brandon can perhaps bring to mind the type of weather Jane might imagine as putting even her and Martha off their beloved walks.

Lizzy Bennet too, scrambling over the fields in the storm, so desperate to get to her sister Jane and enquire as to her health, puts us in mind of Jane and Martha's experience of walking in all weathers. The even better moment where Lizzy braves the drawing room and the shocked examination and scrutiny of the Bingleys, Mrs Hurst and Mr Darcy is a moment of joyous rebelliousness that perhaps Jane and Martha themselves enjoyed. Getting one's petticoats utterly filthy in the process of experiencing the joy, the freedom of being out of the house and away from prying eyes, ears and expectations was a price she and Martha had delighted in paying on many an occasion. Could it have been the Misses Debary that she had in mind as the foolish and haughty, frivolous and judgemental onlookers? It's a thought. Jane certainly used the weather to hope to persuade Martha that a return visit to these, *her* friends, normally expected and all part of the etiquette of the country set, was impossible and oh, so sadly, out of the question. We can just see Jane trying it on with a downcast eye and a sly wink at her friend. Her letter to Cassandra on a day of dire weather gives her away, 'Three of the Miss Debaries called here' (Jane always insisted on referencing that these annoying friends of Martha's seemed to endlessly multiply). 'You know it is not an uncommon circumstance in this parish to have the road from Ibthorpe to the Parsonage much dirtier and more impracticable for walking than the road from the Parsonage to Ibthorpe.'[19] (Cough, cough.) Normally nothing could separate Jane and Martha from their walk. Here she is oh, so cheekily hiding behind a veil of playful politeness and quite literally dragging her feet about going out to visit them.

As soon as the sun was out, Jane and Martha would capitalise on the opportunity. On one such 'Prince of days' Thursday, 17 November 1808, a beautiful break in the grim November grey, 'a soft bright day with a brisk wind,' Martha and Jane break out for a walk, enjoying bumping into acquaintances in the neighbourhood and not wanting the moment to end. So much so that they stayed out and kept on walking and walking, 'Martha and I did not know how to turn back.'[20]

A month later in the grip of December and only three days after they had stayed out till late at the ball in Southampton, Martha and Jane were at their walking lark again. 'Martha and I made use of the very favourable state of yesterday for walking.'[21] It seems that this activity invigorated them and through the physical act of exertion, they lifted their own spirits. They certainly demonstrate stamina and good health with an appetite for being out and about for they did not stop after visiting a neighbour, but carried on with a trip on the local ferry extending their outing and then returned back via this long diversion to their lodgings by foot 'up and over the bridge' and apparently 'were scarcely at all fatigued.'[22]

These walks were not at all sombre affairs, filled with long silences and partaken only to benefit one's body from the activity and to give the soul a chance to 'look upon verdure.'[23] No, there was such a lot of talking and banter, and jokes and gossip and storytelling about their neighbours and family, near and far. One wintry December, Jane and Martha were once again chomping at the bit to get out and stretch their legs in a nice long stroll and their tongues in a nice long conversation: 'Martha has promised to return with me, & our plan is to have a nice black frost for walking to Whitchurch,' a local village of some distance, about five or so miles as the crow flies.[24] A black frost was one that blackened or killed plants but was not associated with snow or any frozen dew, hence no allusion to white frosting. It would have been a cold and reviving air to say the least, and hard ground for stamping out on in search of adventure, yet possibly slippery underfoot, thus planting the idea in Cassandra's head of them squirming about and trying to keep on their feet as they set off at a pace together. This was a walk sure to bring a ruddiness to their cheeks. But Jane is not speaking in all seriousness: '& there throw ourselves into a post chaise, one upon the other, our heads hanging out at one door, & our feet at the opposite.'[25] She continues – in other words 'we have been going stir crazy indoors all cooped up because of the winter weather and we can't wait to be let loose.'

What a wonderful image, we can just hear them laughing hysterically together. This was Martha and Jane – not as they would have been seen in the parlour or about their duties – but when they were just two friends together throwing duty, quite literally, to the wind, especially in their imaginations. Others see this too and suggest that such funny detail rivals anything in her own *Love and Freindship* [sic] and it's true that we can imagine this scene as something being straight out of one of her funny and exaggerated stories of the *Juvenilia*, or even one of the scenes with Lydia in *Pride and Prejudice* or a wild and happy Willoughby and Marianne in *Sense and Sensibility*.[26] Jane firmly associated this sense of humour and freedom of spirit with Martha. Her writing comes alive and the vivacity of the moment imprints itself upon our mind's eye. She associated Martha so strongly with this untamed part of herself, maybe it was Martha who enabled this side of her to feel free and to escape onto the page. It truly was a 'gaiety nourished' by Martha, and Jane felt it and treasured it, not just back when she was a young girl but even over a decade later, and in some measure throughout her life and into her later adult years.[27]

Chapter Seven

Home Sweet Home

A sure sign of how much a friend means to you is how it feels when you are apart. Whenever Jane and Martha were separated, and balls and long walks were put on the back burner for a while, as when Martha was visiting friends somewhere, Jane mentioned her non-stop in her conversations with Cassandra, unable to keep herself from wondering how all was going with her friend. Absence definitely made her heart grow fonder and she liked to know exactly what Martha was doing, and that things were going well with her.

The converse was also true, and Jane liked to let Martha know all the ins and outs of what she herself was up to when she was away, whether she was in Weymouth, Lyme, Bath or Southampton; at Godmersham in Kent with her brother Edward; or on other family visits to places such as Stoneleigh visiting her uncle and aunt. She would count the number of days that she had been away and give Martha an update on her itinerary including, of course, her opinions on the subject. The only thing that she did not mind missing Martha for was the chance to attend a ball, but more often than not, although she worked hard to be happy, nevertheless she could reveal herself to Martha to be a little bored without her friend there:

> I shall have spent my 12 days here very pleasantly, but with not much to tell of them; two or three very little dinner-parties at home, some delightful drives in the curricle and quiet tea-drinking with the Tilsons, has been the sum of my doings. I have seen no old acquaintance I think, but Mr Hampson.[1]

Jane's lack of excitement and the inferred dull comparison of the time she is experiencing with what she and Martha would have classed as a good time is telling. Sometimes an adjective or two can convey such a lot between friends and reading between the lines, Martha would have been sure to pick up on the vibe of Jane's stay and her tinge of disappointment.

Martha and Jane now had a shared history of friends, places and memories, and Jane was as aware of Martha's friends as she was hers. Jane would often pass on her compliments and good wishes to people that Martha was staying with and whilst she was away from Martha, she would pass on to her even private family news, such as the birth of a new niece or nephew.

Jane preferred the idea of hosting Martha to visiting extended family. She felt the pull of the obligatory vacation, the seemingly endless round of duty-bound visits to different members of her mother's branch of the family that constituted their summer holidays. 'I should like to make a compromise with Adlestrop, Harden and Bookham that Martha's spending the summer at Steventon should be considered as our respective visits to them all.'[2] In their associating with Martha, they could technically class themselves as engaged in hosting a guest and this would be a legitimate rebuff to any invitations or expectations from other quarters. Jane must have held some hope somewhere of persuading her mother, but the request put to Cassandra was more in vain and iced with pleading desperation. It was Martha who she wanted to spend the lovely long summer ahead with and Martha who filled her thoughts when the prospect of the warm season stretched ahead of her.

When the chance came to meet up, the moment had to be seized. The pair had to rely so often on transport being provided and they had to strike whilst the iron was hot. One early summer in May, Jane was set on inviting Miss Anne Sharp to be part of a get-together – the one-time governess to Edward and Elizabeth (Austen) Knight's children. 'If you and Martha do not dislike the plan… the opportunity… will be excellent. I shall write to Martha by this post, & if neither you nor she make any objection to my proposal, I shall make the invitation directly.'[3] Jane was the catalyst for many of the meetings to take place and she had a brilliant mind for seeing how a plan might come together, matching up this ride with that person and connecting up this person's journey with someone else's in the most profitable and efficient way. She was often raising schemes and suggesting ways to meet up. Jane and Martha were not ones to be easily thwarted in their plans to be together as 'agreeable inmates' and if there was a hint of a chance of being together, they would seize the day.[4] 'Do not let the Lloyds go on any account before I return,' she desperately instructs Cassandra.[5] Sometimes they had to contend with harsh winter weather, logistics or Martha's other duties, but they worked at it, because making it happen was a primary objective for them both.

What they really liked best of all was to be at home together in one of their houses. If Cassandra could be there too then it was all the better, 'a snug fortnight' in Jane's opinion.[6] Jane looked forward to these planned visits with her friend in the same way that she longed for her sister to return to the fold. 'I shall be very glad to see you at home again, and then if we can get Martha and shirk…who will be so happy as we?'[7] Planning her next visit to Martha was always uppermost in her mind, especially in their younger days. 'I think of going to Ibthorpe in about a fortnight'[8], 'Martha has as good as promised to come to us again in March,' and 'Martha desires her best Love and says a great many kind things about spending some time with you in March and depending on a large return from us both in the Autumn.'[9]

The anticipation, the actual experience of a visit and the recalling of it afterwards brings happiness and cements strong social bonds. Looking forward to being together, as well as the opportunity to take a break from certain people or duties, brought real happiness to them both. Martha coming meant a little light relief for Jane as she was great company and she also brought news. 'I am forced to be abusive for want of subject, having really nothing to say. When Martha comes, she will supply me with matter.'[10] Jane wrote fulsome acceptances to Martha's invitations, just as in the over-written and deliberately decorated sentences of her dedication to Martha in the *Juvenilia*. The playing with the formal language of an RSVP was aimed at trying to prod Martha into smiling and joining in. Jane used joky repetitions of her phrases, her prose acting in the same way as tickling a small child in the ribs or under the arms might.

'You are very good in wishing to see me at Ibthorpe so soon, & I am equally good in wishing to come to you; I believe our Merit in that respect is much upon a par, our self-denial mutually strong.'[11] The emphasis here on their shared humility, the ironic, irreverent reverence of their conduct in the matter, their 'saintly' behaviour and the understanding that this was, in fact, no hardship at all for them, no cross to bear, makes for a very funny note and one that underscored just how very much they were looking forward to being together and how much Jane wanted to make it happen.

Jane often had another scheme or plan afoot to lay out before Martha so that they got to make the most out of any visit. On one occasion she wrote that she wanted to enjoy the 'pleasure' of seeing Martha's mother. Such propriety and good manners in a visitor, and what a lovely thing to write in a letter, and yet Martha would have perceived an underlying, ulterior motive in Jane's words. Her agenda, she finally revealed to Martha, letting her in on the secret; 'that I may have a better chance of bringing you back with me.'[12] Jane would cajole and work on Martha so that she too would come on board, writing again and again about their ideas and suggestions 'till we have tired ourselves with the very idea of my visit, before my visit begins.'[13] We might call this type of friend the Alpha friend or simply 'the bossy one'. She is confident that Martha will be up for accepting her idea. The older years on Martha's side helped in this respect. One can almost imagine the older cat or dog being poked at by the younger kitten or pup, sitting quietly to one side, not bothered by the pesky fretting of the younger one. 'Your promise in my favour was not quite absolute, but if your Will is not perverse, You and I will do all in our power to overcome your scruples of conscience.'[14] Martha may have felt a duty of care to her own mother and their home, and may not have wanted to or felt that she could freely leave. Jane's gentle teasing makes its point but in such a playful way that Martha could not and would not have been offended. The poking of fun at her friend Martha's values and the tenets of her beliefs is an easy target as Martha was so conscientious in what she saw as her Christian duty; but it's also so endearing for don't we just love to tease those parts of our loved ones that we adore the most and for which they are the most notorious.

Jane did so love to stay at Martha's. It gave her the opportunity to tease the garrulous Mrs Stent, out of earshot and in her letters to Cassandra, of course, and no doubt via side comments, quiet gestures and whispers to Martha too. Martha's mother's housekeeper was a little deaf but loved to talk. 'Mrs Stent gives us quite as much of her Company as we wish for, & rather more than she used to do.'[15] The familiarity and routine of the wonderful Mrs Stent adding her two penneth shows just how happy and accustomed Jane was to spending so many leisurely hours in and about Martha's family home. It was so nice just to spend prolonged time in each other's company again. 'I have the pleasure of thinking myself a very welcome Guest, & the pleasure of spending my time very pleasantly,' Jane wrote to reassure Cassandra that she had settled in on one of her visits to Martha at Ibthorpe.[16] The over-exaggeration of the 'pleasantness' of it all, rubbing it in just enough to let Cassandra know that she was having a great time, and although *of course* she would be behaving herself and keeping her good manners, she was happy to hold back with a little hint of glee in her voice again too. Goodness, what on earth would Cassandra have been imagining them getting up to. Jane would have hoped that she imagined away, imagining all sorts of mischief.

In reality their tastes were simple and Jane loved to 'while away the evening chatting with Martha.'[17] They would talk about whatever topics took their fancy, without any interruption or consideration of others who might be listening. In terms of topics of conversation, it would be wrong to assume or to infer that they were simply trivial matters or frivolous, light-hearted topics. Jane would open her heart *and* her mind to Martha. Jane's letters to Martha give us an insight into what they liked to discuss. In them she could flit from topic to topic in brief one-liners, as she was wont to do, knowing that Martha would keep up with her pace and the patterns of her thoughts, just as they would do if they were face to face. Jane could raise and then drop many different and entirely unrelated themes and references in blunt and contrasted juxtaposition to one another, including her own family news, personal enquiries, matters of fashion and also politics and art. 'I have seen West's famous painting and prefer it to anything of the kind I ever saw before. I do not know that it is reckoned superior to his "Healing in the Temple," but it has gratified me much more and indeed is the first presentation of our saviour which ever at all contented me. "His Rejection by the Elders", is the subject. I want to have you and Cassandra see it.'[18] Here Jane first bubbles up with the pleasure she has had in seeing a particular artist's latest painting and she just has to share with Martha that a) she has been to see it and b) what she thought of it. To have someone who she could share that opinion with doubled her joy of the painting. She offers her opinion on it, contrasting it with that of a previous painting and the art critics' and public's conjectured opinion. Jane admits to this being her absolute favourite of this type of picture, which tells us that Martha would have known her other preferences and would now have understood Jane's re-ranking of her likes and loves in the art world.

Martha's religious faith was the cornerstone of her life and this particular painting and Jane's personal comments upon it would have meant so much to her, more, say, than a painting of fruit or a country scene. We are to understand, it seems, that Martha's knowledge of the painting was mutual and matched Jane's as she does not describe the picture but assumes that Martha knows the one to which she is referring. That Jane gives to Martha her heartfelt and personal response to the painting of '*our* Saviour' is a very intimate sharing between the two and shows just how close they were on this matter as in others. These comments reveal an area of their personal and spiritual lives that really mattered to them both individually. For Jane to say to Martha that the image 'contented her', in other words it satisfied her, and she felt it to be such a representation as met with and rested with her view so well that it seemed to therefore elevate the painting for her, in her regard, was a sharing of something deep and meaningful from Jane with her friend. To share views relating to such foundational touchstones of our own lives is a true sign of the closest of friendships. We do not let just anyone in to our own 'holy of holies.' When it comes to the things that soften our hearts the most, we cannot share our thoughts with any other than our most trusted. Usually for Jane, this would mean a particular family member, yet Jane is dying to tell Martha about this precious painting

– Jane loved it and she knew that Martha would – you can feel her urgency and determination for Martha and her beloved Cassandra to see it too.

Yet in practically the next breath Jane jumps ship and brings Martha other news that rises to the surface of her mind. With such a high tempo change from topic to topic, we understand a sort of shorthand between the two. They had such a shared vocabulary and memory together that succinct comments and momentary ponderings were more than enough. They could cover a lot of ground together. Like a stream of consciousness coming through her pen, the words flowed like a river touching different stones, upturning them in its wake. Martha was a friend with whom Jane could share anything, in any form, and the letter implies that Martha was completely familiar with the way that Jane's brain worked.

This was how Martha was served Jane's brother, Henry's view 'and the view of those he mixed with, of Politics.'[19] Martha, we learn, was not unaware then of current affairs and more able than some might think to have a view herself and to want to learn more of other's opinions, especially ones from people that she and Jane held so dear and in such high esteem. The subject matter was not easy to hear either, but rather shocking and brutal in its forecast. Jane was able to talk about all things with Martha, even those that were 'not chearful'. Jane moves on and spells out the topic and the severity of the concerns of Henry and his banker friends 'with regard to an American war I mean; they consider it as certain, and as what is to ruin us.'[20] For two women not particularly of much independent means, and totally reliant on the rule and whim of the men around them in matters domestic as well as State, this must have been concerning news. 'The Americans cannot be conquered... We are to make them good sailors and soldiers and gain nothing ourselves.'[21] This emotionally charged comment has the ring of Jane's own take on the matter. Martha would have known Jane's political stance and would have picked up on her friend's worry and their shared hope. 'I place my hope of better things on a claim to the protection of heaven.'[22]

When all talking had ceased, what they loved to do the most was read together. This was a distinction of Jane and Martha's friendship. Mary, famously within the family and much to Jane's open disgust, did not enjoy reading at all. Jane and Martha's favourite pastime of snuggling cosily around the fire with a book was considered deathly dull by Mary, and only suffered rarely for Jane's sake when they were forced together by the weather or circumstance to do so. When Mary once subscribed to a local library Jane nearly fell off her chair in shock and confusion. They read all manner of things aloud in the Austen family and Jane included Martha in that tradition. This was one of Jane's favourite ways to pass an evening and in Martha, she found a very willing partner. Jane's books, of course, were featured front and centre amongst those that were habitually read and enjoyed by Martha and Cassandra individually or for entertainment as a group together. Jane liked the characters to really come to life and the pace of reading to match what she had written. We can only imagine what it must have been like in this holy huddle – reading with the author herself. Everyone in the family commented on how well Jane read, of course, and Martha got to have this as her regular relaxation of an evening or afternoon. It's tempting now to imagine an audiobook version 'narrated by the author'; how we would love that, and that is what Martha had access to on a regular basis. The added bonus for her was if there were any hidden references or inside jokes, then she would have deduced and devoured them. How Martha must have looked forward to these sessions and craved them when she was apart from her friend.

Sometimes Jane even joked that she thought Martha just a little too willing to read the books that lay about the Austens' home. Jane once received a request from Martha to read *First Impressions*. Cassandra asked Jane on her behalf when she was sending off one of her regular correspondences with her sister. It was just a simple question, and the three often passed on similar demands one to another. Jane often had this request, of course, from Cassandra too. However, this time, when Jane caught wind of Martha wanting to read her book she quickly and quirkily rebuffed her desire. It was the summer of 1799 and the book would have been in an early manuscript version,

perhaps in one of the very early drafts and certainly not in the final
'lopt and cropt' form. The book would not be published, under the
final title of *Pride and Prejudice*, for another fourteen years. 'I would not
let Martha read *First Impressions* again upon any account & am very
glad that I did not leave it in your power. She is very cunning, but I
see through her design; she means to publish it from Memory, & one
more perusal must enable her to do it.'[23] There were so many benefits
of being best friends with Jane, but this was something so special
for Martha. The thought of having early and easy access to reading
these wonderful stories, knowing that you were reading them as the
author intended – being able to talk through the characters and the
plot, and telling her which bits you just loved so much, laughing
aloud and feeling all the ups and downs of the plot together with the
writer. It is no wonder Martha sent this request, for wouldn't we all
have done. How many times have we, Jane's readers, read and re-
read the novels, finding something different to enjoy and admire or
to even discover as we read at a different time in our own lives or in
a different season or circumstance.

Hilariously we have an insight into Jane's canny protecting of her
work from an early age. We find not even Cassandra knew where
the manuscript was. It must have been locked away, either in Jane's
portable writing desk or in her drawer in her room. The sentiment
in the letter is also an example of Jane's runaway imagination in
action – she refuses to accept that Martha simply wants to re-read it,
holding up a virtual hand to stop the tide of her requests. The irony
of Martha having the same level of fiction-writing ability as Jane is
partly what makes the idea of her writing it all out for herself, word
for word by memory alone, so ludicrous and therefore the refusal so
tender and noteworthy. She is not putting Martha down, but she
is teasing her for sure – pretending that Martha's personality is the
opposite of the actual truth. At the same time, she is attesting that in
her opinion Martha certainly is 'cunning' in the sense of the word
back then – that she did have the 'ability to know' and the 'crafty
skill' to 'learn to know.' Jane is pointing to her friend and playing
her 'remember I know you so well' card; she is teasing Martha from
a place of awareness and stating plainly that she knows Martha is

not just a sweet-faced simpleton. But more than that, Jane is stating her ownership with pride – it's mine! It's not so much that she really wants to send the 'hands off' message, although the thought of it being read when she was not there obviously was not something she wanted; she was controlling her readership. It is more than this, it's her making a point of establishing her own authorly happiness and faith in her writing in front of her friends. Here we also have a further revelation of her friendship level with Martha – what a joy to be able to swat her friend away, to leave her wanting more. We learn from Jane that she has let Martha read it or hear it many times already, but here she is going to leave her dangling. She calls Martha out on her 'cheek' for desiring and asking to read the work again – the rotter and what's more, she enjoys all the fun of leaving Martha hanging in her request at some point between agony and ecstasy. Yet, through her humour, she allows Martha and Cassandra (for she knew that Cass would either read out or quote her letter back to Martha) to see her hidden vulnerability towards her work, her own personal goal, her audacious desire for publication; she lets it bubble up in front of her friends and the words come into being. In so giving this admission, so carefully encased in her habitual love of word-play she actually looks 'confident'; perhaps this is her own trust in her skill and in her work, or in the support and conviction of her cause that she receives from Martha and Cassandra's belief in her.[24]

'You distress me cruelly by your request about Books; I cannot think of any to bring with me, nor have I any idea of our wanting them,' Jane writes when Martha and she are in the midst of planning another visit together.[25] We can sense the smirk on her face as she writes and it is almost on a par with a romantic teasing, in the sense that an intimate pair know just how much the other likes to spend far too much time in the eyes of others, on a particular hobby together. Jane goes into full-on lament that she is looking forward to a good heart-to-heart and gossip, a good session of putting the world to rights. 'I come to you to be talked to, not to read or hear reading. I can do that at home.'[26] Ouch! The cruel blow of saying that she can be just as entertained at home with her mother is perhaps the equivalent of admitting that you would rather be in washing your hair. But Jane was surely teasing and definitely shared Martha's enjoyment of reading as part of their time together, even if not necessarily the whole. Jane proceeds to drown Martha under a list of possible and honestly quite improbable topics from 'Henry's History of England' that she will bring to read. 'Of course, you can have it your own way' is the happy shrug of reply contained in Jane's words. She is in full-on racks of laughter now as she promises to 'repeat' the words 'in any manner you may prefer' and she revels in the idea of reciting dry academic industrialised topics: 'The civil and Military, Religion, Constitution, Learning and Learned Men, Arts and Sciences, Commerce Coins and Shipping and Manners, so that for every evening of the week there will be a different subject.'[27] Poor Martha, perhaps for a second she thought that Jane would really subject her to all these heavy topics! But Jane hammers home that she is joking and has loved getting carried away with her rant for she continues until she finally runs out of steam. Jane's words run away with her like a horse out of control, bolting down a hill with a post chaise of passengers on board. She triumphantly blows out of all proportion her scorn at Martha's original request so that now her response seems heightened to an enormous and ridiculous size. Her pièce de résistance is the suggestion that Martha recite 'French Grammar' and dear Mrs Stent burst forth about Cocks and Hens![28] Poor Martha – she may well have been laughing in response as she read, holding up her hands trying to hold back Jane's barrage of words – happily sorry, not sorry, that she asked and looking forward to the knock on the door from her friend.

Chapter Eight

In Sickness and in Health

It was in early December 1800 that Martha and Jane returned to Steventon from one of these happy times. With the triumph of being able to spend time together uppermost in their minds, we can imagine their satisfaction in jumping down from the chaise, pulling off their bonnets and knocking happily on a half-opening rectory door whilst sharing a thought or two over a shoulder. Jane then took a step that would signify a moment in her life where everything changed. Neither she nor Martha had any inkling at that stage of the momentous news awaiting them on the other side of the door. They would remember where they were when they heard the news forever, and for them it would be frozen in time. On stepping over the threshold of her family home, Jane and Martha crossed over into the next moment, one that neither of them could ever go back from. The news meant a fork in the path of the life of their friendship.

For in the interim, in Jane's absence, 'the latent strain of impetuosity in the Austens' was said to have bubbled up and over in her father.[1] He was the master and commander of the family's fate and was free to take and make decisions as he wished, yet we cannot help but believe that no decision could ever have got past Mrs Austen without her approval, and so it was a united front that we assume presented Jane and Martha with a done deal on that doorstep. This moment became a memory for all present and had such an impact that it was embedded in the family consciousness forever. For as soon as they got in the door, perhaps not even having taken off their boots or put down all of their luggage, Mrs Austen was upon them and wasted no time in bringing them up to speed with the news; with barely a word of other welcome, she announced to the two unsuspecting women, 'Well, girls, it is all settled, we have decided to leave Steventon in such a week and go to Bath.'[2] She did not mean for a visit, or to take the waters for their father or even to go for a long stay in the upcoming months with family members there – no, she meant to up sticks, move out of the rectory, hand it all over to James and Mary, and for her husband to retire to Bath, taking Cassandra and Jane with them to live there – permanently. The message was addressed to both Jane and Martha – to the 'girls', they were both to be informed of the news in the very same instant. Both their lives were about to be wrenched in different directions again, beyond their own powers of control and leading to who knows where down the road. Family legend has it that for Jane, 'the shock of this intelligence was so great that she fainted away.'[3] The image of poor Jane lying out in a heap on the floor is upsetting. The framework of her happy routines and the relationships that buoyed her creativity and enabled her to channel her impetus to write were about to be shattered. We can imagine Martha, who must have been reeling from the news herself, trying desperately to process, calm and console her own fretting spirit and mind, being suddenly snapped out of her own private reverie at the sight of her friend needing help.

Mary was also present, perhaps to welcome her sister and to take her back to Deane with them. Whether she was privy to the information in advance or discovered it upon hearing Mrs Austen's exclamation, in that moment the news for her would have been life-changing in a different way. The move to the bigger Steventon rectory and the increase in their income with James becoming rector was effectively a promotion for her husband. She may well have been surprised and a little sad at losing the Austens as neighbours, but maybe not. In reality she was probably delighted. She remembered, however, that Jane was 'greatly distressed'.[4] She could not have failed to notice the pain in her own sister Martha too. Initially it must have been etched on her face, if only momentarily, for she was emotionally strong and unfailingly polite, and would have been acutely aware of being in someone else's house, someone else's life, in that instant. Although quiet at the time, Martha must have been contending with a raging stormy sea inside her own heart and stomach. She had been threatened with the loss of Jane earlier that year, when Mrs Austen had dallied with the idea of sending Jane and Cassandra to the aid of their Aunt

Mrs Leigh Perrot. At the time she had been suffering the indignity of awaiting trial in Bath in the gloomiest of circumstances and Mrs Austen had offered up her daughters in service to her. Thankfully that had all come to nothing, but now they faced more separation for an indefinite period. She was going to need to rest completely upon the rock of her faith once again. Geographical distance was going to contend for her place in Jane's heart. Would it make that heart grow fonder or weaker in terms of her friendship? Only time could tell.

In line with her true essence and nature Martha threw herself into the role of helpful and practical friend. She supported Jane in particular as the news began to sink in and to feel more real. As Jane accepted the situation and began to come to terms with it as much as she could, Martha's instinct was to deal with what was directly in front of them, to bring outer order, which helped her fight the inner chaos that threatened to overwhelm Jane and herself. This was the resilience of their friendship. When the rug was quite literally pulled out from under them, for instance, when she had been forced to leave Deane as Jane was now forced to leave Steventon, Martha and Jane focused on what they could control and moved forward. They had little other choice and it was either find a positive ongoing motion that enabled them to process their emotions and organise events where they could, or wallow and sink and be pulled along anyway, but at someone else's command and whim.

Jane and Martha began spending every day cataloguing Mr Austen's books in his 500-volume strong personal library, as well as other items in the house that the family had decided were to be sold. These included most of the furniture, fixtures and fittings, ornaments and pictures, and even Jane's pianoforte. Some livestock was to be sold off too, and James and Mary were set to inherit or receive a proportion of the home chattels, much to Jane's disgust. In her letters to her big sister, Jane complained about the sad and unseemly dividing up of their possessions, and the terrible return and prices they were being offered upon them. We know that she most definitely would have shared her feelings on the subject with Martha as their leisure time at home together now became diverted into the Herculean task of packing up the Austen house. Perhaps the grumbling somehow helped them all to let off some steam and come to terms with the new impending reality.

The physical packing and the mental work required in the keeping of lists and the preparation of inventories and book-keeping absorbed some of the energy brought about by the anxiety and high emotion of this state of affairs. Martha, too, as we know, was sensitive to the loss of loved ones and would have been rocked by the news, and it most likely stirred up for her feelings of great grief and sadness. But as the days ticked by and come the turn of the month, Jane noted that Martha was feeling better, that 'her spirits are better than they were.'[5] The two set their faces to the wind of their destiny and continually made plans and schemes to spend time with each other – two friends against the world, never to be thwarted – at least not if the strength of their friendship for one another could have anything to do with it.

In any event as time went by and Jane and her family settled in at Bath, other matters of a higher priority than feelings pressed in on Martha's world. Her mother was now ageing, on the threshold of her seventh decade – quite an age for someone to reach back then. Life expectancy for this era is hard to calculate; at birth it was probably 40–50 but many infants died in childhood and many mothers died during childbirth, often after having tens of children, as in Jane's family. Therefore, when Martha's mother looked pale or wan or seemed unwell, it was big news to impart amongst the family and Jane herself communicated it to Cassandra in her letters. Any sort of ailment or injury was news – either because it had not been experienced by Martha or Jane before; or because they were concerned about the recovery of the sick person; or because it had come about in a dramatic fashion; or worse still, because it thwarted their plans to be together. Martha and Jane helped to keep each other and their families abreast of changes on anyone's condition. It was always one of the first pieces of information passed on and Jane was always quick to reassure that Martha was well or to give some details, sometimes very specific, when she was not. Martha too asked Jane to pass on facts about her health to others, such as the time when, one September in her early forties, she wanted Cassandra to know that she had chilblains on her fingers. She had never had them before and working around the house or at her sewing and knitting, or out in the gardens and in the kitchen cooking, she would have really felt the imposition of them on her hands, as well as the discomfort. In her writing about this, we feel her reaching out through the page; wanting to let her friend know what was happening to her, for her sympathy and concern. Knowing Martha's love for figuring out cures and holistic and horticultural health treatments, she most probably wanted Cassandra's advice and for her to seek out that of the older women in the neighbourhood who had come across chilblains or experienced them before.

'A friend in need is a friend indeed', they say, and Martha and Jane were there to help each other when needed. When Martha had a cold and it stopped her from going to church, Jane let Cassandra know. It must have been quite a bad cold to keep Martha from her attendance at her Sunday service. Martha's faith was her highest priority and attending church was an outward sign of her reverence and commitment. Martha really enjoyed going but took her participation in the rituals of her faith very seriously and solemnly. For her to decide not to go pretty much means that the decision was taken out of her hands and that she was truly unwell, hence Jane made a note of telling Cassandra. They would have surely silently and jointly understood that they were both now to keep an eye on her. Indeed, little references to the wellbeing and current strength and status of Martha creep into Jane's letters from time to time, quite unrelated to anything else she was mentioning and signalling that Martha was always on her mind. As a good friend would, she was keeping tabs on how her friend really was and her day-to-day health and wellness was uppermost in some part of her brain or other, squirreled away with other important pieces of information.

'Martha wants me to find out that she grows fat,' Jane passes back to Cassandra, Jane scoffing at the use of the word and choosing not to believe her best friend's negative opinion of herself.[6] We have all been there with a friend – listened to their worries about their bodies, their figures and their appearance, and therefore their self-worth. It is our duty as said friend to chide them and tell them not to put themselves down so, as Jane duly does; 'Martha looks very well', giving us a sense of hope that she looks strong and in good spirits, that her inner woman is glowing with health too; 'I cannot carry my complaisance farther than to believe whatever she asserts on the subject.'[7] Well done, Jane, we all think – Martha did not need another blow to her self-esteem. She was suffering from the ravages of the smallpox to her face, hands, head and body, and would not have needed another niggle in her mind to put her looks and spirits down. The best way indeed was to shut the conversation down by ignoring and rebuffing the negative words with humour, and this was what Jane was an ace best mate at.

Sometimes in mock anger, Jane would use her 'health' as a topic to tease Martha – 'Martha will have wet races and catch a bad cold,' she jests when Martha was off, staying away with a friend and going to a horse racing meet without her.[8] Not so very far underneath the surface was a genuine concern though – a bit like when we scold a child for taking a risk for pleasure, such as going out without a hat on in the sun, or not wearing a jumper or a coat in the cold, or for doing too much too soon after being unwell, for Jane knew that Martha was getting over a rough patch of health. 'In other respects, I hope she will have much pleasure at them – & that she is free from Earache now.'[9]

Other times Jane and Martha turned getting better into a bit of a competition. Humour was their coping mechanism; in playing with words and playing with each other Martha and Jane helped each other – it was part of their emotional toolbox and a way of finding each other. 'I have a cold too as well as my Mother and Martha.' Jane passes on this news to Cassandra. 'Let it be a generous emulation between us which can get rid of it first.'[10]

Just a few years after Jane and her immediate family retired to Bath, Martha and Jane both went through a period of loss. These were earth-shattering and shocking experiences when they came, and if not unexplained, they were to the largest degree unexpected. These trying and difficult periods show Martha and Jane really stepping up when it counted. In the midst of all the pain and anguish, and the hardship of illness of key family members, Jane, Martha and Cassandra drew up their combined strengths and, like the three

Musketeers, they were 'all for one and one for all'. Together they were stronger and together they walked through the practical and emotional fallout that these situations brought with them.

In early September 1804, when she was about 75 years old, Martha's mother, Mrs Martha Lloyd, was taken rather ill and Cassandra, who had been on holiday in Weymouth, raced directly and urgently to Ibthorpe to help Martha care for and tend to her sick mother. Jane was oh, so anxious to hear of her safe arrival and had been tracking and plotting what she thought would have been Cassandra's route. She had estimated that it would have taken Cassandra about two days to get there and that she would have reached Martha in the early evening, so she timed her letter accordingly. The focus was clearly all about getting to Martha as quickly as possible, not caring what time she was arriving – just making haste. Taking the journey in and of itself, and all alone, was a commitment and a task. Jane herself was on holiday in Lyme, caring for her own mother. Jane opens and closes her correspondence enquiring after Martha and her mother too, conveying her depth of feeling and concern, primarily for her friend. Mrs Lloyd's brother, John, had died suddenly of an illness in June and the burden of this, as well as Mrs Lloyd's age and constitution, had obviously caused Martha great concern. We can feel Jane in her letters wondering silently at the depth of distress that Martha must be in and the difficulty of the work involved. 'I need not say that we are particularly anxious for your next letter, to know how you find Mrs Lloyd and Martha.'[11] But Jane knew in her heart what Martha must have already confirmed. 'Say everything kind for us to the latter. The former I fear must be beyond any remembrance of, or from the absent.'[12] In the very next lines, she tries to think of other ways to buoy up and distract Martha, using fun and humour to bring the spotlight off the dire circumstances and back on to lighter-hearted affairs in teasing Cassandra together.

In the meantime, disaster struck elsewhere. In December of the same year, Madam Lefroy died after sustaining injuries in an accident that occurred when she was riding her horse home. She had been shopping in Overton and bumped into James there, who was running errands and going about his business himself. He was the last of the Austen family to see her alive. Headed home up the steep hill, her horse had got into difficulty and the groomsman running to catch a hold of him had made the horse bolt further still. Poor Madam Lefroy, who was a competent horsewoman, was eventually thrown from the horse. She died on Jane's birthday. Yet death crept closer still, this time to Jane's family. Her father, Reverend George Austen, died peacefully yet unexpectedly from a short illness at his home in Bath on 21 January 1805 with Mrs Austen, Cassandra and Jane at his bedside.

At the end of March, Cassandra returned to Ibthorpe once again to assist Martha in nursing Mrs Lloyd. There was no knowing when the end would come but a certain acceptance of the inevitability of her death was felt by them all. Jane wrote regularly to cheer and accompany both women as they continued in their difficult task of caring for Martha's elderly and frail mother. She referenced the pretty spring weather, and talked of her day-to-day happenings, suggesting the two get out and walk if and when they could. She did her best to raise their spirits. Jane and Cassandra were the perfect pair of friends for Martha at this time, knowing her and her family as well as they did, and having just dealt with and experienced the passing of their own father. Jane knew that Mrs Lloyd was a fighter and she hoped that nature would take its course as a mercy to her, to release her from her suffering, but she almost banked on Mrs Lloyd reviving herself for another bout of struggling. Jane was full of empathy for her friend and wished that the end might be 'peaceful and easy, as the exit we have witnessed.'[13] Apart from that, Jane was not sure what to say; Mrs Lloyd was falling in and out of consciousness, she was frail from experiencing 'repeated and paralytic seizures' and as all the women were well aware, 'had been failing in mind and body for some time past.'[14] Martha and Cassandra; the faithful Mrs Stent (who perhaps was out of her depth with the grief and worry of it all, for Jane writes 'Poor Mrs Stent! it has been her lot to be always in the way; but we must be merciful, for perhaps in time we may come to be Mrs Stents ourselves, unequal to anything and unwelcome to everybody'); and as much as she was able at this time, Mary (who was due to give birth to her daughter Caroline in June), had done all that they could.[15] All were now waiting, and hoping that nature would take its course as calmly and as kindly as possible.

When the end finally came on 16 April, Cassandra was with Martha in person and Jane was there in spirit. Letters had been flying back and forth on a near daily basis. Jane was sure that they must all be worn out, but she was full of gratitude for her sister being there and being such a rock for her friend. 'As a companion you will be all that Martha can be supposed to want.'[16] Jane knew how Martha would be feeling and responding, and she was so sure and heartened that her sister would know Martha so well and be able to supply all her needs so fully. This gave Jane peace too. 'Your presence and support have the utmost value,' she wrote – knowing that Cassandra's friendship to Martha meant so much, not only to Martha but as a reassurance to Jane herself too.[17] 'Your account of Martha is very comfortable indeed, & now we shall be in no fear of receiving a worse.'[18]

Cassandra stayed on with Martha for over a month, and her help was indeed invaluable, not only to Martha and the family and for poor Mrs Stent the housekeeper, but also in keeping Jane as well-informed as she could possibly hope to be if she was able to be there herself. Jane was with her mother in Bath, it only being a matter of months since their father died. Jane though was not as practical a home keeper or household organiser as Cassandra; she was, of course, full of feelings and care for Martha, and sending Cassandra to help was the best gift that she could give.

The Sunday after her mother's death, Martha had felt able to attend church. This was the very same one at Hurstbourne Tarrant where her mother was buried and her sister had married, with the local congregation around her in attendance as on every usual Sunday. This would have been a huge milestone for her and the clearest indication to Jane that she was going to be okay and that she was already getting back on her own two feet. 'This day if she has gone to church, must have been a trial of her feelings, but I hope it will be the last of any acuteness.'[19] She tried to cheer Martha up with teasing and laughs over a possible interest in Jane from a Mr Hampson, whom she had met on the way during one of her walks through the streets of Bath. Calling on their romantic jokes and japes of the past, she

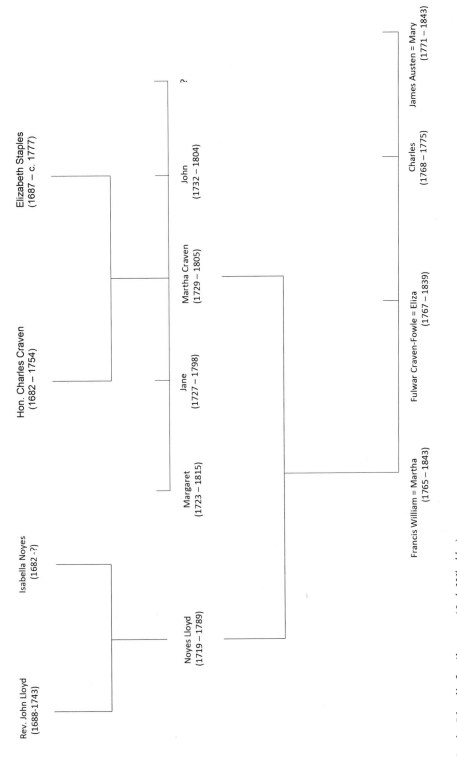

Martha Lloyd's family tree. (*Josh Wheddon*)

View of Enborne countryside. (*Author's own photograph*)

Front elevation of St. Michael and All Angels Church, Enborne. (*Image used with permission*)

Rear elevation of St. Michael and All Angels Church, Enborne. (*Image used with permission*)

View of Deane countryside. (*Author's own photograph*)

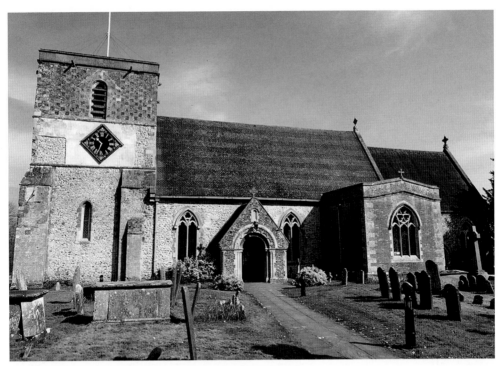

St. Mary's Church, Kintbury. (*Image used with permission*)

St. Nicholas Church, Steventon. (*Image used with permission*)

View of Steventon countryside. (*Author's own photograph*)

Image of Martha and Jane in a post chaise. (*Lucrezia Fyvie H.*)

View of Ibthorpe House, Hurstbourne Tarrant. (*Copyright Sarah Basden*)

Front elevation of Ibthorpe House, Hurstbourne Tarrant. (*Copyright Sarah Basden*)

Front of Chawton, Jane Austen's House. (*Image reproduced courtesy of Jane Austen's House*)

Martha's bedroom window at Chawton, Jane Austen's House. (*Image reproduced courtesy of Jane Austen's House*)

Martha's kitchen at Chawton, Jane Austen's House. (*Image reproduced courtesy of Jane Austen's House*)

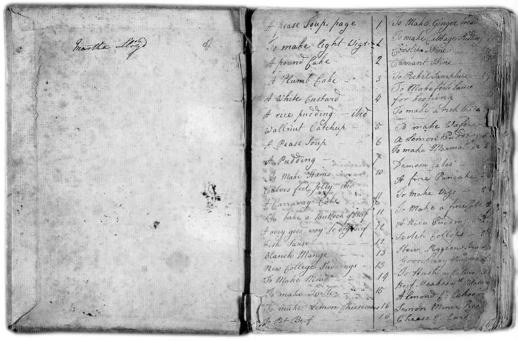

Martha's signature at the front of her Household Book. (*Image reproduced courtesy of Jane Austen's House*)

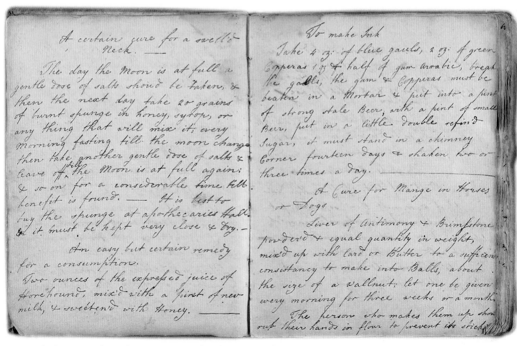

Martha's recipe for ink. (*Image reproduced courtesy of Jane Austen's House*)

Barton Court, Kintbury. (*David Hill, Barton Court Estate*)

St Maurice Church covert, Winchester. (*Nicky Liddell Photography*)

Drawing of Portsdown Lodge, near Portsmouth. (*Image reproduced courtesy of Jane Austen's House*)

View from Portsdown Hill, near Portsmouth. (*Author's own photograph*)

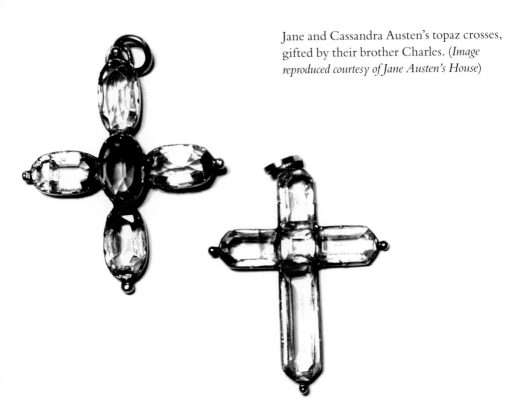

Jane and Cassandra Austen's topaz crosses, gifted by their brother Charles. (*Image reproduced courtesy of Jane Austen's House*)

St Peter and St Paul, Wymering Church, near Portsmouth. (*Image used with permission*)

Martha's grave at St Peter and St Paul, Wymering Church, near Portsmouth. (*Author's own photograph*)

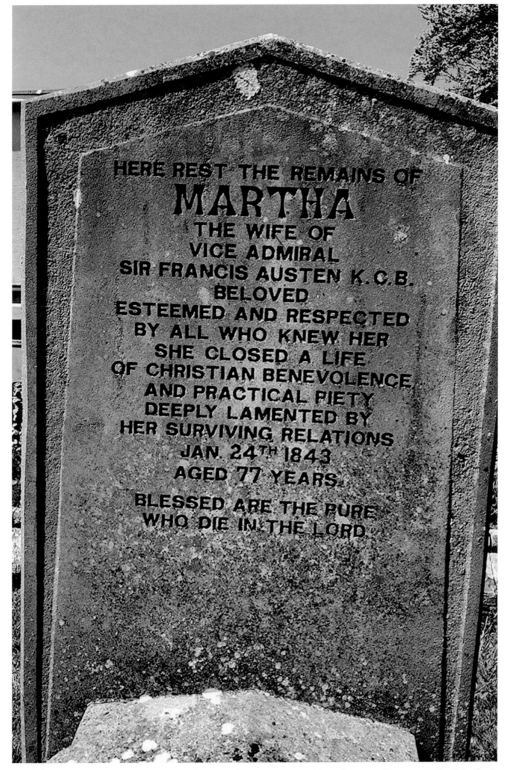

Martha's headstone at St Peter and St Paul, Wymering Church, near Portsmouth. (*Author's own photograph*)

Tombstone for Martha and Francis Austen at St Peter and St Paul, Wymering Church, near Portsmouth. (*Author's own photograph*)

paints a picture of waiting for him to pay her mother and her a visit, but alas he has not called upon them – 'I trusted to his forgetting our number when I gave it him in Gay St & so I conclude he has, as he… not yet called.'[20] We can just see Jane trying to coax a smile on her friend's face. In her self-deprecating joke, she is gently getting back in Martha's face – using her talents for making her laugh and reassuring her that all is well and will be well again in time. That she, her friend and their friendship, were waiting for Martha and would be there for her in her recovery.

Never out of touch with the roots of her writing and with Martha so carefully entwined within those roots, it is not unsurprising, but adorably touching, that Jane and her mother wrote one of their witty poems to Martha in this moment, to entertain her and lift her spirits further. Although some uncertainty exists as to whether the poem was sent at this time, Jane's closeness with Martha, their penchant for silly jokes, their preference for sincerity and honesty, and their habitual need to talk about anything and everything, alongside some enigmatic references in Jane's letters to Cassandra, hint that it is more likely that it probably was. 'The Nonsense I have been writing in this & my last letter, seems out of place at such a time; but I will not mind it, it will do you no harm, & nobody else will be attached by it.'[21]

The poem itself with its lively humour and clever play with words and rhyme would have surely been a blessing and a salve to Martha. Furthermore, receiving something that was somewhat part of an Austen tradition – the passing of notes and stories in poetry form amongst themselves and their inner family circle – would have been really touching and moving for Martha. Jane's verses, like others of the Austen family, are 'a small and essentially private part of her work,' 'a fascinating and revealing aspect of her art,' for their literary qualities but they also show just how she communicated her personal side, within her own life with family and friends.[22] Many believe that these little poems show the 'importance of the family's literary pursuits in the development of her writing.'[23] So, being the muse for one of these verses perhaps had the double-edged outcome of supporting her friend's writing career and progressing her creative talents too.

Receiving one of these poems, directly and personally, was truly a clear indicator of a special friendship. This was an inclusion of Martha into Jane's family unit, and being the recipient of such a precious item is a validation of the prominence of Martha in Jane's everyday life, of how much she mattered to Jane's heart, as well as her writing. Jane wrote poems when she was feeling a particularly poignant emotion and at times where she had a great many feelings. On the fourth anniversary of her friend Madam Lefroy's death, for example, she penned a long poem lamenting the loss of such a lovely lady and honouring the memory of her friend. On the birth of her brother Frank's first child, she wrote a sweet, intimate poem in congratulation and praise of her beloved brother and his son. Writing and posting this poem was a way of Jane sending Martha a hug in an envelope – like a prettily embroidered handkerchief or someone's signature bake. It was personal on so many levels and a way of Jane reaching out to Martha and making her feel included, giving her a sense of belonging – as well as making her laugh and feel entertained.

These verses were 'often suggested by domestic matters' and the words of Mrs Austen and Jane would have leapt off the page at Martha chiming with her in a familiar and comforting way.[24] The words and wit meeting Martha in the moment, just where she was at – giving her a reminder of the firm foundation that friendship had laid for her, helping her to laugh at the situation – wherever she could, as was her and Jane's way. The words were sent to help lessen the loss a little, to acknowledge that sense of loneliness and sadness, but with a palpable message of solidarity from Jane and the women in her immediate family too. It was something that would help Jane and Mrs Austen feel that they were contributing to Martha's restoration. At such a distance there was much that they could not do, but this little poem was something to engage their hearts and skill, and was something that they could provide, thus easing their angst to help and passing on something positive of themselves as part of Martha's and their own grieving process.

The poem addresses Miss Green, a dressmaker, either imagined or perhaps real, whose delay in making up the required mourning clothes for Martha has disappointed. Jane writes the first verse and is seen standing up for her friend in empathy and understanding of the many trying, practical aspects put upon a daughter in the midst of coping with the death of a parent. Some have said that the direct reference to mourning was what made the poem less likely to have been passed to Martha, but it is unlikely that the subject matter or words used would have offended her. The friends were in the habit of reading out entire letters to each other and Martha had been present at the writing of the *Juvenilia* stories and attended family reading sessions at Steventon, so the tone of the poem would not have been in any way unfamiliar to her or offensive in her eyes. There was no subject that Jane and Martha could not talk about – and no words or language that was ever out of bounds. The poem was completely in line with family tastes and makes it highly likely that it was sent and intended for Martha to have. This is the surprising and long-lasting effect of their friendship. This is the freeing influence that their close partnership brought with it and is perhaps one of the keys to its longevity and success.

Jane Austen writes the first verse, voicing Martha's part of the suffering customer:

> Miss Lloyd has now sent to Miss Green
> As, on opening the box, may be seen
> Some yards of a Black Ploughman's Gauze,
> To be made up directly, because
> Miss Lloyd must in mourning appear-
> For the death of a relative dear-
> Miss Lloyd must expect to receive
> This license to mourn and to grieve
> complete, er'e the end of the week
> It is better to write than to speak

Mrs Austen sends Miss Green's reply:

> I've often made clothes
> for those who write prose,
> But 'tis the first time

I've had orders in rhyme
Depend on't fair Maid,
You shall be obeyed;
Your garment of black
Shall sit Close to your back,
And in every part
I'll exert all my art;
It shall be the neatest
And eke the completest
That ever was seen–
Or my name is not Green.[25]

In December of the same year death struck again, this time upon General Mathew, father of James Austen's first wife; grandfather to little Anna and godfather to James Edward. This generous man had continued to pay an allowance to Anna all her life, and Mary and James stayed regularly at his home, Clanville. With a new 6-month-old baby girl in the house, and James's income set to dwindle, this branch of the Austen family would have truly felt the blow of his passing.

Chapter Nine

Home Is Where the Heart Is

With all of this unsettling change and particularly with the loss of key members of their respective families, Jane and Martha had more in common than ever. As the horizon of their lives changed, the two of them looked about them at the totally new and unchartered landscape. A cross-roads appeared before them both – there was no going back – but how could they all move forward? They had no one to provide for them and with the death of both parents, Martha was particularly vulnerable. What was she going to do next? Where were she and Jane both going to be living? How would she provide for herself? There was only one thing for it: Martha would have got down on her knees and prayed. In the meantime, her best friend had been hatching another of her plans and Cassandra was fully on board.

'I am quite of your opinion as to the folly of concealing any longer our intended partnership with Martha.'[1] Jane's plan was for Martha to team up with her, her mother and Cassandra. The situation was clear to Jane and one that she and Cassandra had discussed at length, proposed to Martha and worked hard in all quarters to smooth the way for it to happen. As women of their time, they had little influence over their own fates even when it came to where they might live, breathe and have their being. Jane – pushing forward their plans, carefully, tactfully, thoughtfully and leaving no room for obstacles or hindrances – had taken an unusually bold step in seeking and settling approbation for her idea. Less than a week after the death of Mrs Lloyd, the circumstances now helped rather than curtailed a plan that Jane had had in mind for many years – a plan that would bring her and Martha into closer daily contact. And so, 'as Martha was now almost alone in the world, it was agreed that she should presently come to live with Mrs Austen and her daughters.'[2] 'None of <u>our</u> connections I think will be unprepared for it; & I do not know how to suppose that Martha's have not foreseen it,' wrote Jane.[3]

There may not have been much room for Martha to live at Steventon Rectory with Mary and James and their three children, even if she had desired it. Mary, practical but not brimming over with empathy and joy, was not as close, as a sister, as Jane was to Martha as a friend. In her pocketbook diaries of the time, meticulously kept, year in, year out, Mary always respectfully and customarily refers to her sister with a title, yet never on simple first name terms. Mary may well have even resented having to contribute to her sister's as well as her own family's upkeep. They had just lost the income from General Mathew and James was inclined to turn down the opportunity to take on another living offered by her sister Eliza at nearby Hampstead Marshal Vicarage, on moral and ethical grounds. He could not come to agree with the wording and statement of faith that he would need to make based upon the liturgy of that branch of the Christian church, which was different in tone and denominational leaning to his own. James could not bring himself to accommodate the values of this other parish, and honourably declined the invitation and the salary and increase to his household income that would have come along with it.

It is easier for us to understand Martha's partiality for living with Jane rather than her sister, even if her income and lifestyle were to be less comfortable. In moving in with her friends, she would perhaps feel more at ease and more able to experience a freedom to live according to her own rhythm of life amongst the atmosphere of this home than in the other. She would be living with adult women, rather than a husband and wife and young family, and the difference in lifestyle choice is easy for us to comprehend. The pull of living with her intimate, long-term friend must also have been as strong as it was exceptional and unique. But like all things in Martha and Jane's domestic lives, it was not all as clear and plain sailing as this original scenario sounded. The Austen women were left without their breadwinner and Mrs Austen was now under the care of her four sons. The friends were forced to spend time sofa-surfing with acquaintances, family and relations, participating in a long round of extended visits and holiday residencies, unsure as to how exactly their plan would come together. When the friends were separated, they kept up their repartee through the sharing of letters and news as always, and in their hearts, they held onto the assurance that somehow they would be together at some uncertain point. They knew that they both wanted the same thing and that it had been sincerely and openly shared with all their family, and better still it was sanctioned and accepted as a mutually beneficial arrangement.

Meanwhile, Jane's time would be taken up in visits to support and help with her extended family, whilst Martha went off and stayed with friends. On other occasions, Jane and Martha visited Steventon and sometimes Martha was alone with Mrs Austen awaiting Jane and Cassandra. This was surely a relief and a help to the Austen women, freeing them up to see to other needs and also a boon to Martha, who would have rejoiced in taking care of Mrs Austen and in having the opportunity to match and reward the kindness shown to her own mother by Cassandra. In August 1805 they were in lodgings together in Worthing with Edward's family set to join them. Whilst Jane was delayed in her arrival, there is palpable relief in her voice when she confides in Cassandra that 'we are sure of my mother and Martha being happy together.'[4]

Martha had still had the respite of Ibthorpe, which her mother had left to her in her will, but the time was coming when Martha would have to prove and confirm all the arrangements for her mother's final wishes. It was a difficult time, so it was helpful for Martha to have distractions and obligations, and it was a time when Martha really needed a friend, someone who she could count on to stand with her in her hour of need. On 4 November 1805 Martha appeared in person in the parish of Broadwater, Sussex to swear to the truth of her mother's last will and testament. Who was there to help her and to steady her – signatures sit silently on the page in witness to Martha's sworn affidavit and show most movingly all we need to know. Whose name appears? Why, Jane Austen's, of course.

Mrs Lloyd had bequeathed everything to Martha for her 'absolute use and benefit if she shall be single at the time of my decease.'[5] There was no one else who could support Martha and her mother was well aware of that. She had taken real care to list all of her belongings and worldly goods that she wanted Martha to be able to utilise. She asked that Martha make an inventory of all her remaining monies and household objects, furniture and provisions to be given to her executor Charles Dundas back at Barton Court, so that all her debts could be paid and her will carried out. It is unclear how Mary felt about this arrangement. All Mrs Lloyd's personal effects were 'to be shared amongst my three daughters... in equal proportions' – 'share and share alike,' she wrote in a way that must have evoked her mother's voice in Martha's head, just as surely as if she was there.[6] In giving that order to her daughters, we wonder which daughter may have needed to have been prompted in such a way.

We do not know many specific details of what her personal effects were, or who got the valuable ring that she bought from Charles Dundas, her executor for twenty guineas in May 1802. We do know that Mary was separately left her mother's eight-day 'Tompion' clock. This would have been a mantel, or a free-standing grandfather clock, and it was a worthy piece of furniture to be left as it was of both monetary and cultural value. Thomas Tompion (1639–1713) was known as the revered 'Father of English Clockmaking'. This piece may have been a family heirloom and it may have sat in their rectory at Enborne when she was a child. It could have been in her mother's family but as her mother escaped with few possessions, this is perhaps more unlikely, despite her aristocratic connections. It may be this sentimental link that made Mrs Lloyd Senior think of leaving it to Mary. The clocks had an unequalled reputation and only limited editions were made – the highest quality materials were used but the quality of the piece was in the undoubted, unquestioned and exemplary skills of the craftsmen who built them and the engineer who designed them. To this day an example stands in Buckingham Palace. We can be sure that the officious Mary with her eye for order and precision in the running of her parsonage, along with her social airs and graces, would have been very happy to offer it a home.

Constantly on the move, the little group of friends were now fervently hoping, praying, plotting and patiently waiting for the family to provide a more substantial base and an appropriate permanent home, alongside the agreed allowance that the Austen men were making for their mother and sisters. In the summer of 1806 Martha took lodgings near the family in Bath. Their scheme was very nearly ready to hatch, and it was agreed outright once and for all that she would join them as a fourth member of the household wherever they settled next.

On 2 July 1806 Mrs Austen, Cassandra and Jane finally left Bath for the last time and Martha travelled with them. They made their way as a party to Clifton in Bristol. Martha was waiting there to be transported to visit friends at Harrogate. The difficulty of their situation, as Martha hovered in the balance, uncertain if she would be able to secure transportation, had Jane thinking about their day-to-day inconveniences. Jane once again picked up her pen to raise Martha's spirits – inventing a little ditty addressed simply 'to Martha' to make her friend laugh at the ridiculous situation that they found themselves in, once again waiting on a lift, waiting on the whim and fancy of their male friends and associates to help them.

Martha was hoping that a 'Mr Best', perhaps a real contact known to the group or perhaps a mythical 'made up' rescuer straight from Jane's imagination or the pairs' conversations, who might be on his way to Harrogate, could accompany her as she attempted to visit her friends Mr and Mrs Morton there. Perhaps she was off to help care for Mrs Morton in the birth of one of her thirteen children, or just to help her with her young brood. In the poem, Mr Best's 'lack of gallantry is teasingly rebuked' in Jane's signature style and in the laughing language that she and Martha so loved.[7] Jane appeals to the funny images of men vainly following the lure of the waters to heal and help their bodies and minds, and once again we are taken back to the little room upstairs at Steventon where Jane delighted her young audience with tales of vanity and bawdy, base behaviours in her *Juvenilia*. The topics touched upon so hilariously are quite clearly 'a joke intended for an intimate family friend.'[8] Jane boldly refers to the lingering power of death, unafraid as ever to bring up any subject, no matter how raw or how personal. Tact was an unhelpful hindrance to humour.

Yet in the poem Jane touchingly depicts her friend too, conjuring up words that sweetly define and compliment Martha and reveal qualities in her friend that Jane sets aside for special mention. The love and warmth in the words, allegedly being used to persuade and tempt the hero of the hour and poke fun, actually work as a soothing balm encouraging and tenderly reaching out to her friend. Jane depicts herself as the protector, as one standing up for her friend, pestering on her behalf – playfully proving her friendship and the happy bravery she is willing to put on show in defence of Martha's honour. We learn so much about Martha in these words; they spotlight her, putting her under the microscope, allowing us to magnify what Jane knows about her and helping us to piece together a more detailed sketch, a more accurate portrait of the woman Jane enjoyed spending time with and wanted to keep closely about her in everyday life. The 'friend of all', 'her converse sensible and sweet', how 'lucky' one was to be in her company – all of these musings are the heartfelt sighs accompanying the melancholy anticipation of the absence of her friend and all the lucky gain on offer to the poor, put-upon Mr Best:

> Oh, Mr Best, you're very bad
> And all the world shall know it;
> Your base behaviour shall be sung
> By me, a tuneful poet.
>
> You used to go to Harrowgate
> Each Summer as it came,
> And why, pray should you refuse
> To go this year the same?
>
> The way's as plain, the road's as smooth,
> The posting not increased;
> You're scarcely stouter than you were,
> Not younger Sir at least.
>
> If e'er the waters were of use
> Why now their use forego?

You may not live another year
All's mortal here below.

It is your duty Mr Best
To give your health repair
Vain else your Rienard's pills will be,
And vain your consort's care.

But yet a nobler duty calls
You now towards the North
Arise ennobled – as Escort
of Martha Lloyd stand forth.

She wants your aid – she honours you
With a distinguish'd call
Stand forth to be the friend of her
Who is the friend of all.

Take her and wonder at your luck,
In having such a Trust.
Her converse sensible and sweet
Will banish heat and dust.

So short she'll make the journey seem
You'll bid the chaise stand still.
T'will be like driving at full speed
From Newbury to Speen Hill.

Convey her safe to Morton's wife
And I'll forget the past,
And write some verses in your praise
As finely and as fast.

But if you still refuse to go
I'll never let you rest,
But haunt you with reproachful song
Oh! wicked Mr Best.[9]

In October 1806 the Austen women, accompanied by Martha, were on the move again. The group made their way via Steventon to Southampton with the newlywed Frank and his young and pregnant wife, Mary Gibson, with whom he had met and fallen in love whilst on a posting from the navy in Ramsgate. They took up lodgings of a short-term nature whilst they all looked for something that fitted Frank's budget and their allowance, and whilst they discerned where exactly in the city, that to Jane smelt so much of stinking fish, their needs would best be served. Jane and Martha were not always together as their familial duties still heralded them from afar and journeys had to be undertaken. In the small accommodation and in the strange configuration of relations new and old, this was sometimes a boon to both the household and the person filling a bed elsewhere. Fitting everybody in was like putting together a jigsaw puzzle and arrangements had to be carefully thought out. For Christmas, Martha went to stay with her sister Eliza at Kintbury whilst poor Jane had to host James and Mary over the yule-tide break which, in regard to her sister-in-law and the children, continued well into the new year.

Mrs Francis William Austen fell easily into the family habit of reading aloud together and enjoyed hearing old family favourites just 'as one could wish', even though they were entirely new to her.[10] Martha's sister Mary, on the other hand, was a lost cause to Jane in this regard and Jane had given up trying to change her. Her disinterest was no longer of any surprise nor shock to Jane but that didn't mean it would go unmentioned. 'The other Mary, I believe, has little pleasure from that or any other book.'[11] Oh, how Jane missed Martha's company and her sister too was away in Godmersham; what a strange passage of time this was for her. Mary was not in her good books at all. Jane blamed her for changing James's opinions and conversation too much, and that Mary had corrupted his ways for the worse, so much so that she could no longer enjoy his companionship either. In the meantime, Jane tried to engage the two Marys writing little plays and notes on raising a baby. Her solace came in these jottings which provided a little escape in her mind. When Mary invited Jane to accompany them back to Steventon, Jane tellingly pauses and drolly passes the retort, 'I need not give my answer,' for by now Jane was desperate for Martha to return and in the same letter begs for reassurance of her release from the situation. 'You must have heard from Martha by this time. We have had no accounts of Kintbury since her letter to me,' she laments.[12] We can almost hear her kicking her own feet and see her face in a pout. Jane busied and cheered herself with whatever contact with Martha she could make, sending baskets of fish and welcoming the same basket back into the house full of poultry and game, but it was no substitute for seeing her friend and she had yet to sit it out for a few weeks more.

Their care and provision for one another was not simply emotional though, but was often completely practical in nature. Finally, in the early spring of 1807, the troop began preparing to move into a house in the shadow of an elaborate abode in Castle Square. Martha had her own room and Jane shared with Cassandra as she always had. They needed to add some carpet to their rooms for warmth and care of the floor, especially underneath the dressing tables, and Jane took charge of making sure that this was organised. In Martha's absence, as a distraction to cover her loneliness for her and as a way of making the time go quicker, Jane tried as hard as she could to make Martha's room comfortable. A rug was knitted for Martha, probably by Mrs Austen, who offered to make one up for Cassandra too. The rug was looked over and inspected by Jane; she was quite pleased with it but had hoped it would look even better. 'I see no fault in the border, but the middle is dingy,' she commented at the time.[13] We do not know if Martha had chosen the colours as Cassandra was going to do for her own rug, so the colour scheme may well have suited Martha's tastes perfectly well. The concern Jane shows for Martha, wanting the rug to be just right for her, is a kindness of the most homely and intimate. Jane was definitely excited about making a home with Martha and making it as welcoming as possible.

Jane took an equal interest in the planting up of a beautiful little garden and shrubbery in readiness for Martha's arrival, which she hoped would be by the end of February. Martha confirmed with heartfelt 'best love' that their 'wishes are answered' and that she was truly filled with 'peace and comfort' here with Jane.[14] As soon as they were all able to return and take up residence, which in the case of Cassandra was not until April, the Austen women gathered with Martha alongside them with the new Captain and Mrs Frank Austen, and together they all set about readying the house and equipping it with all they and a baby could need.

Frank was particularly helpful, whipping up sets of curtains and making anything they required with his carpentry skills. He was so practical and useful to have around the house. Mary, however, did not glide easily into her pregnancy, finding the trials and changes in her body quite overwhelming at times, much to Jane's chagrin and sly amusement. Jane was convinced that she was, on occasion, a hindrance to herself and perhaps tended to exaggerate her situation, ignorant of how she was a major influence on her own experience. The women with young Mary were probably more help than she knew she needed, especially when Frank, who was on active service, had to leave to take up his new commission. They were fundamental in supporting her on her journey into motherhood, an experience that Mary would go on to undertake eleven times.

Chapter Ten

Charity Begins at Home

For Jane and Martha, the community around them had always held special significance. Apart from the expected etiquette of receiving visitors and paying calls in return, the pair really did focus on '3 or 4 families in a country village' as it were.[1] They knew about the needs in their surrounding neighbourhood and it was very much part of their individual characters and an identifying feature of their common bond, to think of others. Martha acted from a place of Christian service and duty, and Jane too had a real sense of stewardship and leadership alongside her self-awareness of place and standing in the social order. Martha was generous and noticed when people were in need, anticipating their feelings and wants. She was always looking to share what she had, and her upbringing really did express itself in her adult life in this way. Brought up in a rectory, just like Jane, she knew, understood and deeply respected the primary role and responsibility of the local church to care for the poor and the needy. This centred purposefulness never left Martha but only grew and her generosity continued to seek out worthy recipients which Jane enjoyed partnering with her in.

As an example of this, it is worth pondering on the loyalty to Martha's mother of dear Mrs Stent. She was actually a spinster originally from Hungerford and the title of Mrs was probably applied to her out of respect and deference to her age, and because of her position in the household. She had been part of Mrs Lloyd's household for many years and had devoted herself to the role. So much so that even after Mrs Lloyd's death, she was considered a family friend. Her own reduced circumstances due to previous 'family misfortunes' in her past would have been well known to Martha, and the 'narrow means' which she lived by would not have escaped Martha's notice or consideration going forward.[2] The witness to all of Mrs Lloyd's wishes in her will, Mrs Stent had verified in the eyes of the law that they were written in her mistress's handwriting and that she could testify, having known her 'character and manner', that they were indeed Mrs Lloyd's views and desires.[3] Mrs Stent had been there until the end. It is impossible not to think of Martha looking out for her as best she could for the rest of her life, for she lived another seven years after her mistress. She was hosted on the Highclere estate, home of Martha's grandfather, in a little cottage next to another of the family employees, Mrs Criswick.[4] Her health weakening, she was on Martha's mind until the end, even in the midst of her other charitable work. 'Poor Mrs Stent I hope will not be much longer a distress to anybody,' Jane writes with more of a mind to the pressure on Martha than for the elderly lady for whom Jane saw passing from this life to the next as a merciful release for all.[5]

The acts of kindness carried out by Martha and Jane were not only in response to personal circumstances such as births, weddings, injuries and illness, but were often dictated by the gentler routine patterns of the church calendar year and the seasonal periods of giving as laid out by this order. The weather often triggered needs too. Jane and Martha were always up on the news of the needs of their nearest citizens.

The interweaving of Martha's relations at Kintbury spread far and wide and relationships with kin, some of whom that with the passage of time were now quite tenuously linked, were still felt. It was in Martha's nature to reach out and think of what she could do to be a blessing to others and to lighten their burden in some way. A Miss Murden was one such lady to fall into this category. Another Jane, she was distantly connected to Martha via her sister's marriage into the Fowle family. She visited with Jane and Martha but did not entirely impress Jane. Jane made her welcome for Martha's sake, even though she turned up on occasion having previously refused the invitation 'sitting very ungracious and very silent with us.'[6] She was always on the move, with no real set direction or plan, from one set of uncomfortable circumstances to another. She was often complaining, unwell or seemingly unhappy with her lot and Jane did not vouch highly for her, wishing that there 'were more stability in the character' of her personality.[7] Yet Martha was not one to judge people or to only help the gracious, kind and seemingly deserving by their behaviour and merit. Martha saw it more her duty to help the unlovable and the rejected, those who seemed therefore to have a greater need. Jane was surprised at the difference Martha's charity made to the constitution and the personality of everyone whom she helped. It was like she gave them a makeover, and there was a definite sense of before and after. 'Miss Murden was quite a different creature this last evening from what she had been before, owing to her having with Martha's help found a situation in the morning which bids very fair for comfort.'[8] Martha, it seems, could see right into the heart of a person, beyond their outward behaviour, past the symptoms to the reason for their behaviour and responses – and she was often the one who found the cure.

One of Martha's oldest and most precious of friends was Mrs Dundas, née Ann Whitley of Barton Court, Kintbury. Heiress of the beautiful and sweeping estate, she was about thirteen years older than Martha and was married to the MP for Berkshire. Martha most probably first made her acquaintance when the Lloyd family were living at Enborne and would go over and visit their aunt and the Fowle family there. Later, when her sister was settled with her own home there, the probability of them getting to know each other and indeed to build up an attachment would have increased. Mrs Dundas often needed Martha's help and the impression given is that she was neither strong in nerves nor body but oh, so powerful in other ways. She was not a woman that Martha could readily refuse, but Martha also really seemed to love going and staying there with her. She went often and would never delay in responding to the clarion call of her Mrs D. Whether completely out of a sense of duty or due to the lure and pull of the friendship and her social scene it is hard to tell, but Martha always seemed to go willingly. There is just the slightest hint of jealousy from Jane at the speed and frequency with which Martha answered Mrs Dundas's bidding. 'Martha desires me to communicate something concerning herself,' Jane writes to Cassandra with her tongue in her cheek, perhaps a little put out by Martha's enthusiasm as the something 'is affording her very particular satisfaction; she is to be in Town this spring with Mrs Dundas.'[9] Martha may have been just as excited at the prospect of spending time in London in the lap of luxury as well she might, as spending time with Mrs D. There were few chances to enjoy such a lifestyle and when they came, it would have been wrong not to have looked forward to them. Jane knew this full well. As in all such opportunities, there were mutual benefits and sometimes an offer like this could come just at the right time, the optimum solution for someone who normally had very little control over their day-to-day direction. Jane was quick to acknowledge the power of Mrs Dundas's offers to her sister: 'you understand enough of the whys and wherefores to enter into her feelings, & to be conscious that of all possible arrangements, it is the one most acceptable to her.'[10] Sometimes being faced with the prospect of a visit elsewhere or being called upon to help someone else, a woman's feelings could get lost in the mix. Her true friend, Jane, recognised Martha's feelings and emotions; she always noticed them and felt for her. Maybe the other option might have been going to help her sister's family, enough to send a little chill down Jane's spine, hence the shared frisson and thrill that all Martha's sewing of service had harvested for her a little blessing. Jane could be big enough to wish goodness and happiness on her friend, even if it meant sacrificing her company in the process.

Martha showed the same empathy to others. When a mutual friend, Catherine Bigg, was to be married, Martha became unusually agitated on behalf of Mrs Dundas; so much so, that Jane passed on a message for her about the new Mrs Hill to Cassandra to ensure that a piece of her special wedding cake be shared with Mrs Dundas as per tradition in polite society. 'Do you recollect whether the Manydown family send about their Wedding Cake? Mrs Dundas has set her heart upon having a piece from her friend Catherine & Martha who knows what importance she attaches to this sort of thing is anxious for the sake of both, that there should not be a disappointment.'[11] We learn a lot about the character of Martha's Mrs D from the tone of the words used here, and we can just see why Martha might have picked up her fretting on her radar. This is a woman with clout who is used to getting her way and can make waves in local society if she doesn't. It is no wonder that Martha sped to her side when beckoned. Martha knows both parties full well and even if Catherine is not particularly one of Mrs Dundas's friends, to be snubbed in this manner was obviously going to matter a great deal and Martha was at pains to look after both. She was quick to spot a potential clash and faux pas, and together she and Jane moved quickly to avoid anyone being upset or disappointed, thus preventing any ugly consequences.

Martha herself felt duty-bound by the expectations of this woman and although she hoped to stay at home with Jane and Cassandra for Christmas, she had one ear and eye out for Mrs Dundas. Jane felt sure herself that the call would come: 'I do not think however, that here she will remain a great while' and Martha herself did not think that Mrs D 'will be able to do without her long.'[12]

Martha was such a dear help to her that in the latter days of the winter of Mrs Dundas's life, her family called upon her to wait upon the dying matriarch. Perhaps Martha was one of the few people that Mrs D could tolerate helping her in this state. Martha tried to write as often as she could, and Jane kept up a cheering correspondence with her from the sidelines. Sometimes Martha wrote such long letters that Jane declared herself 'forced to eat humble-pie' and teased Martha, 'I am really obliged to you however, & though it is in general much pleasanter to reproach than to be grateful, I do not mind it now.'[13] For Martha, writing to Jane must have been a way to keep her spirits up and to feel a little less isolated from her normal world and from her friend, with little or no one else to confide in or talk to. The lengthy letter, which appears to be longer than the norm between them, is a sign of just how much contact with Jane meant to Martha and how great her need to talk to her was.

Jane wasted no time in writing back, nor in encouraging her friend. For all her acerbic wit and pithy observations, for all her fearlessness in cutting to the chase and telling it how it is, Jane was eager to bear witness to happier truths too. 'We shall be glad to hear, whenever you can write, & can well imagine that time for writing must be wanting in such an arduous, busy, useful office as you fill at present.'[14] In acknowledging the difficulty of the task in front of Martha, she was also admiring Martha's strength and dedication

to what she herself would consider her Christian duty. Martha
would have so appreciated the shared understanding of the full-on
unrelenting nature of the task, but would have been buoyed up by
being reminded of her deeper values and the reason why this task was
so important.

'You are made for doing good & have quite as great a turn for it
I think as for physicking little Children.'[15] The kindness in these
words is so tender, like a gentle stroking of the hand or arm and
in them, we learn so much about the soft-hearted, caring nature of
Martha and the phenomenal combination of this with her excellent
communication skills, her intellect and understanding of medicinal
and holistic care. 'The mental Physick which you have been lately
applying bears a stamp beyond all common Charity, & I hope a
Blessing will continue to attend it.'[16] Here we see that Martha has
been able to describe accurately the range of symptoms that Mrs
Dundas was facing in her final days of her life. Clearly, the anxiety,
fear and confusion she was experiencing was extreme and Martha
with her understanding of natural science and the ability she had
for applying natural healing methods, alongside her deep Christian
belief, was obviously needed in full force.

This must have been very draining, and Jane recognised the acute
intensity of these final few days. Jane's prayer for support and grace to
be poured upon Martha to sustain her and that her help may continue
to be so effective is truly supportive, and just what Martha needed to
hear on what would turn out to be the eve of Mrs Dundas's death.
Still Jane knew that there was nothing that gladdened Martha's heart
more than being of use in this way and that she somehow became
a different person when using her super powers – a confident and
glowing friend, right in her element. Jane shows herself a true friend
in her encouraging praise.

She cannot help but wish Martha home though, and for the respite
of boredom, of the natural rhythms of their life together to work
their magic on Martha's mind and body, even if her soul and spirit
were quite happy. 'I am glad you are well & trust you are sure of being
so, while you are employed in such a way; I must hope however that
your health may e'er long stand the trial of a more common-place

course of days and that you will be able to leave Barton when Mrs D. D [Mrs Dundas's daughter, Mrs Dean Dundas] arrives there.'[17] I cannot help but imagine that Martha loved reading these words and as she closed her eyes in moments of rest, she too imagined the scenes of her home where her heart was. The closing lines of the letter, 'Pray give our best compliments to Mrs Dundas tell her that we hope soon to hear of her complete recovery' were on the outside of the address panel, and thus could be read by anyone transporting the letter to Martha.[18] The sentiments were undoubtedly sincerely wished and maybe Martha even said the words to the ailing lady as she came in and out of consciousness or sleep. However, the two friends must have known that the end was near. In this shared acknowledgement was a little message from Jane to hang on in there; it would not be much longer and they both knew it. Indeed, Jane was mightily relieved to soon learn that Martha would be able to come home and not have to return to Barton until the end of the next month, and that Martha's health would be able to recover within that time.

It wasn't long before she was off there again though and Jane didn't know how she felt about it at all. She was shocked that Martha might risk her own health again so soon, but knowing her friend as well as she did, she was not surprised. She had been half-expecting her to go back sooner, although she had hoped against hope that she might remain with Cassandra at Steventon. 'As far as one may venture to judge at a distance of 20 miles you must miss Martha.'[19] Jane knew that she would have been and she wrote hinting at the little wonder in her mind that Cassandra let Martha get away, leaving her alone there with Mary and James. 'For her sake I was glad to hear of her going, as I suppose she must have been growing anxious, and wanting to be again in scenes of agitation and exertion. She had a lovely day for her journey.'[20] Jane can't resist adding a tiny barbed flick of her tongue; she was clearly a little miffed with Martha for sacrificing herself again, in the way we are with a friend when we know it will all come to tears, and that we can well recognise their need to slow down even if they as yet cannot. Yet we know their nature and that it would be in vain to try and stop them on their chosen course. Mary's diaries confirm that Martha had indeed gone to Barton on

3 February, probably to assist the old lady's daughter in clearing her things after her mother's death and dealing with other administrative and household tasks. There may well have been community events to host at the house in honour of the deceased and to allow visitors to call and pay their respects to the family.

Women's needs were something that Jane and Martha, as spinsters without a certain steady income, were acutely aware of. When activating their kindly Christian antenna and stirring each other up to love and good works, it was the women's needs that were most often uppermost in their minds. Alongside old people and children, vulnerable women formed the greater part of their plans. As they had little money of their own to bestow, Jane and Martha were often apt to share provisions or make things as gifts. Martha made up a little parcel for Mrs Digweed, a farmer's wife and mother of three children under the age of 4, who was a local acquaintance of Jane and Martha's from Dummer. For many generations her husband's family had occupied the manor house at Steventon. Jane did not have a lot of time for the Dummer set, but the pair never ruled out anyone from their charity. The means would have been tight for this family, which would soon welcome a fourth little mouth to feed. Their pity for Mrs Digweed's plight would have been strong on many levels. 'I gave Mrs Digweed her little parcel, which she opened here & seemed much pleased with–& she desired me to make her best Thanks &c to Miss Lloyd for it.'[21] Jane and Martha knew what people needed and what their reaction might be – it needed no words. 'Martha may guess how full of wonder & gratitude she was'; this may have been true and a sincere feeling or perhaps an example in Jane's humour of the opposite view – either way, the friends gave graciously regardless of what the response of their audience might be.[22] Jane and Martha were always on the lookout for people to help. Just as they organised their shopping for each other, they made each other aware of needs and remembered if one or other had a donation to give or a worthy recipient in mind.

'You have sometimes expressed a wish of making Miss Benn some present,' Jane comments in a letter to her friend.[23] Miss Benn's brother was a Reverend, but he had some thirteen children and a wife to provide and care for. Miss Mary Benn was unmarried and very poor, and was often moved around with no hope of holding on to accommodation of any quality or for any real length of time. She could be turfed out of even the most 'wretched abode' with only a few months' notice and no clue of where she would settle next.[24] Martha and Jane took her under their wing, feeling sorry for her predicament, making sure that the community looked out for her and inviting her to come and eat with them as often as they could. She was typical of the type of person that Jane and Martha never failed to notice. They were constantly aware of the detail of others' needs but also respectful of their sensibilities. The friends tried to take great care to make an appropriate gift, that could be both of service and of a seemly proportion so that the recipient could not feel offended or obligated by accepting. 'Cassandra and I think that something of the shawl kind to wear over her shoulders within doors in very cold weather might be useful, but it must not be very handsome or she would not use it. Her long fur tippet is almost worn out.'[25] Within a few weeks Miss Benn was sporting this very gift, Martha jumping at the opportunity to fulfil a need and mindful of the advantage of her having it as soon as possible, before the winter weather really bit. With no money or abundance of heating, in what was most probably a small and roughly made cottage, Miss Benn would have been particularly vulnerable to the cold and her health depended on provisions such as the one Martha made. Jane delighted in passing on praise and congratulation to her friend; she knew that Martha would not be seeking it, but would be gratified indeed to know that the older lady was benefiting as they had all hoped she would. 'Miss Benn wore her new shawl last night, sat in it the whole evening and seemed to enjoy it very much.'[26]

But in terms of real importance, first and foremost, Martha and Jane's charitable works really did start from home. From the earliest days of their friendship, they were passing on compliments and care for members of each other's family and this desire to nurture one another's kin was a great draw in bringing them closer together. Two years after they became official 'sisters-in-law', Martha wrote to Jane and made her very happy in passing on news about her brother

Charles and his reception in society. We know that this praise of her 'own particular little brother' would make her heart sing, as she had revelled in the joy of her friend and neighbour Madam Lefroy's comments that she 'never saw anyone so much improved in her life' and thought him 'handsomer than Henry'.[27] This was saying something as Henry was always lauded as the charming and sociable bonny lad of the family. Often people said that Jane looked more like him than any other sibling, so maybe this comment was an inside joke with Jane. Martha passing on the news as a sort of positive gossip that Charles was 'very much admired at Kintbury' by her sister Eliza and the Fowle family, with whom the Austens felt a familial connection, was a report of the kindest sort.[28] It helped soothe Jane's fears for him and to reaffirm to herself that her brother was doing well. She had witnessed and half-winced to herself at the pains he went through at Godmersham trying to fit in with and impress that set; bending and changing himself so much that he was 'oppressed by a pain in his face or powder in his hair.'[29] Martha clearly knew her friend so well and that this particular type of news would go down well with her and build her up.

The family's offspring were a preoccupation for Jane and Martha, each being concerned in the comings and goings of each other's relatives. This was either when things were going badly, as in some case relating to a 21-year-old Fowle, 'Your nephew William's state seems very alarming, Mary Jane… writes of him as very uneasy; I hope his Father and Mother are so too', or when the news was better.[30] The children of the family were a constant joy and occupied a great deal of Jane and Martha's thoughts and time. They were called upon as single adult women to take care of the children either at their homes or as a stop-off on their journeys to and from school. When the boys were at Winchester College in Hampshire, visiting with them was more than just a familial chore, and Martha and Jane adored spending time with them. When Jane once suffered as many as five boys staying over with her and her mother on their way to start the new term though, she couldn't help but let Martha know how she felt at the thought of being 'all alive' and how much she would be 'not sorry' when it was all over.[31] Martha visited the same group one October, once term was underway, making a detour on her way back to Southampton so that she could visit them at school. She spent an hour and a half with them, 'walking about' with 'the three boys' (her nephew, Eliza's son, and Edward's sons) and notes Jane making a stop 'at the Pastrycook's'.[32]

Jane revelled in the fact that Martha knew the children so well and that they loved her back in return. 'Pray give my duty to grandmamma and love to Miss Floyd,' writes little Elizabeth, Edward's daughter, using the inflection that Mrs Lloyd had tried so determinedly to inculcate amongst the family, insistent that it was the true Welsh pronunciation of their name.[33] Another sign of the happy entwined lives they lived together was the way Martha was able to comment to Jane on how the little ones had changed – passing on news of healthy, growing children. That Martha was able to see a likeness for Henry in the young George was also a lovely link between the two women. They came to know each other's families so well that they could remember back to how they once were and notice little details and signs in other family members. These subtle details are not the type to be picked out by acquaintances only, but by close and intimate friends who have spent a lot of time with one another. This is a touching detail and that Martha mentions it makes it even more tender still.

Jane was delighted that Martha 'speaks with the same admiration as before of his Manners' in reference to Edward.[34] She knew how much manners and polite behaviour meant to both of them and, of course, she revered Martha's high standards. In mentioning his manners being so good, Martha was esteeming their little relative in both their eyes. This sort of comment always caught Jane's attention and her heart. 'My mother and Martha both write with great satisfaction of Anna's behaviour,' she noted with warmth and pride of their little niece.[35] It was always so much more fulsome and heartfelt with such goodwill and hope for Anna than any news she ever received in that regard from Mary. The fact that the family's children had drawn such praise from Martha was praise indeed in Jane's eyes, and she found this point so gratifying that she had to pass it on as news to her sister.

The strength of these family bonds was to be truly tested when the sad news reached them in Southampton, via a short and hastily written letter from Martha's sister Mary, that Edward's wife, Elizabeth – so helpful to Martha at the time of her own mother's death – had died shortly after the birth of her eleventh child. Cassandra, thank heavens, was already at Godmersham, having gone there to take care of Elizabeth in her confinement and to help with the new-born baby boy. Martha mourned for the boys dreadfully. No doubt the loss of their mother touched a raw nerve with her, as she had lost her own parent only a few years before, and knew the sadness of losing a parent in one's younger years. They had returned to Steventon with James and Mary, and Martha and Jane's heartstrings were severely pulled. For all their praise and sanctioning of the decision for the boys to be picked up as soon as possible, and by James who had the means to do this, they were itching to take care of the poor souls and must have wondered how Mary would console them beyond her practical care. They believed them to be 'more comfortable at Steventon' but Jane was in a quandary as to if they would be better with her and Martha (certainly, she knew that Cassandra would understand her 'feelings' about this).[36] 'I own myself disappointed by the arrangement; I should have loved to have them with me at such a time.'[37] Being with her meant having Martha's watchful and caring eye too, and Jane would have been assured of their emotional wellbeing and care. Jane did not hold out the same hope of Mary. Less than ten days later, she got her wish.

Jane, full of her grief and sympathy for her immediate and extended family and Elizabeth's friends and relations, was also prompt to relay that Martha was in sync and tandem with their grief and that Cassandra must tell Edward 'that we feel for him and pray for him.'[38] She does not hesitate to make sure that Cassandra is aware 'with what true simpathy [sic] our feelings are shared by Martha'; we can almost see her eyes brimming with tears as it all starts to sink in.[39] The power and strength of her language in communicating not only her own but Martha's grief, and her emphasis on Martha's jointly sharing any good news from the family quarter in Kent, is unusually direct in its reference to female emotions. Jane is quite sure that Cassandra would not even need the news of Martha's mourning to be imparted to her; she would not need any convincing or even telling of how Martha might be feeling right now – she would just know. 'You need not be told,' she confirms with Cassandra as she touchingly includes, 'she is the friend and sister under every circumstance.'[40]

Martha and Jane instantly changed into mourning clothes to signify to the outside world their solidarity in their grief with their family. They both wore the same 'bombazeen and crape', wanting to be seen to be showing respect in the most publicly acceptable way, and as they had noted was 'universal here' in their neighbourhood in Southampton as it surely was in accordance with 'Martha's previous observation.'[41] They even tried on some appropriate shoes in the hope that they would be a suitable match for Cassandra. Jane believed in and wanted to follow just what her sensible and knowledgeable Martha thought was the best thing to do and as always at critical moments, she trusted in Martha's opinion and values, and relied upon her good judgement.

Jane and Martha helped each other and tried to bring relief by being a hub of communications with all branches of their family. In constant and frequent contact with Cassandra at Godmersham, whose health they were keen not to suffer under all of her extra unexpected responsibilities and trials, and the family in general, they passed on news and all the goodwill and kind words from other parties and lightened the load with tales and titbits from their friends in Hampshire. They were particularly anxious to know how the other children were coping and once under their roof, they kept a careful eye on the boys' impressions of the situation, most notably their tears and outward signs of grief on show. Jane turned to Martha for reassurance that both boys, in their personal expressions of their understanding, were alright considering the terrible circumstances and that they were appropriately channelling and processing their feelings, most notably their comprehension of their sadness and shock.

Martha used her perceptive natural skills for nurturing and caring for the sick and for young children, putting to the test all that area of awareness and intelligence that she had practised over the years. She monitored and checked them, using those first twenty-four hours to ascertain the mental and physical state of both boys. They had been sent from Steventon in late October unaccompanied and without coats – a sign that Jane and Martha were indeed right to bring them both under their watchful and more nurturing gaze. It seemed that Mary had not had time to fetch them many clothes, and that neither James nor herself had considered these needs. The poor coachman had leant them his own coat to share.

Jane clung for comfort to Martha's evaluation of the suffering children. Her assessment of them left her mightily relieved and comforted. 'Miss Lloyd, who is a more impartial judge than I can be, is exceedingly pleased with them.'[42] The boys were able to be sincere and authentic under their care and to express their grief and shock in a healthy way in a safe environment. Jane and Martha distracted and cared for them with a mixture of fun and entertaining indoor games and gentle outdoor strolls in nature, sitting alongside the river. Martha and Jane's faith was foremost in their mind as a tool for caring for and calming the boys, and they centred them at their hearth with the rituals and routines of their religion. 'In the evening we had the Psalms and Lessons, and a sermon at home,' a tradition that both women would have practised in some form or another since childhood.[43] The setting must have been extremely peaceful and gently soothing, probably shared by them both, no doubt with a large input from Martha whose faith was her bedrock and would have been in her eyes the greatest gift she could have shared with the boys, and perhaps even incorporating some of Jane's own prayers. The boys responded in kind, their spirits stilling; these two growing and active young boys who had come to the house at a time of high confusion and huge distress remained 'very attentive' and the moment shared had a huge impact on them. 'You will not expect to hear that they did not return to conundrums the moment it was over,'[44] says Jane with a grateful heart.

Edward and his 'Harem' of little daughters, as Jane and Martha nicknamed them, would often visit with their grandmother and aunts when on an annual visit to Edward's estates or on short stays timed to coincide with either collecting the boys from or dropping them off at school in Winchester.[45] Jane would make sure that Martha knew of 'their safe arrival and happiness.'[46] Martha was always kind enough to allow her rooms to be let out to the family in her absence, and the little ones and not so little ones really appreciated it. 'Lizzy was much obliged to you for your message, but <u>she</u> had the little room. Her Father having his choice and being used to a very large Bedchamber at home, would of course prefer the ample space of yours.'[47] Jane was always keen to let Martha know how the little posse had got on and to compare a visit with themselves in a favourable light – especially when contrasted with a return to school or a visit to James and Mary. This tongue-in-cheek teasing of Martha over her sister must have been a shared opinion and acceptable in their conversation – Jane getting away with it, another sign of the confidences they shared, that words could be said or written between them for their eyes only, without a hint of recrimination or offence. 'The visit was a very pleasant one I really believe on each side; they were certainly very sorry to go away, but a little of that sorrow must be attributed to a disinclination for what was before them. They have had favourable weather however, and I hope Steventon may have been better than they expected.'[48]

Most of all, Jane liked it when Martha was back at home with her, her mother and Cassandra. Jane did not at all tolerate it well being left in sole charge of the house, housekeeping or daily routines, and worse, if her mother had taken one of her turns, triggered either by real or imagined illness, then Jane liked it even less. More than anything in these situations, she would long for Martha's sympathy and for her to return and spotlight her practical help on them all. It brought such relief to Jane. 'I will not say anything of the weather we have lately had, for if you were not aware of its' being terrible, it would be cruel to put it in your head,'[49] she says, emotively paving the way for a little tea and sympathy and a tug at Martha's heartstrings before she drops her next hint: 'My Mother slept through a good deal of Sunday, but still it was impossible not to be disordered by such a sky, and even yesterday she was but poorly.'[50] The implication being that her mother has been quite demanding, and that Martha would well understand what that meant. Dark skies and intense air pressure could easily trigger a migraine and being trapped in such a dull scene, with little light and perhaps incessant storms, Mrs Austen could have been subjected to one of her headaches. The prisoner here was not simply Mrs Austen; Jane was clearly meaning for her friend to realise the awful truth and come home to rescue her too, to return to where she was needed more than anyone else could possibly need her. Jane was laying on her hints with a trowel. Everyone in the family knew how well Mrs Austen got along with Martha and how much lighter Jane felt being able to leave her mother in Martha's care. She could be released to go and enjoy herself in the comfort of knowing how well they got along and how well Martha understood her mother and could handle her – far better than she felt she did herself at times. 'We four sweet brothers and sisters dine today at the Gt House. Is that not quite natural? Grandmama and Miss Lloyd will be by themselves, I do not exactly know what they will have for dinner, very likely some pork?'[51] The cheeky implication here, being I don't know, and I don't much care – Martha will sort it and it will not be my problem. Although in her heart of hearts she really did care, Jane delighted in the lightening of her load, the freedom that Martha afforded her, even the freedom to think in this rebellious way; it fired her imagination and allowed her the permission to just be herself and Jane adored it.

Chapter Eleven

Our Chawton Home

And so it was that Jane's need for Martha and her friendship continued. As plans and schemes emerged in the aftermath of Elizabeth Knight's death, Martha was unquestionably included in Jane's vision for her own next move. There was no doubt in her mind that any change for her was going to mean a change for Martha too, that she would be included. Most intriguingly and unexpectedly, Edward offered a choice of his own cottages to his mother, for her and his sisters to live in permanently. One of these was in Wye, Kent and seemed most appealing to Mrs Austen and her inmates, although it unsettled Mary, Martha's sister, which did not bother Jane in the slightest. The other was a cottage in the village of Chawton, back in the boundaries of their beloved Hampshire, close to Alton. Jane was hopeful but also desperate for the whole idea to be nailed down, for her mother to be convinced and for Edward and Lady Bridges to consent to the whole plan. She felt quite sure that all could and should be well, however, there was a bubble of excitement within that she might let the cat out of the bag and jinx everything. 'We scarcely feel however, to be in suspense, or only enough to keep our plans to ourselves,' she writes of her mother, Martha and herself at home.[1] 'We have not yet mentioned them to Steventon,' she muses with a mix of a little trepidation and stubbornness, but 'we are all quite familiarised to the idea ourselves,'[2] emphasising the 'we' and the closed circle of her decision-makers. Jane had by now pulled Martha closer into her camp and was convinced that their claim on her would trump anyone else's approval or even disapproval.

Jane had been careful to point out to Edward at the time of Elizabeth's passing just how caring, interested and totally supportive of everyone at Godmersham Martha was. The timing of her reminder was poignant – could it be she felt the need to praise Martha in his presence and to smooth away any chance of doubt he might have about including her in the lodgings – their new home? She could not bear other alternatives creeping in and gaining hold in his mind. She used emotional and unusually bold language in addressing and appealing to Edward, almost directly, but from standing just behind the shield of her big sister Cassandra's lips as trusted messenger in this deed; 'Martha begs my brother may be assured of her interest in everything relating to him and his family, and of her sincerely partaking our pleasure in the receipt of every good account from Godmersham.'[3] Jane would have been devastated to lose her and no joy could be found for her in a permanent home without Martha in it.

There were a few suggested dates floating hither and thither, and questions and enquiries were batted about like flies. Mrs Austen, Jane and Martha, along with Cassandra at Godmersham, were listening out for and gathering together any snippets of information from Henry and Edward and different friendly sources who knew the neighbourhood, or who at least thought they did. Gradually the image of their Chawton home came into view, with its six bedchambers – but what would there be of a kitchen garden or cellars? Mary, too, kept her ear to the ground and whilst she was in nearby Alton, caring for Mrs Frank Austen in her confinement, her family record notes that on 7 July 1809 they 'took possession of their new home at Chawton' finally moving out of Southampton.[4] Jane and her family went to Godmersham for a long stay as Martha left for Barton and the highly anticipated trip to London with her friends. This left plenty of time for excitement to brew and the house to be put in order ready for their habitation. All these plans and events lay ruminating in Jane's mind and must have been hotly anticipated by both friends.

In the days that followed, Jane wrote one of her cheering poems to Frank to congratulate him and his wife on the birth of their little baby boy. In the poem she also touched on the shores of their own lives, mentioning her happiness and determination to be grateful for their new home. But Jane, true to her wit, could not resist a little knock, knowing that the larger house that Edward owned was just a few hundred metres away and that they, however happy, were in a smaller cottage that had seen many uses and was now being cobbled together into one dwelling from previous incarnations and configurations, including once having been used as an inn. Charles did indeed move in to Chawton House for a while and one of his daughter's signatures can be seen scribbled as an autograph on one of the paintings in a touching reminder of the young family's presence there.

> Our Chawton home – how much we find
> Already in it to our mind
> And how convinced that when complete,
> It will all other Houses beat,
> That ever have been made or mended,
> with rooms concise or rooms distended.
> You'll find us very snug next year;
> Perhaps with Charles and Fanny near
> for now, it often does delight us
> To fancy them just over-right us.[5]

For Jane, though, the greatest gift of all, was that there was room enough in the place and in everyone's hearts for Martha to live there with them too. By now, Martha had been living with Jane for over five years and they had been friends for over twenty – more than half of Jane's life. Martha was now known throughout the family as more than just an acquaintance or friend of Jane's, or even more than just her association to the family via James and Mary. To even the youngest members of the family, Martha was now defined as a most 'near connection,' which meant being part of the 'circle of persons with whom one is brought into more or less intimate relations.'[6] She was closer and nearer than other friends might be and their friendship was seen as special, even more so now after all these years, and it was binding Martha together with Jane almost as if they themselves were closely related by kinship. They were now replanted 'inmates', having made their home together for more years than the youngest ones of the family had memory of, co-habiting companions in what felt like a more permanent arrangement in a more fixed abode.[7] It was a home, this time organised by the family for the family and made to work by Edward as 'a labour of love'.[8] In this place, settled at Chawton, Jane had found a 'real home' amongst 'her own people.'[9]

The house was along the road that led one way to Alton and the other to Winchester. Jane and Cassandra shared their bedroom as always and were settled near to their mother. With another room available for visiting family, Martha had her own room set around the corner from the others, in a little more private part of the house. The room was of good proportions, with 'ample space' as Jane remembered to tease Martha about.[10] Jane had always been most keen that Martha should feel settled and comfortable in all their homes together. She thought ahead and always checked up that things were suited to Martha's needs and tastes. She wrote to Cassandra about provisions for her rooms and helped smooth over every anticipated crease in Martha's happiness. When Martha couldn't open her drawers as Cassandra had left her the wrong key, Jane made sure it was dealt with: 'Martha does not find the key, which you left in my charge for her, suit the keyhole-& wants to know whether you think you can have mistaken it. It should open the interior of her High Drawers – but she is in no hurry about it.'[11] It was in these little details that she showed her continued concern that Martha be included and treated as an equal. Wherever it was that they lived together, she simply wanted her to feel at home.

Martha's Chawton room had a chillier aspect, but she did have a window which, like that of downstairs, 'opened at the side which gave view only to turf and trees,' except that as it was a floor up, Martha would have been able to see over 'a high wooden fence and hornbeam hedge' and witness the hurtling post-chaise and its passengers as it trundled by.[12] Happily, Martha would have also been able to turn her eyes to look upon verdure as she could see the parkland of Chawton House in the distance and their very own garden set out around her. From her side of the house 'trees were planted each side to form a shrubbery walk' and directly below her bedroom was the little kitchen with herbs and plants around the door. The young family remembered in their older age Martha being part of a very 'comfortable and ladylike establishment, though the means which supported it were not large.'[13]

Now a new routine was put happily into place. Jane would get up early and practise the pianoforte, which she was delighted to have once more so that she could play 'little country dances' for their nieces and nephews.[14] Then she would lay out the breakfast things and be done with her household duties for the day. Martha and Cassandra took charge of all the remainder; they 'did all the rest' as the younger ones put it, sharing the housekeeping together and directing any home help that they were able to have.[15] Here Martha was to really come into her own, and her skills and ability to run a house would have been really appreciated. All that she had begun to contribute to their lives together in Southampton whilst caring for their friends or hosting younger relatives could now really come to the fore. She was all set to have a truly positive impact and would prove her worth as an asset to the family, as if that had ever been in doubt.

Here, it seems, was the recipe for creative freedom. Jane, who had experienced the contrast of different homes in Bath with her parents and in the jam-packed rooms in Southampton, was now able to recreate those early country-life days with her friend and that familiar atmosphere in which 'she had talked with Martha, dined with her, slept with her, walked and joked and found her available to renew civil intimacies.'[16] For as well as being a generous, community-minded person dedicated to her charitable duties, Jane was also still 'a very private person' who needed to feel that she was 'having easy relations with the Austen's' and that her 'strong psychological defences' were all shored up.[17] Jane still had her ever-pressing need for Cassandra, present since childhood and treasured the happiness that she found in Martha; in Chawton, the atmosphere became once more conducive to freeing and feeding her imagination.

The quiet, calm and generously controlled atmosphere of the house helped build a screen of security around Jane. She famously asked her family not to repair the squeaky door that opened within earshot of the approach to the room where she wrote, enjoying the warning sign when someone arrived in the hall and allowing her time to either finish a thought, jot a note or pop her things clean away. This tiny matter is a symbol of how 'feeling right' and eliminating any 'feeling bad' was so key in producing the elements required for Jane and her 'atmosphere of growth.'[18] With Martha there as part of her nurturing group and with no other elements to cater for but themselves, Jane could rely upon their 'simple and sane routines' and let herself relax into whatever world she wanted to go and explore.[19] Now Jane had her audience from that upper room back again, she had her own little forum with whom she could try out ideas or pitch scenarios. She could fire an idea off in perfect secrecy; she could gauge their precious reaction once again and see if she could make them laugh and thrive on her delight in their laughter in return. Once more, she had the space and time and the ones she could 'rely only on' 'those female friends who laughed with her.'[20] Madam Lefroy had now passed and the Bigg sisters were more engrossed in their own lives, marrying and involving themselves in the world of their own families. Martha, however, was still there, she was the one that Jane had kept close and drawn closer still, the one that she kept coming back to. Now her 'old inspiration' was no longer far, she was within the same four walls of the special citadel that was Chawton.[21] Now that Jane had her close friend and companion accompanying her on a daily basis and co-creating the perfect home environment, Jane could allow her vulnerabilities and creative sensibilities to congregate and rise to the surface of her mind and her will. Their long friendship, now giving a different perspective and comfort to Jane, became even deeper than before and therefore the impact of Martha's atmosphere and the emotional ambience that she created was more symbiotic.

In this period of her life, Jane was highly influenced by both the energy and the stillness that Martha could help to create with her and for her. At Chawton in the physical space of the safety of their home and with the emotional space that being with her sister and Martha created and cleared, Jane settled back to her writing like never before. Creativity had tried to surface in the meantime in the form of keen observations whilst Jane juggled the commitments to her everyday life as part of her local society, and in the midst of milling about with new faces and new scenery, with all those different people and locations to enjoy. Her writing talents had appeared again, even when Jane had found herself caught up in the midst of the upheaval and fall-out caused by the loss of loved ones. During their time in Bath and Southampton, she had been picking at the seams of her earlier works, re-copying out and editing little pieces here and there of *Susan*. She had even attempted to allow new ideas to form and take shape on paper, but the death of her father in 1805 put pay to the story of *The Watsons* – the subject matter mirroring life too closely for the comfort and the solace in writing to be enjoyed and dampening all Jane's desire for this story and any effort to entertain with it. In these 'intervening' years, in hindsight Jane 'seems for a while to have given up writing.'[22] However, as soon as Jane had the move to her new home with Martha, Cassandra and her mother confirmed to her, a strange transformation began to take hold. She was seized with the conviction and confidence to seek to claim back the rights to the still unpublished *Susan* from the lacklustre and unhelpful publishers that had acquired them six years before.[23] Unfortunately, their response, a stubborn clinging to the manuscript unless she could buy it back for the same price she was paid for it, put her off. It must have been a bugbear for her and one that she talked with Martha about. The work was now definitely in her sights; she had a clear goal for it and a more confident determination to get it back in her possession and under her will once more. If women cannot work if they are not happy, then the converse by implication is equally true; if Jane now found a new impetus to create, then she must have been very content and perhaps more so than she had been for a very long time.

Even Jane's family recognised the chemical reaction that happened when the household at Chawton first formed its ranks. The spark that had been lit up in the little room at Steventon had ignited again. Jane 'rediscovered her earlier manuscript notebooks' and the feelings they stirred up collided with who she felt she was in that moment and what, with the support and encouragement of her significant others, she now believed her work could become.[24] 'The intense burst of creativity between 1810 and 1817 was the necessary consequence of the recreation in the Chawton years of the emotional and environmental security that Steventon had represented' is what Jane's family later accepted and believed to be the truth of this

period.[25] In other words, at this exact and particular moment in time
of the coming together of the household in Chawton, there was
an inevitability in the outpouring of Jane's writing; it was a perfect
storm of inner confidence that created a combustion of ideas that
came to life immediately, once certain key elements were in place
– fundamental foundational parts of a whole that had once come
together back at Steventon. The emotional stability way back then
had stemmed from the banter of key people; the fun and freedom
had been instilled in the place by particular individuals and habitual
routines. 'The unusual and stimulating home' acknowledged in the
past, was being recreated, 'with all the fun and nonsense' of before
resonating here now in the present.[26] The common denominator
at Chawton, apart from her mother and her beloved sister, was her
special and precious friend Martha; the aforesaid 'environmental
security' was created by these pillars, the creators and upholders of
her new world, distinctly in the persons of Cassandra and Martha.
They created a sort of 'island from the world' and the sea around it,
now was the ebb and flow of their daily life around the kitchen table,
just as it had been in the upper rooms at the rectory in Steventon.[27]
Jane *could* now set to work with intent and consciously affect all
her desires on work old and new. Truly it was the 'vigilance', the
watching over her of these 'older women that left her secure so that
her imagination and recollections were free to interact.'[28] Away from
these relationships whilst living in the extended and disrupted family
homes of Bath and Southampton, Jane was separated, interrupted
and semi-estranged from Martha, yet here cleaved together again
she could become fully reunited with her and the joy of their daily
rapport, and importantly, as a result, she could get back in touch with
herself.

Now that Jane was part of a 'real home' at Chawton, she launched
into writing full-length novels.[29] She set herself upon her 'old'
ones, reordering and rewriting them, making what she saw as key
'alterations and contractions' to ensure she was writing a message to
suit the later times, and to fulfil the vision that she now had for her
older stories.[30] She renamed the novels begun back in the days of
Steventon. *Elinor and Marianne* now became *Sense and Sensibility* and

was no longer to be a story told in epistolary form. *First Impressions* was retitled and reset as *Pride and Prejudice*. What had once been known in the family as a 'confidential publication read and discussed with the extended Steventon household' which included her friend Martha, now in Jane's mind became something she was brave enough to share and to pursue on the public stage.[31] In this wonderful new world of revisiting, reinventing and revamping earlier writing between 1811 and 1816, Jane also wrote new novels entirely from scratch; *Mansfield Park, Emma, Persuasion, A Plan of a Novel* and in 1817, the unfinished draft later named *Sanditon*.

It is widely acknowledged that this period of renewed determination to write with concentrated application and vigour represented a resumption in Jane's writing career almost unequalled to any that had happened before. There is a noticeable spike, a peak in her writing timeline during this period that it is linked so obviously and coincides so precisely with the move to the house at Chawton that renders it a marker for us to take note of. Apart from the volume and quality of the editing, re-writing, 'cannibalising' and the sharp, considered and relentless focus on each of the works in turn that she wrote at this period, the metamorphosis that takes hold of Jane is stark leading some to reflect that in this period, 'Austen underwent a sort of personal and authorial revolution.'[32] Jane needed the balance of powers around her to align in order to create; she needed conducive circumstances such as these. Some believe that having 'the society of some young relatives interested in writing, helped to free Austen's mind and restore confidence' but without the combined efforts of Cassandra and Martha in creating the climate for this new season of Jane's writing, even the children and their needs could not have helped Jane plumb the depths of her own consciousness and creative source.[33]

Martha was a key part of Jane moving from unpublished to published author. She was a catalyst and influence on Jane's immediate environment and lifestyle, part of the charge that created the current that helped Jane to reverse the tide and direction of her creative ambitions. Martha co-created the conditions which enabled Jane to see and make the changes she wanted to make in herself. Martha was a friend when Jane needed her most. She helped her friend to get her mojo back and helped her to take the stopper out of the bottle of her creativity that meant she could finally find her voice and let her words and ideas flow. As a by-product of her presence, Martha helped Jane to pin down and capture the spirit and meaning of what she wanted to express – she held the stillness with Cassandra so that Jane could get quiet enough herself to hear the ideas and form them into the shapes she needed to, to express herself. Jane could now move from having fleeting ideas, from 'giving herself in small drops' to her art and now allow a whole 'pitcher-full' to accumulate.[34] It was Martha and Cassandra who allowed Jane to find substantial and routine solitude. They removed many of the household duties, the traditional 'roles' and obligations from her shoulders in the full understanding, as perhaps only women and women of their generation could, that this would make a huge difference. It would help leave a store of energy for Jane that she could then draw upon, but it would also help to open up a portal for Jane to pass through into her 'creative solitude.'[35]

This practical help is cited as the main benefit attributed to Martha and Cassandra at this time, but alone time was not the only necessary requirement for Jane. She could have got up earlier, gone to bed later, turned down invitations and carved out time to set aside for her own needs, even in Bath or Southampton. No, it was this and something more that Martha helped to create – she changed the atmosphere, and she and Cassandra understood Jane's need, giving her permission to make as much time for it as she needed. They helped settle her spirit with their approbation and mutual goodwill. They took the burdens from her and moreover, they did not judge Jane for needing this time or shame her away from it, because they knew that 'certain springs are tapped only when we are alone.'[36] They knew that it was in the quiet, in the unrationed stillness that Jane could work through and puzzle out all her thoughts and find opportunity to finally and fully, as every creative type needs, 'turn inward for strength.'[37]

For Jane, writing from her own observations and her own opinions required a great deal of self-awareness. Martha being her mate and hanging around with her in the meantime, in the gaps in between her thinking, helped her find and subsequently tap into her true self again – something which solitude and energy alone had been unable to do. Knowing that Martha would be around at some point and in having refreshing conversations with her over lunch or in walking to visit a neighbour or run an errand, Jane knew that she had found a way to release and distil her spirit, that essence that she needed in reserve for those moments of muse and of writing. When Martha was back in her life on a day-to-day basis, in the hundreds of mundane, simple routine-like interactions of their day, interspersed with their own history, perspective, humour and trust, Jane had something even more – she had someone to help feed her soul. Martha, alongside Cassandra, was part of the fuel to the fire; she was a sustainer of her friend and when she had not been there like this, then Jane's well had been left to run dry.

In Bath and Southampton, Jane was constantly giving out, to her family, the relations and the social expectations upon her. It had always been Jane's plan to have Martha live with them. Perhaps like all truly close friendships, Jane noticed early on, not what Martha did, nor even what she had to say, but the way that she made her feel.[38] She became aware, perhaps more acutely of the loss of this anchoring force, when they were apart, when Martha was in Barton or there were too many people crammed into the house in Castle Square. Jane loved being at Henry's lodgings in Hans Place for the solitude and peace, or the library at Godmersham when she had it all to herself, but it was Martha who nourished Jane, even when she was not conscious of it. Even the types of household task that they undertook together at Steventon and Ibthorpe, times of happy flow in writing for Jane, were 'conducive to a quiet contemplative drawing together of the self', and when these were enlarged and warped into other shapes, perhaps it was then that Jane noticed that Martha was the missing piece – the missing peace.[39] The absence of Martha was a major part of why Jane was 'simply fretted with removals and uncongenial surroundings and unhappy.'[40] Martha was the cog in the wheel that produced congeniality; she was the gilder of happiness that Jane missed, and it affected her ability to write.

In the absence of this power Jane lost heart and therefore grew fonder of Martha. Perhaps we see now why Jane always contrived and chivvied, petitioned, pursued and pleaded for the plans that she had for her and Martha as a unit. Martha helped Jane feel more like herself than any other friend of her age. Martha fostered in Jane a sense of her true identity. Martha knew the 'real' Jane and when they spent time together, Jane was filled with that self-identity and awareness too and it made her feel great. In the curated calm of their Chawton home, Martha helped roll back the malady that had afflicted Jane in her early thirties when she was 'not in health of body and spirit' and now Martha helped hugely in creating that which had been lacking, a 'sufficiently settled and sympathetic' environment.[41] With the correct soil and conditions now prepared and in place, seeds of creativity could be sowed and harvested. Here we see perhaps why Jane had previously shunned the married life, in order to pour her whole self positively into her writing. Martha was the other necessary influence she needed to bring to bear on that life, so that her focus and her goals would be free from fetters and fragmentation, from duty and distraction. Jane may have chosen and even needed to be someone who 'really lived remote, in great reserve' but it was more a case of her living near to her well, her source; without it she would have withered and run dry.[42] When Martha was around Jane found she made her feel truly alive and that her creativity was more vivid and within easier reach. Martha was key to her happiness, and she found happiness in writing. Without Martha's support and presence, would such 'astounding fecundity' have taken place at this time and would the 'three supreme efforts of her maturity' have pushed through?[43] Jane had become fully conscious and aware of this need to have her friend around. Perhaps it was even for many years now that Jane had 'hungered nostalgically' for the 'original pattern' of their early friendship together when writing and laughing with Martha were her only cares.[44] Now they were back together, every day creativity could flourish in the security of knowing that Martha was nearby along with her beloved sister; the writing could finally find a way out and it was immediate and decisive in its appearance.

This outlet that allowed passion for her writing to flow once again was no flash in the pan or overnight obsession that fizzled out. Two years into her life with Martha, her mother and sister in their private quarters, despite the continuing family visits and day-to-day life and responsibilities, Jane was still happily ensconced in her commitment to her creativity. 'No indeed I am never too busy to think of S & S. I can no more forget it, than a mother can forget her sucking child,' Jane asserts to Cassandra in the midst of her editing of the work.[45] Now her brother Henry was involved and acting as her agent from London. He was busy touting for deals and drumming up interest and once he had secured Jane a publisher, he was then wonderfully active on Jane's behalf, chivvying the printers and hurrying the process to publication as much as he could, and in truth, more than a woman doing the same could expect to achieve. Jane did not much like delegating this role to Henry, and her shyness pressed upon her the weight of the expectation that this placed on her brother and on his health. She was always conscious of any strain upon him, of taking him away from his priorities and business. Jane did not like the feeling of being the one behind the imposition, yet she also felt the strain of the frustration at being powerless to speed up the publishing conveyor belt.

Thus we see reiterated the importance of the discreet layering of comfort and support from Martha and Cassandra – the creative process was a fragile one that took its toll on the caring sensibilities of the author, who disliked the feeling that came with being obliged to others, their efforts and their timetables. Yet with this support for and coaxing of her inner strength, her confidence in participating in outward activities, for example, in sharing her work with others, grew to match her inner convictions and her steel began to show. Now she could share her pride and joy with others, enjoying their praise and keen interest. Extended family members began to wait with bated breath for the publication of *Sense and Sensibility* and Jane grew excited for their responses. Martha and Cassandra were helping Jane at home, stoking her own fires and helping to push her towards the achievement of her great dream of being a published authoress. Jane felt free and confident to speak of herself in these terms with

Martha, talking about and referring in familial and yet authorial ways to her about her unpublished works, including her poetry, 'as it stands in the Steventon Edition' carrying on the tradition she set with her friend long ago in her earliest works from the age of 13.[46] The buzz that Jane had felt back then and the frisson that Martha had shared with her continued.

Jane shared the journey to publication with Martha; she was a vital part to Jane's courage and a close confidante in the whole business side of all Jane's dealings with the publishers and agents. Jane had no hesitation in sharing even the most private details of the economics of the situation. 'P & P is sold. – Egerton gives £110 for it.'[47] Jane is eager to relay the outcome of the deal and her tone is conversational, as well as most confidential. 'I would rather have had £150, but we could not both be pleased, & I am not at all surprised that he should not chuse to hazard, so much.'[48] *Sense and Sensibility* had been published at Jane's own financial risk but here Jane rejoices and laments the difficult dilemmas faced when closing a deal. She would know that Martha would be interested in the details and the finer ins and outs of her feelings on the matter, that Martha would be rooting for her and praying for the benefit of a good final outcome for her friend. In stark contrast, Jane was not prepared to go public with her identity in the beginning, aware of a hullaballoo that would follow and unsure of the reception her work would have. It was too nerve-wracking to allow light in on her writing process, too scary a thought the notion of how being known as an author might affect her talents and routines. Her shyness raised its head again and the fear that went with it meant that only those that were really close to her knew what was happening and who 'A Lady', ascribed as the author, actually was.

Jane was already aware of the heavy pressure, of the ramifications of it all, even on her brother Henry: 'Its' being sold will I hope be a great saving of trouble to Henry, & therefore must be welcome to me.'[49] When she could breathe a sigh of relief and not have to worry any more about further conversations or plans, she could not wait to rejoice with Martha. 'The money is to be paid at the end of the twelvemonth,' she informs her sensible friend who she knew would be deeply interested in making sure that all agreements were in place and that the commitments to Jane were confirmed and clearly stated.[50] Running a tight ship was as important in business as it was in housekeeping and Jane, always trusting in Martha's judgement, would appreciate Martha's interest in all areas of the arrangement. What is more, earning an independent income was of vital importance to Jane and perhaps part of the impetus for her finally becoming serious about submitting her work for publication at all. 'I am in some hope of getting Egerton's account before I go away – so we will enjoy ourselves as long as we can.'[51] Her happiness and delight in being paid earnings for her work was more than a little piece of good news to share with a confident nod of her head to her friend who would be pleased for her. Money was no dirty word between them, but a practical necessity and the earning of one's own income was something to be celebrated.

Martha, along with Cassandra, helped out with fact-checking, assisting Jane as she researched details that added credibility to her observations and her settings in her novels. 'I am obliged to you for your enquiries about Northamptonshire,' she remarks to Martha. Jane had wanted to know about the countryside there and was previously interested to know if it was a 'Country of Hedgerows', perhaps for *Mansfield Park* or *Persuasion*.[52] She adds that now she has changed her mind, something has spooked her, 'but do not wish you to renew them, as I am sure of getting the intelligence I want from Henry, to whom I can apply at some convenient moment "sans peur et sans reproche."'[53] In other words, she loved Martha for helping her, but she was keen to keep her questions as low-profile as possible, to avoid other unwanted questions and a crescendo of interest from other parties. Jane trusted Martha to ask for her, but she liked to keep herself and her works out of sight, to keep them away from the attention, from prying eyes. She needed the information and was happy for Martha to know this, but being able to pick the brains of Henry 'without fear or criticism' was a quieter option and one that at that moment Jane clearly preferred. Dipping into her cousin Eliza's French tongue, she shields her words further, using humour and deliberately cloaking her meaning, letting Martha know it wasn't personal and that she knew Martha would hear her heart. Mary's family always thought that Martha and her sister knew no other language but their own, but either way Martha would have smiled at the point Jane was making. Martha would have wanted to help Jane and would have understood where she was coming from, knowing her friend, her temperament and how much her privacy when writing meant to her.

Martha being privy to the details of her situation was one thing, but Jane was thankful that her own personal copies of *Pride and Prejudice* that she was sending out to family, including Steventon where Cassandra was staying with James and Mary, were going to be delayed past Cassandra's visit. 'For your sake I am as well pleased that it should be so, as it might be unpleasant to you to be in the Neighbourhood at the first burst of the business.'[54] Jane had wanted to keep her identity secret, but there was no telling what Mary, with one eye on her social standing in the place, may have done with her copy. However, perhaps James uncommonly flexes his influence here and triumphs on the matter for Jane reflects on Cassandra's feedback that, 'The caution observed at Steventon with regard to the possession of the Book is an agreeable surprise to me.'[55]

Martha's friendship was so special as to be able to steady Jane, to help her find herself, to help her feel grounded. Martha had been a constant from 'the burlesque trifles and entertainment pieces of her childhood to the writing of her full maturity,' and the recreation of their tight-knit homelife and the flourish of writing that this created is no coincidence.[56] The mishmash of fun and seriousness, of frivolity and maturity in their friendship kept Jane centred and brought her back to herself. Martha allowed her a freedom in life that meant Jane could therefore suffer the straitjacket necessary for the publishers and the public. Now that Jane was cushioned in this new world of Chawton, her friend closeted away with her, a new enthusiasm and belief came together and took Jane over, kindling a new flame that burnt stronger perhaps than ever before. But just as their relationship changed and grew, allowing them to hold on and let go and then come back together, Jane's writing is also seen as metamorphosising and evolving; there is no revolution, even though publication meant a certain framing of her wit and work. 'There is no seamless division into early, middle and late writing' such as a set of circumstances might evoke, or a change of scene or home in itself might delineate or even dictate.[57] No, scholars believe that there was 'a vital and unexpected revision of material over a considerable time.'[58] In other words, it was the influence of key relationships around her that helped to rock the cradle of Jane's 'children.' Through the pulsing of the sustaining flow of friendship and love around her at this time, Jane was finally able to organically progress, explore, create, innovate and develop in her own natural way and at her own pace.

Chapter Twelve

The Character of Friendship

J ane was grateful for all and any feedback in relation to her books, and she soaked it up, noting everyone's ideas down for her own interest and enjoyment. Jane remained glad of the support from Martha's friends too. The Dean Dundas branch at Barton were just one such set: 'Pray give my best compliments to your friends. I have not forgotten their particular claim to my Gratitude as an Author.'[1] Perhaps they had offered information in the past; as Captain Dean-Dundas was in the Navy, it has been thought a possibility or perhaps they subscribed or bought copies of Jane's books.

Jane 'evaded the lionising that lesser women covet'; she was wary of fame and scrutiny by others, the sheer attention that would be directed her way when her identity as the author became known.[2] She was concerned as to what the fallout of this would be, not just nationally but more locally, for her family and for herself. Her shyness perhaps became tied to a creative vulnerability and she did not want to mix with either the infamous or the celebrities of her day. At the same time, however, with her ambition high, she was caught in a circle of emotion – she wanted to know what people thought and revelled in capturing and sharing different people's reactions with her family. If those readers were prominent people of good standing, she was excited that they were reading her work and she wanted them to like her characters, particularly Lizzy Bennet. She still wanted to please her audience, even when that audience began to grow.

However, of all the opinions that crop up, Martha's meant so much to her and keeping Martha's good opinion of her mattered more to Jane than sycophantic new fans, even if they were in positions of influence such as the Prince Regent's librarian James Stanier Clarke. Jane cared about Martha's judgement of her in all matters relating to her writing career and when important decisions arose, she was keen for Martha's favour to be upon her. For example, Jane became insistent in her hope that Cassandra had made clear to Martha her thoughts about the possibility of making a dedication to the Prince of Wales in her forthcoming publication, *Emma*. Jane had been in quite a quandary about it, not caring for the Prince as Martha well knew, but feeling caught by the expectation of public duty, of the publishing world and the current readership. All of this was on top of fearing what the royal circle might think of her if she did not publish a dedication, as it had been hinted directly to Jane that this should be very much to the liking of the royal household.

In previous times, Jane had made her feelings about the Prince of Wales well known to Martha. She felt that he had behaved most improperly towards his wife, the Princess of Wales, and that any downfall on her part or of her behaviour since could be traced back to his treatment of her. 'Poor woman, I shall support her as long as I can, because she IS a woman and because I hate her husband... I am resolved at least always to think that she would have been respectable, if the Prince had behaved only tolerably by her at first.'[3] Now with the dedication looming, Jane wanted Martha in the loop and it was her confidence that she sought. 'I hope you have told Martha of my first resolution of letting nobody know that I <u>might</u> dedicate &c- for fear of being obliged to do it,' then with her customary humour just below the surface, Jane adds, '& that she is thoroughly convinced of my being influenced now by nothing but the most mercenary motives.'[4] Jane's tongue is once again planted firmly in her cheek, but the grain of truth is also there, that Jane was over a barrel and at the end of the day, as well as wanting to entertain, Jane was ambitious for her 'children' and wanted them to succeed and excel, to reach the highest of heights. Jane Austen, it seems, had also come to a realisation, albeit an unpalatable one to her, that she had 'to change to a regency writer.'[5] Hilariously, she quickly pulls the discussion back into the heart of their friendship and humour, the Martha and Jane comfort zone, adding in her note, 'I have paid nine shillings on her account to Miss Palmer; there was no more oweing.'[6] Jane points the finger back at Martha – well, she had a need for money too, and Jane's money has just done her friend a favour, so she must not complain or sit in any harsh judgement of her, for after all, all is fair in love and independent living.

Jane knew that her friend would land on her side whatever her decision, that her Martha was completely behind her in her ambition. There is an 'altered tone' to her later works that can be recognised side by side with Jane's comments to Martha about the dedication to the Prince Regent.[7] Her newer novels manage to hang on to and to allude to her original wit, to retain some language and joky quirks of her earlier works, but at the same time acknowledge that her audience's palate was now different and so her work had to be too. Jane was at pains to make sure that Martha knew that she had not changed, that her values remained unaltered, but that she now had to be wily and wise and approach her publishing with a sensible business head on. There was no benefit in being zealously idealistic; realism was what would help her achieve her dream of entertaining and earning.

And so it was that Jane collected together and copied down all of the opinions and criticisms that she received from her nearest friends, family and neighbourly connections. Their views did seem to interest her a great deal, the contradictions and contrasting opinions appealing to her intellect and to her personal amusement. Mary's opinions of *Mansfield Park* tickled Jane, 'Mrs James Austen is very much pleased,' and 'She Enjoyed Mrs Norris Particularly.'[8] It is often believed that aspects of Mary's character made it into the shaping of Mrs Norris – so perhaps Jane was laughing inside at the lack of self-awareness, yet there is a clear personal identification of Mary with the meddling, officious, socially-conscious and controlling Mrs Norris. Martha, she noted, 'preferred it altogether to either of the others' (*S&S* and *P&P*) and she was 'delighted with Fanny' – who, of course, is the charming, pious and positive example to all of her new family and the unlikely heroine of the piece. Hilariously, Jane noted that Martha 'Hated Mrs Norris.'[9] So, no love lost there then! Captain Austen, Frank, her brother, found Fanny 'a delightful character' also.[10] In regard to *Emma,* Mary complained that it was 'not so easily read,'[11] but Jane did not write for such 'dull elves' and we know that she found Mary's approach to reading lacking in both passion and taste.[12]

Martha, it seems, had just the right balance of praise and personal opinion for Jane to be satisfied with her friend's views: 'Miss Lloyd thought it as <u>clever</u> as either of the others but did not receive so much pleasure from it as from P&P and MP.'[13] Jane herself had owned at the start, when writing the novel, that she would probably be the only person ever to really like her heroine so she would have been delighted that Martha had confessed her own likes and preferences towards the book. Some have viewed Jane's friendship with Martha as similar to that as Emma with Harriet – although they quantify their own speculative comparison and acknowledge, 'her regard for Martha was deeper and more considered.'[14] I believe that Jane was full of admiration and love for her friend and often inspired by her mix of intelligence, creativity and Christian kindness. Jane looked to Martha for fun and for dependable emotional and practical support, and she was more like a rock and a touchstone to Jane than a project of charity or friendly interest. Jane did not find Martha wanting in any way and apart from meddling from time to time in her love life, her major scheme of all was simply to have Martha living with them all under her roof.

Jane and Martha lived more a life of earthy fun and frolics than sitting in drawing rooms sipping tea together and looking at sketches. It was Martha's character underlying her fun personality that had clicked with Jane all those years ago. In her works, Jane's concern was 'primarily with character unfolded through love' and the same could be said of their blooming and blossoming friendship, that allowed space for them both to expand and contract as necessary, yet held and captured within an intrigue and an interest in each other that deepened in sympathy and gratitude for one another as life progressed.[15] Their human natures responded to one another's and what Jane observed in Martha drew her nearer and closer to her. Jane and Martha could do everything or nothing together; they had been through the ups and downs of life, through thick and thin, and as reflected in her novels, Jane could attest that with her and Martha 'in the supreme moments, humanity becomes inarticulate.'[16] They had a friendship that was also comfortable in silence – living amongst one another, they could rise in their friendship to just a wonderful sense of being. Jane loved the sparkle and lightness of her laughter with Martha, but there was something deeper in Martha that resonated with Jane too. The difference in years was added to layer upon layer with Martha's natural reflective qualities and inner maturity and strength. Some picture Jane through her writing as 'standing aloof from the world, she sees it, on the whole as silly. She has no animosity for it, but she has no affection.'[17] Yet, in her real life she was blessed with the silly, the raucous and the still waters that run deep and touch the meaningful. Martha encapsulated all these qualities and her faithful friendship was an antidote to the frivolous and distracting insincerities of others in the world. The passion permitted to pass through the freedom of fellowship with a kindred spirit was a strong and rewarding social bond of the highest order for Jane. She knew Martha inside out and Martha knew Jane to perhaps the very same degree. Jane did not suffer fools and Martha, we therefore can deduce, was the very opposite, the very best of womankind in Jane's eyes or she would not have chosen her, nor have identified with her so strongly, nor wanted her to be her friend as badly as she did, nor for as long.

Jane's 'intense preoccupation with character' pushes us to reflect on what a marvel Martha must have been and how well their commitment of nearly thirty years of friendship must have tested this truth.[18] Truth is the foundation, and honesty and trustworthiness are cornerstones of friendship, but sharing the same truth is what binds best friends together. Knowing that you can own your personal truth, good and bad, warts and all and not be judged but be welcomed, not be patted on the head with patronising platitudes, but frankly be told where you stand and still be loved, just as you are and all the better for being real. Scholars have noticed that 'All the women that Jane Austen commends are absolutely honest and well-bred in mind.'[19] This was the friend that Jane found in Martha. 'Not only the truth, but the whole truth, must be vital to any character of whom she herself is to approve,' and Martha was full of empathy and kindness yet most openly and blatantly living her life on a firm belief in the truth of her Christian faith; that was the crux of her own identity.[20] Martha spoke truth in love, and she had been able to take the heat of

Jane's passionate truths as spurted out onto the page in her *Juvenilia*. These were two women who could handle each other's truths and could be trusted with them. This conviction of the importance of truth, coupled with the pleasant reality of Martha's kind nature, was a winning formula for friendship with Jane.

Martha and Jane did not grow apart over time, instead they grew alongside one another. Their friendship was a healthy source of help and soul food for both of them equally. They may have grown in different areas and at different speeds, but this only served them both better. Their friendship was like a web, stronger over time from the building up of the many threads of their lives. They were attached but not in a swamping, smothering sense. They were able to be interdependent and independent but not overly dependent on one another to the detriment of either one. They had day by day overlapping shared experiences, acquaintances and a perspective built upon shared memories. They developed loyalties and points of view. Their strands were woven individually to form something together, equal partners in their friendship, people in their own right. They didn't do everything together, and they allowed one another space for their own interests, duties and friendships to flourish. They gave each other the permission and freedom to follow their own arrows and their own gut reactions and instincts. Routines helped both of them, but they also enjoyed the delights of spontaneity. They both tried new things, but they loved to fall back into their old ways and the homely, comfortable activities of walking and cooking, serving others and being in nature that fed both their souls and where they found companionship that meant more as the years passed. In a funny sort of way, the changing of their homes and the ebb and flow of periods of being apart and coming together enabled the form of their friendship to naturally mould to a new shape, and to change as they both matured. These bases then became the hooks on which the threads of their lives were secured and the points to which in their memories they could wander back to and locate themselves.

For Martha to sustain her friend, she needed oxygen for herself – and for her this was found in her Christian faith. It was a history and a bedrock that she shared with Jane, a foundation stone for their friendship from which they both looked out together. Martha found her solace in spending time reading her bible and attending church. In the hours there away from Jane and Chawton life, she fell back into her familiar routines and her personal space. With no one permitted to call upon her or interrupt her, she could feed on the sustenance of her own spiritual practice. Everyone knew how fundamentally important this aspect of her life was to Martha and the priority it held in her daily routine. Out of love and respect for Martha, this was always made room for and Martha was always free to adhere to it. This was where Martha came for refreshment, where she was 'renewed' and her 'springs were refilled.'[21] This was how Martha sustained herself from within so that she could give herself so completely in her Christian duty and to her sense of purpose in life. For her, supporting Jane and loving Jane through her cooking and household service was her act of friendship, her proof of her commitment to her friend and with it, she lived out her sense of usefulness in her world and gained a sense of identity and self-esteem.

'Jane sums up her ideal woman, not as a 'good natured unaffected girl' but as a 'Rational creature.' 'Rational' being 'her highest word of praise.'[22] Using this word to describe someone of the time would have been defining them as being 'endowed with' or actually in their self being 'from or belonging to reason'; as being a part of calculation and reckoning, speaking as if it was a physical evolution from a source of character, springing up holistically from within, being something innate and not added on by someone or something else.[23] Jane valued and preferred a heroine to have 'a real education in character.'[24] She was not convinced by her own experience of formal education or the judgement upon others who had not received it, that the outcomes of a different type of schooling – more homemade and organic than the revered female pedagogy of the time – were not actually as good. She wrote into the upbringings of her purist heroines a countryside educational experience that she and Martha shared. In her mind, Martha had grown up with this natural good sense within her, yet she had not been schooled formally or to the highest of worldly standards.

In her friend, Jane saw reflected many of the qualities that she would later imbue her heroines with – thus pointing us towards her admiration for and the inspiration she found in her friend. For Jane, 'Breeding is not a matter of birth or place, but of attitude towards life,' and she brought out this truth in her writing and saw it reflected back at her in the friend that she had chosen.[25] Miss Bates, for example, found within the novel *Emma*, is pictured sympathetically and like the motif of the 'mad woman in the attic' of literature, underneath a layer of exaggerated froth, 'in her humble, quiet, unassuming happinesses, she is shown throughout as an essentially wise woman;' qualities that Jane truly admired in Martha and whom she would defy anyone to underestimate at their peril.[26]

Many believe that 'character becomes more and more the very fabric of her works' and as the friendship and comradeship of Chawton became the air that Jane was breathing, the background atmosphere and ambience, perhaps the qualities of the pair's friendship were forming part of Jane's observations and reflections on what made for a happy life.[27] The pervading essential oils that were wafting around Jane at this time may have influenced the scent of the stories and the makeup of these wonderful heroines who are now timeless to us, even though they were written to be very much an observation of the time in which they were created. Perhaps it is the qualities, the human nature, the personal attributes of the heroines and their outlook and relationships, the qualities that Jane was enjoying with Martha, that reach out and speak to us now as if we were in a room with them both. When we read and re-read the novels, perhaps it is the personal characteristics residing within each heroine that deepen our attachments to them. Could it be that we are experiencing reflected fragments of the friendship that Martha and Jane were enjoying, and that the spirit of their friendship can touch us still.

Martha was a faithful family member in life who 'kept up a cousinly correspondence' with the Lloyd relations in Norfolk, the oldest branch of her father's family; she was the one who made sure that they were 'apprising each other of family events,' 'the last who had the clue to our family connections in that quarter.'[28] It was she who held dear the long and lengthy pedigree of the Lloyd and Noyes family whose surname became her father's own Christian name.

Martha also held to thinking the best of people, for no personal gain, gossiping in a good way of neighbours: 'Martha has heard him very highly spoken of' was her comment upon the character of a rumoured local newlywed.[29] Martha came from perhaps even more humble beginnings than Jane, not having had the benefit of good health or a father who lived on into her young adult life to encourage her own ambition or to point her towards his own library of literature. Perhaps Jane didn't see Martha, as some have, as an 'unambitious' friend but one who lived on a plane above ambition with her heart and mind rooted in a better place.[30] Jane admired Martha's wisdom, her personal grace and goodness, her innate class and she shared some of Martha's qualities as she perceived them with the heroines who appeared upon the pages of her novels.

Jane depicted female friendships, as a thing in and of themselves, quite negatively in her novels, showing up the falsehood and fake friending amongst closely coupled women, especially when her work is 'compared to other women writers,' for 'aside from sisters, there are no good friends' scholars have found.[31] Therefore, knowing what we know about Martha's character and how we can see elements of it portrayed and personified in aspects of Jane's heroines, could it be that she considered Martha above the rank of mere friend? 'Friendship' is an over-used and undermined term in Jane Austen's novels, the screen onto which selfish behaviours are projected and a relationship often carrying spiteful and untruthful undertones. In the novels, this relationship for some is a mask worn in polite society, that people hid their true feelings and motives behind. For Jane, her relationship with Martha was based upon mutual respect and honest dealings with one another over a lifetime. Martha was much more than this common and misused term could define; she was more akin to a sister for Jane. Living with her at Chawton, Martha, 'a friend of her own tastes and background', brought with her joy, happiness and practical help.[32] Alongside Cassandra in the house with a shared love for Jane, they could, as sisters would, 'afford to indulge the youngest in the cottage.'[33] As close-knit as a family unit together, Cassandra, Mrs Austen and Martha 'shielded and favoured' Jane and they were happy to act as such 'indulgent companions'.[34] For them it would not only have been the publishing of the novels and their relative public success that 'confirmed the rightness and worth of her labours'; they knew and understood Jane more deeply than anyone else, more than even a friend might and taking care of her in this way seemed the most important and yet the most natural thing in the world to them – the greatest testament to their own character and kinship.[35]

Chapter Thirteen

Anything You Can Do...

Living with Jane, Martha was not freeloading. She both made and paid her contribution to the household, 'Though the means which supported it were not large.'[1] Chawton life was largely paid for by the four women that resided there. Mrs Austen was made an allowance jointly by her sons although this fluctuated as to their means. Jane and Cassandra had allowances and gifts made to them by family members, but these too were subject to whim and alteration as the donor was free to change their mind and could not be counted upon to make a similar gift the following season or year. Charles once gave Cassandra and Jane beautiful Topaz crosses when he fulfilled a well-paid and successful commission, and Jane often remarked at the discoveries of money and good fortune that he seemed to make by happenstance. The impetus for Jane to earn her own money was clear; she was motivated to bring stability to herself and her home group of women and just like Charles did, she loved to treat them when her money flowed in.

Martha had some resources of her own: her mother left her a third share of all her worldly goods and her uncle John, who married an heiress, may well have shown her care in his lifetime, even though he died suddenly at a young age the year before her mother's death. Eliza and her husband Reverend Fulwar-Craven Fowle also shared from their own household abundance with her when she was orphaned, which was reciprocated by Jane and Martha from both Southampton and Chawton. Other Craven family members were also in close contact and others remembered her after their death, leaving her a share of their money, though these larger settlements were rare. Mostly the family allotted one another a share of their own harvest and looked out for the provision for one another in smaller, more measured, practical and seasonal rations.

Martha would have made a financial contribution to the household as some sort of return for rent and for food and she was in the way of making them gifts as well. She once bought a Wedgwood breakfast set for Mrs Austen and settled the account for the group's other purchases there. Even if they had paid her back, which the group were in the habit of doing on their shopping trips, this would still have required sizeable means to be available so Martha must have had the funds at the ready at least at certain points in her life. Jane was so excited about this particular gift. 'It is certainly what we want, & I long to know what it is like,' she writes, almost hopping up and down in anticipation of her friend's generosity and great shared taste, '& as I am sure Martha has great pleasure in making the present, I will not have any regret.'[2]

Martha was certainly able to pay her share of bills and had a bank account at Henry's bank from which she made payments on her own behalf. 'Martha sends her love to Henry & tells him that he will soon have a Bill of Miss Chaplin's, about £14 – to pay on her account.'[3] That was quite a lot of money back in 1808, the equivalent to over £1000 today. Miss Chaplin, according to author Deirdre Le Faye, is believed to have been a shopkeeper, either in London or Manchester and some sort of supplier of lace, cotton or fabric.[4] The material may have been for clothing for Martha, Jane and the other women or a contribution for materials needed for the sewing of bedding, tableware, curtains or soft furnishings for making the house both elegant and comfortable as it was known to have been.

Martha, it seems, was also paid by other sources and it can be assumed that this was for acts of care and service that Martha made, perhaps of the type rendered to Mrs Dundas. Awaiting payment was always a tricky affair, for as women and single women at that, they could not easily press their case to be paid and had to wait upon the money. Sometimes money could be owed over the course of a year and in any case, it was anticipated with bated breath in hope rather than expectation of its arrival date. This could either scupper or make their plans and Jane was well aware of Martha's plight. On one occasion, Martha was waiting to travel to spend time with Mrs Dean Dundas and her husband as they were moving from a house in Bath to a place at Clifton in Bristol. She was hoping to travel in that direction with Mrs Craven – her widowed aunt who lived close by at Speen Hill in Newbury. Transport now secured, Jane was yet fretful, as she wanted Martha to be able to make her summer trip before the weather played its part and made it more uncomfortable, 'to go on from Berkshire and visit them, without any fears from Heat.' Her lack of funds, though, was a spanner in the works and Jane drily noted, 'I wish she could get her money paid, for I fear her going at all depends upon that.'[5]

When money finally came through, it was rejoiced over and something to be congratulated upon and what is more, thoroughly enjoyed. Receiving any payment, perhaps especially when Martha had been looking out for it and looking forward to it, was another happy source of teasing and delighted prodding of Martha's ego by Jane, 'you are too busy, too happy and too RICH I hope, to care much for letters. It gave me very great pleasure to hear that your Money was paid, it must have been a circumstance to increase every enjoyment you can have had with your friends and altogether I think you must be spending your time most comfortable.'[6]

When Jane had her money come through from the sales of her books, she too delighted in the happy feeling of it all; it made her quite dizzy with joy, even if she knew deep down that the prospect of more was a flighty or flimsy one. The chance to be giddy in the moment, revelling in travelling in style in an open carriage or splashing out on gifts for her family and friends and refusing any payment or guilt in return from them, was something to be enjoyed, perhaps all the more because of its unlikely occurrence. 'Instead of saving my superfluous wealth for you to spend, I am going to treat myself with spending it myself,' Jane once wrote back to Cassandra.[7] Not all their money had to go on bills and surviving – Jane was excited about money too.

It seems that Martha had the happy possibility of winning another unexpected and totally amazing windfall in the early summer of 1813. Jane was out in 'Town' with Henry (in a particularly buoyant and sprightly mood as she gadded about collecting purchases, ferrying little nieces and visiting all sorts of beautiful places along the way), when she made a surprising statement, full of confidence and self-assured happiness. She was halfway through making practical and pleasing plans to benefit them all, dovetailing her ideas for her next day alongside what snippets she had heard of her brother Henry's itinerary. She was quick to foresee the prospect of her cashing in on the serendipity of being in a particular street at a particularly convenient time to pick up her mother's pre-ordered gown. In detailing her own plans, she makes the following admission, 'so, by 3 o'clock in the afternoon she may consider herself the owner of 7 yards of Black Sarsenet as completely as I hope Martha finds herself of a 16th of the £20,000.'[8]

The implication here is that Martha had very high hopes of being the lucky winner of the lottery. The jackpot was worth £20,000 and tickets were bought and sold as whole, half, quarter, eighth or sixteenth shares.[9] Imagining Martha to be the recipient of £1250, the equivalent today of £85,000, is just mind-boggling. No wonder Jane was hoping that Martha would be as likely to win as her mother was to get her dress. That sort of money would have been life-changing. The understated goodwill towards Martha here is wonderful in its matter-of-fact delivery, with not a spark of jealousy and every hope and wish for good fortune for her friend. Jane is in a really good place – all is well in her world when all is going well financially for them all.

Whether or not Martha really did come into this money is never confirmed. In her normal everyday life, Martha was sensible with her finances; well-known and appreciated for her frugality and excellence in finding value for money. Martha was an asset to the homemaking at Chawton because she was able to cook and what's more, to make something almost out of nothing. Using her knowledge of herbs and plants, she could make substitute household products as well as plan seasonal recipes at a fraction of the cost.

The little family-type group at Chawton grew their own flowers, vegetables and fruit, with Jane sometimes accidentally overseeing the killing of a plant or two. Cassandra kept her own bees and Mrs Austen their own chickens. At Chawton, as it had been when they lived together at Southampton, setting up the kitchen garden and the outside planting had been a matter of great care and concern for the group. Knowing how much Martha liked to experiment and use her own home-grown products, Jane's queries and anxieties that there be a kitchen garden there had been as much out of concern for her friend Martha as for her mother and sister. From time to time they received seasonal fruits, livestock to kill or fish and meat from relatives, such as James and Mary at Steventon or from the Fowles at Kintbury – and Martha knew just what to do with it.

Jane trusted Martha's tastes in food and they both gained the same satisfaction from eating quality produce. Their little household always sent for Martha's turkey of choice from her friend Mr Morton. Jane once again finding an opportunity to tease her friend, hinting and pretending that the rest of them couldn't possibly get the turkey themselves and that without her, they would be in a total mess for Christmas, 'If you do not return in time to send the Turkey yourself, we must trouble you for Mr Morton's direction again, as we should be quite as much at a loss as ever. It becomes now a sort of vanity in us not to know Mr Morton's direction with any certainty.'[10]

Jane and Martha loved experimenting in cooking together; it was something they had most likely enjoyed playing about with since their early family duty days back in the parsonage kitchens at Deane or the rectory at Steventon. 'I am very fond of experimental housekeeping,' Jane once pronounced to Cassandra, 'such as having an ox-cheek now and then; I shall have one next week, and I mean to have some little dumplings put into it, that I may fancy myself at Godmersham.'[11] Martha was partial to spruce beer and whenever she was coming home, Jane would busy herself and make sure that it was ready and waiting: 'You know of course that Martha comes today; yesterday brought us notice of it, & the Spruce Beer is brewed in consequence'.[12] Jane herself loved orange wine but loved the company of her friend even more. She could joke about spoiling herself whilst away from their modest household menus at Edward's Godmersham Estate with 'Ice' and 'French wine & be above vulgar economy.'[13] Yet she preferred her home with Cassandra and Martha, even above the delights of such good food and drink – the way to a man's heart may well have been through his stomach, but Jane flattered her friends that she was happily willing to forego and sacrifice all these pleasures in exchange for time spent with them. There is laughter in her words but a seriousness in her heart when she writes of her Chawton posse, 'luckily the pleasures of Friendship, of unreserved Conversation, of similarity of Taste & Opinions, will make good amends for Orange Wine.'[14] This was high praise indeed, the biggest luxury in life for Jane was being at home, with her sister and with Martha.

It was well-acknowledged within the family that Martha, alongside Cassandra, had control of the housekeeping at Chawton. Mrs Austen preferred the younger generation to take over the day-to-day running of the house as she tended to her passion projects such as her potatoes and chickens. For many years now, Martha had begun to compile her own work of literature – not a novel, but a household book. Collecting and noting down little ideas for recipes may well have been an interest of Martha's that started when she and Jane met way back in Martha's early twenties. Seeing Jane writing out her ideas in her little notebooks may have helped to forge the idea of a portfolio collection in Martha's mind. The inception of the idea may have already been there but being in so much contact with her little author friend, it seems likely that Martha might have become even more enthused to make a permanent note of the ideas that were coming to her. Martha's careful collecting and copying into her 'quatro notebook, bound in white vellum' may have continued in earnest in the days at Ibthorpe, when Mary moved out after her marriage to James.[15] There may well have been a need for it then as Martha quite organically, in the reshuffling of their family unit, superseded her mother as the chief organiser and began to run the household on Mrs Lloyds' behalf. She may have fallen further into the tradition of keeping her own collection and compendium then, as many of her generation felt the need to do. If not, then it would seem likely that she definitely compiled it in the days of living in Southampton. Martha found herself cohabiting with a new group of people who had come together as a larger household from a range of different routines and habits; leadership and order would have been needed. Being such an innate and natural talent of Martha's, as well as of such interest to her, she would have found her niche in this area of family life and may well have started it then. With a need for such a compendium to be called upon again and again, it would have been a way of saving space in her own head as well as a method for collating everyone's ideas. Some have deduced the date of the book by working out the timeline of the deaths of the contributors. In any event, Martha's household book was definitely something that she regularly updated and continued adding to over time, referring to it periodically throughout her adult life. The little book included recipes for meals and other culinary delights, and also for household remedies and home-made alternatives for routine domestic, health-related and occupational tasks.

Martha signed her name on the inside back cover, numbered the pages and included an index, just like Jane had done in her little volumes of her *Juvenilia*. Turning over the book in one's hands, the tanned leather-like cover feels soft and well-used. Several of the pages have now fallen out and gone missing over time with others, which have aged as one might expect, changing colour and now frail to the touch, though they are still quite clear enough to make out if you are familiar with the font used. The handwriting itself is for the most part careful, well-spelt and considered; in other parts it is a little wilder, looping and more rushed, yet it too can mostly still be deciphered with some patient scrutiny. When reading it, it was not as littered with stains from food or smudges from spills or sticky fingerprints as many of my recipe books are. In holding the book, one feels close to Martha's heart and on reading it one cannot help but agree that it holds for us a 'timelessly true insight of character' and of her essence.[16] It is wonderful to know that it meant as much to the family, that it was treasured by the younger generations as a piece of Martha's history, special in its connections to her beloved Austen family and as an expression and personification of her. As such, it was handed down as an heirloom until it was deposited with the Jane Austen Memorial Trust where I was able to visit to see it with the kind permission of the Jane Austen's House team.

Martha became known amongst her and Jane's friends and relations for this pursuit and they readily sent her their best-kept secret weapons, lists of ingredients and top tips for the best methods for achieving greatness in the kitchen or with a sick or injured patient. The book reads like pieces of advice, for someone else other than Martha to follow too. It may well have been used to teach their succession of cooks and help-maids in the home as 'the planning and a good deal of the work must have been in the hands of the ladies,' (Martha and Cassandra).[17] It may well have been something that Jane and Cassandra pulled down from the shelves and referred to themselves when looking after the children in her absence. How reassuring for them that when a 'What would Martha do?' type thought occurred to them, they could check in the tome, read through a relevant section and feel like Martha was there talking to them, like being on the end of a phone feels to us now.

Some have noticed in regard to the entries that Martha 'includes some which oddly enough are word-for-word repeats (was Martha very busy, or absent-minded?)' they question.[18] I think this may mean that Martha's collection was not one that she actually read frequently or referred to often herself. I rather believe that she held most of it in her head and that the notes were more to help others who were either in need of the information or at a loss as to where to start. What the recipes do reveal is Martha's competency and vast knowledge of all that went into running a house – the little book's scope is all encompassing. It's clear from the sheer number and range of contributors that Martha was known for being a font of all knowledge and having a hunger for and interest in this area, and that she was keen to keep abreast of innovations and imaginative ways to create all that was needed to run an efficient household. Jane even approached their friends on her behalf, and she was delighted by, and eager to support, Martha's special collection.

In regard to the instructions for preparing dishes for the table, Martha did not note down easy, everyday recipes that would have been so familiar as to not have needed inclusion. Martha's collection reflected her household's shared 'same tastes and pursuits,' similar in essence to those of the grander, richer classes, perhaps those Jane and her family might experience at her brother Edward's table or when visiting Mrs Austen's relations, but with a twist that reflected the difference in their female, more middle-class budgets.[19] Martha may have referred to the more specialised recipes for particular occasions. She included a range of different courses from soups and starters to meat, vegetables, pickle and sauce preparations for main courses, to desserts, cakes and biscuits, with a special section set aside for drinks too. Indeed, one of these stands out – not a recipe for spruce beer because there isn't one (if Jane could prepare it, then we are convinced this recipe was so much part of their cooking DNA that they didn't need it written out). No, the recipe was for making orange wine – now we wonder who Martha might have had in mind for that little rascal!

Martha writes with similar scientific precision in the culinary section as she does in the medical, and shows an in-depth knowledge and understanding of a range of spices and sauces, the longevities of different concoctions and the subsequent knock-on effects of using substitute ingredients.

In reading the book, we hear Martha's voice and better understand the network of her friends, her contributors. Others have noted that, 'In some cases, Martha gives the name of the person from whom she received the recipe and in a few other cases the donor herself wrote the entry.'[20] Further study of those names gives us a wonderful insight into the years over which Martha collected the content and the extent of her circle of acquaintances. There are recipes forwarded to her by the people that she and Jane met and moved amongst together during the course of their friendship and in the duration of their domestic partnership which spanned more than twenty years. Just that thought alone, captured in a simple household book, is a little window for us into Martha and Jane's worlds, notifying us of how much these overlapped and interlinked. One of the best ways to meet people and to make friends is by being introduced as a mutual acquaintance – you are sure to have so much in common. The converse is also true, so looking into their shared links we learn more about the background of Jane and Martha's friendship. We see it rooted in their local community, the network of religious households and the fact that they drew so heavily for friendship from their inner circle and friends from the neighbourhoods of their youth. Jane's family too leant Martha many ideas for the book including

Mrs Austen Senior, Captain Austen and the wives of Jane's brothers, thus signalling in this little book that Martha's area of expertise and interest were known about and indulged by Jane's nearest and dearest, as well as her own. Recipes too came from their mutual friends, such as Miss Sharp (whom they met when she was governess at Godmersham to Edward and Elizabeth's children), showing just how much these ideas must have been a matter of conversation and correspondence between Martha, Jane and their friends. Jane, who was enthralled by the language, culture and personality of her French cousin Eliza, la Comtesse de Feuillide, also had a particular liking for her brother Henry's French cooks such as Madame De Bigeon, whom she remembered fondly throughout her whole life. It could well be that they discussed food and recipes influenced by French cuisine when Jane was visiting Henry in London. This would have been of great interest to Martha who would have delighted in passing on and swapping ideas with this interesting French connection.

Martha's own family also loved to share their ideas with her and all generations found this a topic of mutual interest and support. Recipes are included from her mother's sister (who married Reverend Thomas Fowle at Kintbury), Mrs Jane Fowle; Eliza's sister-in-law, Mrs Charles Fowle; and her Uncle John's second wife, Mrs Craven. We all have someone in our family who is 'the sporty one' or 'the artistic one'; Martha was 'the scientific one' who loved to experiment with new flavours and techniques, who had great skill in this area, and found delight in providing wonderful meals or hosting social dining occasions. She was the one who generally loved to be relied upon as the practical, common sense solution-finder and problem-solver in all and any domestic situations. Martha was the one that everyone turned to when they needed a judgement or help in this area, and the person they sent their best ideas to for safe keeping.

There were plenty of her own friends who contributed too, which perhaps is more expected as they met more frequently and would have been more inclined to talk about day-to-day matters and the habits and routines of everyday life, and with whom Martha may have shared her menu ideas for upcoming events. The Debary sisters and the inimitable Mrs Dundas, who Martha tended at Barton Court and who would have participated in many fancy and higher society meals, also lent her their best recipes. There are a range of other contacts who contributed too including old family friends, doctors, curates and the wives of local Reverends who moved in Martha and Jane's social circles.

What stands out most of all is that this collection indicates 'the dishes which the family enjoyed,'; they were meals and ideas for high days and holidays, for celebrations or for adding that extra touch that elevated their shared meal into an occasion.[21] It gathers together the experiences of their contacts, showing them to be well-travelled and to have quite sophisticated and varied palates. It proves that Martha and Jane are willing to try unusual combinations as the recipes reveal a penchant for the experimental. The book showcases a rainbow of gastronomic creativity and in this we learn the flavour of Martha's approach to cooking, and the household's openness to new ingredients and cuisine. Just as Jane was thrilled by the new elements of the theatre, exploring new ideas in word play and the freedom of throwing caution to the wind when it came to confiding in her friend Martha, so we see echoed, 'By the subtle use of wine and flavourings', Jane and Martha's exploration of 'a multitude of fresh culinary experiences.'[22] The recipes are not tricky to assemble but do have elements of the gourmet about them and definitely give the impression that the little group took an open view to food, and enjoyed taste for taste's sake and loved savouring 'new' and novel seasonings.

This little book is another wonderful testament to Jane and Martha's shared domestic way of life. In it we see portrayed tacitly their shared tastes and values. We all have a family pattern or routines with friends that turn into traditions and then memories and nostalgia. The memory of food around a particular person's table always stays with us. No one can cook our favourite childhood dish like Aunty so-and-so can and this is what this book represents. Indeed, it has been felt that the Chawton household could have afforded to have further domestic help, in addition to the small select few that they hired, but Martha and her friends 'were perfectionists regarding household management' and kept the oversight to themselves, enjoying perhaps a higher level of involvement than they necessarily needed to.[23] This was the way that Martha felt she could give back to those who had so readily included her and helped to provide such a roof over her head. This was her domain, where she felt useful and that she had a purpose, and this was a way in which she could use her talents to bless her beloved friend. Perhaps also they could not afford to sink their limited and unpredictable means into hiring someone extra, or there really was no one else, or very few that Mrs Austen felt could live up to the high standard that Martha had set. Perhaps even Martha herself did not find anyone else that she felt she could delegate to. In their local vicinity there may have been very few cooks who could interpret her recipes to her exact liking.

For the sake of her family, Jane shouldered her responsibilities in this area when she had to and although on the whole she enjoyed the conversation, company and repartee of their guests, she was always relieved to get back to the 'comfortable disposal of my time' to 'ease my mind from the torments of rice puddings and apple dumplings.'[24] Jane did not have the same flair as Martha for overseeing the kitchen or the same easy way of welcome; she lamented that afterwards she would probably be left with a great awareness of her lack and 'probably to regret that I did not take more pains to please them all.'[25] In fact Jane was known to tease herself about her lack of housekeeping skills – even in the early days, when she was first left in charge whilst Cassandra was away and when Martha was out of reach at Ibthorpe. She joked about her mother's good opinion of her work in this regard, mocking herself openly, 'I really think it my peculiar excellence, and for this reason – I always take care to provide such things as please my own appetite, which I consider as the chief merit in housekeeping.'[26] Maybe Martha was one to scat and banish Jane from the kitchens with good reason. If there was a larger social occasion, Jane may well have been a warm and interested but ultimately unhelpful and cheerfully distracting influence.

Mrs Austen demonstrated her great faith in Martha with a contribution, a 'receipt for a pudding' in her own inimitable style, introduced by way of verse – of course:

If the vicar you treat
you must give him to eat
A pudding to his affection;
And to make his repast,
By the Canon of Taste
Be the present receipt your direction.[27]

Being part of the rectory circuit and set, Martha did indeed 'treat' many vicars and some wonder if this directly refers to Reverend George Austen, thus dating it before his death in early 1805. However, with her brother-in-law(s) also frequent diners at her dinner table, it could well date from a wider period. The familiar tone taken by the style of introduction, the tenderness in sharing a note of this sort is touching and being from Mrs Austen herself makes us feel that she really did consider Martha as a daughter, as she once promised her she would be regardless of her not marrying James. This is just the sort of way that Mrs Austen communicated when she wished to show affection – she once wrote a touching witty poem to a boarding school pupil of theirs who felt she favoured another pupil, and on another occasion, she wrote a little poem to encourage a truant back to school. Highly personal correspondence, the verses denote the type of wish that was wrapped up in the exchange of these little recipes and the nature in which they were given.

  This little book is an insight that survives, a record of an intimate part of Jane and Martha's everyday life together. It is not just the facts, the recipes themselves, it is the spirit of home that they represent. Through these recipes we can find an emotional connection between the two friends. We see Martha's character and heart, her talent and her aspiration, and we see her Christian desire to serve and be useful to her family and friends. This was an age when the visiting male family members, especially those that moved in wealthier circles, may well have been 'addicted to the pleasures of the table', and this was Martha's way of making them feel welcome and to ensure that the best levels of hospitality that they could manage would be afforded by this little household.[28]

Dr Chapman, who first collected together Jane's precious family letters and who was present at Jane and Martha's Chawton home when it was restored and opened as 'The Jane Austen House Museum,' reflected that 'without deliberate characterisation certain people in Jane's letters become conspicuous for their amiability: Cassandra herself, Edward Knight, the two sailor brothers, and Martha Lloyd.'[29] It is in scenes such as these around the table, that Martha created, that spread her agreeableness and warm-hearted cordiality. Making their guests feel settled was an important part of sharing her natural love and generosity towards them all, but it was also a way of ensuring that their own way of life in their little Chawton cottage was preserved and shored up. When Martha arranged for this quality of food to be served, she was also looking out for her friend and protecting her and their lifestyle. She knew that for Jane, everything rested on the continuation of the pace of life as they knew it. It was this foundation upon which Jane depended and thrived. As a woman with no other outlet for her skills and natural enquiring mind, we also sense Martha channelling her brainpower, her self-taught scientific acumen into these recipes and exercising her intellectual curiosity and her God-given abilities as a creative, rational creature.

Her lifetime studies of the medicinal qualities of plants, the natural cycles of the seasons and the physicking capabilities of ingredients, her very own study of medicine, feels to be contained in this volume. The little encyclopaedia is well-organised, thought out and written mindfully; the layout on the page is fairly neat and meticulously spaced, every element of each sentence or measurement assiduously noted down yet all in a friendly handwritten font revealing interest and personality in the pieces. At pages 88/89, the little logbook is turned around and the register now changes into handy hints for assisting ailments and household labours. In her 'receipts to cure...', Martha carefully instructs what dosage should be used and how far apart it should be administered for the best health effects. Martha understood ingredients and natural healing processes, and she worked with and alongside nature's way – even timing some doses by the cycles of the moon. The remedies have a tried and tested feel, and reading them one acquires a complete trust in their reliability.

If you had 'the staggers' or 'worms', a swelled neck, toothache, something in your eye, a sore lip or had suffered the 'bite of a mad dog', there was advice to be found. There is something for nearly everything and anything one might come across in the course of the most accident-prone life. As one reads on, one's own confidence in Martha grows and it becomes clear that Martha was someone whose judgement nobody would ever question. If Martha wrote or said it, you followed it to the letter. There were even antidotes and palliative solutions for illness in animals around the house and on the farms nearby. These included cures for wounds in cattle and for mange in horses and dogs. It is not beyond all stretches of the imagination to see the locals calling in on Martha for her help and advice.

Of great interest are her own potions, mixtures and brews for carrying out domestic chores or caring for one's own toilette. There are recipes for her favourite lavender water and other powders for the face and body. Martha noted how to make soap and pot pourri, lovely beauty-enhancing additions to the mistresses of the house. Ever practical, Martha thought about the tougher tasks too; she collected methods for making black for shoes, and even how to make varnish for tables – she was always on the hunt for ways to add elegant touches to improve the ambience of their home. Miles away, perhaps from a similar product in a shop or simply without the means to purchase something ready-made, Martha enjoyed hours of experimenting, thinking and trying 'a little bit of this and that' to accomplish her own solutions for household dilemmas, duties and desires.

However, the recipe that excites everyone the most, even to this present day, is, of course, her recipe for making ink. How thrilling to think that Martha supported her friend Jane's writing by supplying the ink to the very quill that allowed her ideas to flow forth. How special too to wonder that perhaps Martha's own book was written, even in part, in that very same homemade ink. What we would all give to be able to bless our own words with the ink that wrote the words of Jane Austen.

Chapter Fourteen

The Spirit of Friendship

Jane and Martha's friendship was more than skin-deep. It was more than the sum of the daily tasks that they carried out together, the laughs they had, the confidences they shared, or even the activities that they filled their free time with. Together they experienced the intermingling of their hopes, dreams and sorrows. Martha's 'one fault' in Jane's eyes perhaps 'lay in her goodness or in a slavish running off to those in need.'[1] But like any fault in a friend, we can raise it, talk to them about it if it serves for their harm, but mostly we overlook it and accept it. When we gaze upon someone with a best friend's eye, we can only see their good. 'The precious intimacy of talk and feeling' with Martha was never underestimated by Jane.[2] This friendship was on a different level to any other that either of them enjoyed elsewhere. Jane could leave her secrets and her deepest, darkest thoughts with Martha with absolute assurance that they would be secure with her, and that there would be no judgement on Martha's part. Jane could share her hopes and her dreams too and every detail about her precious 'children'. This, in itself, shows how special Martha was to her, how trusted a confidante, for Jane was someone who so loved to conceal and then reveal her work, who enjoyed the sense of protection from others and their enquiries that a pseudonym or a squeaking door could give her. That Jane could ask Martha to help her with daily domestic chores and leave both her home and her mother safe in Martha's hands is one thing, but that she could also involve her in secret scouting and fact-finding missions for her as-yet-developing plots is another entirely different measure of their friendship.

As the years went by, Jane needed to call upon Martha's practical help increasingly frequently, for Mrs Austen had 'determined to go no more from her own house.'[3] She had made a final visit to James's home at Steventon in the summer of 1812 and after staying for a fortnight there with Jane, she had returned with a decisive flourish to Chawton. From that point on, things changed and as a result, 'It had been ruled in the family that Mrs Austen was never to be left alone.'[4] Martha got along well with Mrs Austen and was fully aware of her health concerns and the foibles of her personality. Mrs Austen, in turn, felt comfortable with Martha and enjoyed her company. To the outside world, Mrs Austen therefore maintained her dignity, for it seemed to them that she was 'perfectly well able to take care of herself, and she was free from nervous fancies, as any creature that ever breathed.'[5] Yet we know from the constant stream of updates from Jane to Martha and her family in her letters that Mrs Austen could 'turn', and that they all carefully watched her moods and wellbeing. Mrs Austen could be disrupted by any source and her sensitivity to change was as unpredictable as the weather and sometimes the veracity of its vicissitudes unverifiable. In other words, Mrs Austen seemed to be up one minute and down the next in regard to her health. She was susceptible to disruption from the temperature and precipitation, from travelling, from strange food or air, from bad news or from overthinking on events in the family. The family really did try to protect Mrs Austen and to keep her way clear and calm. There was always a pervading sense of relief when they managed it, for example, in hiding concerns over a birth in the family until all was over, 'We were clever enough to prevent her having any suspicion of it.'[6]

The concern and worry for Jane regarding her mother's health was always present, lurking in the back of her mind, and a lack of awareness amongst the family provoked rare moments of her undisguised anger. Abrupt revelations or ill-timed family updates that would exacerbate Mrs Austen's preoccupations or interrupt her plans were better kept away from her and thoughtless slip-ups were unwelcome. 'How can Mrs J. Austen be so provokingly ill-judging? – I should have expected better from her professed if not her real regard for my mother. Now my mother will be unwell again.'[7] Jane lets rip her displeasure and impatience with Mary, her low opinion of her sister-in-law in regard to caring for Mrs Austen in stark contrast once again with her feelings towards Martha. 'Every fault in Ben's blood does harm to hers, & every dinner-invitation he refuses will give her an Indigestion,' huffs Jane.[8] Mary must have updated Mrs Austen on the bumpy road to Anna's engagement to Ben Lefroy, and Jane was indignant that Mary didn't think that this would upset her mother and leave consequences that they alone would have to deal with.

This woman after all was the woman who, when Jane fell ill herself, she would not dream of taking the sofa away from. 'The rule (of never leaving Mrs A alone) was scrupulously observed.'[9] It was a huge relief to Jane, then, to know that her mother would be looked after with great skill and care and pastoral support by Martha. No one else other than Cassandra could have done this so effectively. There was no nurse nor anyone in their employ as capable as Martha and in this instance, Martha moved way past simple 'friend' status. As Jane had stated clearly before, Martha was 'the friend and sister under every circumstance.'[10]

Mary, on the other hand, or rather her attitude, was a consistent thorn in Jane's side. By her early thirties, Jane had begun to lose patience with Mary, no longer hiding the fact that she was not wooed by her or in the business of cultivating a closeness like the one with her sister Martha. She could not ignore how much married life, living with Mary and her prevailing opinions day in and day out, had impacted her brother's personality, in her view, for the worse. She was sad about this change and it provoked her to anger, not an emotion that she usually gave full vent to, normally tending to use icy humour and black but comic thoughts to display her displeasure. Mary's behaviours and misdirected, seemingly self-centred priorities on the other hand really irked her. She could see her strong-minded brother bending and submitting, desiring to contain his true self and run away to other friends and family, preferring to flee and avoid confrontation with his wife and choosing to let himself become spoilt. James professed real love, admiration and gratitude to his wife in poetry over the course of their marriage, but Jane felt a lot of contempt. 'The company of so good & so clever a Man ought to be gratifying in itself;-but his Chat seems all forced, his Opinions on many points too much copied from his Wife's, & his time here is spent I think in walking about the House & banging the Doors, or ringing the Bell for a glass of Water.'[11]

Jane was often disgusted at Mary's lack of patience, warmth and nurturing love towards her own children; she noted that pregnancy did not sit well with Mary who she felt was quite ready to have it all over and done with, and that she did not make any enviable preparations or good judgements that made Jane want to copy her choice in life in any way, shape or form: 'Mary does not manage matters in such a way as to make me want to lay in myself.'[12] 'Mary, who is still plagued with the rheumatism, which she would be very glad to get rid of, and still more glad to get rid of her child, of whom she is heartily tired.'[13] The lack of warmth continues with the maid seemingly more 'in raptures with the child' than Mary herself.[14] This was a trait that Jane had noticed before in regard to little Anna, her stepdaughter, 'Mary writes of Anna as improved in person, but gives her no other commendation.'[15]

Jane felt that Mary was too concerned with one's position in society, of being one of the fine ladies, of conforming herself in order to become one of the in-crowd. She felt her conversation too scheming and ambitious, too focused on gaining money and securing their status with the wealthy. Mary's pocketbook diaries were religiously completed and filled by her, with all of her household expenditure and shopping, her social itinerary and that of the family clearly labelled next to each date in turn. The titles of the diaries themselves give a hint to her personality and state of mind, with names such as, *The Lady's Useful Repository*, *The Lady's Useful Memorandum Book*, or *The Lady's Museum*; they strike at the heart of her need for organisation and, indeed, her considered opinion of herself. *The Christian Lady's Pocket Book* includes a printed quote inside the front cover from conduct mistress and writer Hannah More, the choice in itself an indicator of her personal, pious religious taste.[16]

There are no opinions or comments in the books, as even her own daughter noticed when she consulted them years later. They are, however, neatly written and kept up to date. What they are full of is almost weekly dining invitations with the local movers and shakers, the Chutes at the Vyne estate, the Lefroys at Ashe, General Mathew and his new young wife at Clanville, the Manydown set and Lord and Lady Portsmouth. She refers to her own husband as 'Austen' and her sister by her title, a regular respectful way of writing about someone in a letter, but such formality was not necessary in a personal diary; this is another revelation into the way Mary thought and categorised her life and everyone in it. Jane despaired at this focus on formal relationships. When Mary visited the new Mrs Mathew, Jane noted that Mary, 'by no means disposed to like her' (as she was now perhaps higher up the pecking order than Mary's family in General Mathew's financial generosity), 'was very much pleased with her indeed. Her praise to be sure, proves nothing more than Mrs M's being civil & attentive to them, but her being so is in favour of her having good sense.'[17] When it came to them taking care of poor Miss Benn, Jane spikily retorted, 'As I know Mary is interested in she not being neglected by her neighbours, pray tell her that Miss B. Dined last Wednesday at Mr Papillons – on Thursday with Capt. & Mrs Clement – Friday here – Saturday with Mrs Digweed & Sunday with the Papillons again.'[18] This seems a little on the catty and sarcastic side – Mary may have been more sympathetic towards Miss Benn in regard to general and specific care – but perhaps where Mary was concerned, Jane saw through her veneer and could only see an ultimately ungenerous selfishness in her enquiry. If Mary was inclined towards a more self-absorbed and ego-centric way of life, perhaps as a matter of survival and in the interests of her own family, her juxtaposition with Martha, as Jane's friend and her sister, is stark. Jane's close-up observations of her were clear, leading some to conclude 'It seems possible that some of Mary Lloyd's less attractive characteristics reappear in Mrs Norris' – not something that any of us would like as our reputation amongst our family and friends.[19]

Martha choosing to live with Jane seems somehow even more logical in this light. In seeing the distinction between Mary and Martha, we not only learn more about the sisters' own characters but also Jane and Martha's friendship. We feel a push away from the one sister which serves to highlight the magnetic force apparent in the pulling and knitting together of Jane and the other. Like all of us though, there is light and shade, good and bad contained in our personalities. Jane had to find a way to get along with Mary for James, Anna and the other siblings' sakes. She also had to find a way to tolerate her in front of Martha so as not to hurt her feelings. Mary's personality would have spoken for itself and the grievances Jane had would have been obvious and perhaps shared to a large degree by Martha. But family is family, and the Christian thing to do would be to forgive and to extend charity and love to the individual, and to be a mercy-giver. Their sense of humour must have helped, and Martha would have been able to tolerate Jane letting off steam about Mary – perhaps laughing together about her helped them both. At least lucky Jane could get away from Mary when she needed to – Martha was joined by blood. But for all their tensions and scraps, Mary's records show that Jane visited them at Steventon fairly often, perhaps even more regularly than Martha, as Jane accompanied various Austen relatives to the rectory.

For Martha and Jane, there were no such bumps in the road. They hit it off from the beginning and theirs, as we have seen, was no passing acquaintance, no ordinary friendship; it lasted for nearly thirty years, which is longer than some marriages. Indeed, if Jane Austen had experienced this length of relationship, and this level of shared intimacy with a man, we would have all been drawn to it with great interest, an interest that Martha has thus far not attracted. People who enjoy this type of close coupling and can count on a 'best friend' describe their moment of meeting as 'almost like you already know that person'; they say that 'there is something about the way that they carry themselves, that you immediately just know.'[20] It would seem for Martha and Jane that they didn't need long in one another's company to see that spark and to become such firm friends. They immediately latched on to one another, and with the age gap, it could not have been just a convenience thing, where the frequency of contact was the only compelling attraction. With each new thing that they learned about one another, their bond only strengthened. Best friends in the modern era say that it can actually feel like a bit of a 'girl crush feeling, where you really admire a friend and you are really learning from someone that you think is amazing and brilliant' and you almost worry that they might not like you as much as you want them to, because you really are 'quite a big fan already.'[21] Jane and Martha showed no hesitation but were drawn to spend as much time as possible together, almost from the instant that Martha moved into Deane Parsonage.

Maybe due to the fact that Jane had grown up with brothers around her and Martha had mixed every day with her male Fowle cousins at Kintbury, there was a spark of recognition of the one in the other. The pair of them had loved spending their youth outdoors, in all the elements, exposing themselves to the seasons and nature. They had both spent the free time of their childhood active and alert outside, with ruddy reddened cheeks 'burning with happiness,' rolling down the hills behind the rectory, exploring the countryside and 'getting their skirts and boots muddy in the wind and the rain, 'scampering' after their family and 'hanging out of trees.'[22] This was the way that both of them had been brought up – not simply sitting idly sewing with the girls in the parlour but spending lots of time in the garden and the fields, scouring the hedgerows and enjoying the great outdoors. Maybe they were both quite tomboy in that respect, adventurous and never happier than when outside in nature.

It is easy to gloss over the fact that when Martha moved to Deane, the reason for all the upheaval in her life was the death of her father. At 23, this was still a young and formative age at which to lose a parent and especially one who was held dear and respected, who signified not only a loss of material wealth and security but of emotional devastation too. Her father's death would have reopened the feelings that she had experienced when her little 8-year-old brother Charles had died, and would have affected her regardless of the strength of her Christian faith or her mature outlook. Moving to a new house is stressful, moving area even more so and losing your father is a sadness and grief that is hard to deal with on its own, let alone on top of all the other changes.

The shared experience of being in nature, their joint compulsion to get outside, that natural urge and impulse to get into the great outdoors drew them together and would have been part of the healing process for Martha. As she already had a thirst for knowledge of plants and herbs, fruits and flowers, perhaps this was something that Jane helped to nurture and perhaps they both knew that they felt better in the freedom of the fields. These romps would have been soothing for Martha and truly responsible for grounding her and bringing her back to life after death. Taking her out into the open air would have given Mother Nature a chance to work her magic on tragedy and trauma. The power and force of nature, the open expanse of the fields and sky, and the little changes and nuances that they noticed in their surroundings would have been uplifting in a spiritual way. Taking Martha outside and giving her a change of scene away from the melancholy atmosphere back at the parsonage was a key way of helping her get herself back to normal. The opportunity to talk or not to talk and to raise any concerns or dark, negative thoughts would have had a positive and dramatic impact on Martha's spirit. Getting out and walking over the fields, getting a sweat on, figuring out a path, having the wind in her face and a new area to explore and be shown by Jane would have been cathartic. It would also have forged a friendship, out of the ashes of the sadness of losing her father. Jane showing Martha love and support, getting her blood pumping, introducing her to the local landscape, seeing her love for the outdoors bloom in her and bring a smile to her face would have been re-invigorating soul food for Martha. Martha found a friendship with Jane that began to flourish from that point on. Knowing that your friend is there for you at your lowest ebb, not just a shoulder to cry on but there with 'their heart and their love', their physical presence and their whole personality as well, just when you needed someone the most, is something that no friend ever forgets.[23]

This is how truly deep friendships are forged, and trust and gratitude are laid down. It cannot be underestimated what Jane's friendship, her sympathy and her adventurous spirit meant to Martha at this time. It taught them both that they could be vulnerable together, that they could notice in themselves and in the other when life was getting a little overwhelming. They developed a trust, the one in the other, that they would look out for one another and help each other. They agreed either aloud or implicitly that they had each other's backs and they learnt from situations like this, that they had each other's best interests at heart.

It is no wonder that Jane and Martha continued to nurture these experiences and always sought to go hiking and rambling about together all their lives. Walking gives a proven boost to health and wellbeing that we are only just beginning to understand better today. Jane and Martha made sure to revive this element of their friendship as often as they were able, and it became a key part of their shared identity. One can imagine that if they needed to clear their heads, then a walk would do it – and if they needed to feel close, then a walk out in the fresh air would immediately renew that connection. Out in the wilds of nature, marching along, pausing to pick some flower or to examine some leaf or hedgerow, they could talk about anything, the good and the bad – because out there in the fresh air and fields, they felt safe and secure in the freedom that their friendship had brought them. They could speak freely without worrying that they were treading on each other's toes or what impression their words would create; together they could say how they truly felt, about anyone and anything, without fear of recrimination or judgement. They could speak as they found, even if others would have been shocked at their conversations. They could also muck about and have a laugh, totally alone and in their own world, just the two of them, just like things used to be up there in the little upstairs room at Steventon, and they could let it all go.

In the modern era it has been proven that we just need one person that we feel we could turn to at any time, who we could ring at 2am and know that they would pick up the phone, or would come around or come and fetch us back safely. Jane had her beloved sister, but Martha too was a set of listening ears that she could trust. This was a friendship that was mutually supportive and special – it fulfilled a powerful role in each woman's life and, for Martha, it was born at a milestone moment. In all the future moments that happened in their lives too, Jane was there for Martha and Martha was there for Jane when it counted the most.

Jane had, all in all, lived in good health most of her life; sometimes she experienced colds and illness and sometimes her eyes played her up, although sometimes feeling under the weather was partly self-inflicted as she admitted to enjoying the wine at parties a little too much on occasion, but mostly she was well. However, in the summer of 1816, she experienced a bad patch, not being able to walk about like she was used to doing and feeling totally out of sorts. Her back had been giving her pain and the doctor had added her to his rounds. Humour was her weapon of choice for fighting off this attack, and she laughed off all talk of illness as simply due to the circumstance of Cassandra going away. In the spring of 1817, Jane was eager to report to her younger family that she was 'tolerably well again, quite equal to walking about & enjoying the Air; & by sitting down & resting a good while between my Walks, I get exercise enough.'[24] She had a scheme to have a little donkey cart to use for getting about and taking the air with Cassandra in turns with Martha by her side. By the middle of April, however, she was still particularly poorly, and the family began to grow concerned for her health. Attending and nursing Jane became a priority to them all and even James visited. The family's fears were so much aroused that Mary noted it in her diary when Jane started to feel a little better on 26 April. The relief was felt by them all, not least Jane who, a month later, felt well enough to write to her friend Miss Sharp but was full of her own palpable concern for her recent suffering of 'an attack of my sad complaint' – 'the most severe' experience of 'feverish nights, weakness and Languor' she had ever had.[25] She wrote from her sickbed and admitted that she had been 'very ill indeed'.[26] What she didn't divulge was that less than a month before on the day after Mary's sigh of relief, she had actually written her own last will and testament.

Martha had been with her throughout and we can pick up on how full of care Martha, in sync with Jane's family, must have been. 'Miss Lloyd too has been all kindness. In short, if I live to be an old woman, I must expect to wish I had died now, blessed in the tenderness of such a family, and before I had survived either them or their affection.'[27] Jane remembers Martha's sweet care and attendance upon her, including her in the reference to her family – an almost automatic inclusion that Jane writes without hesitation, allowing her subconscious thoughts towards Martha to float to the surface through her pen. 'You would have held the memory of your friend Jane too in tender regret I am sure,' Jane consoles, intimating at the same time the level of sadness and concern that she had seen reflected back at her in Martha's eyes.[28]

By the end of May, Jane continued to hope that she would improve further, and she removed to Winchester in order to give herself over to the trust and care of Dr Lyford and her sister Cassandra. That Mary was permitting her to travel in *her* carriage was not lost on Jane – even in her sickness, she railed against Mary – not believing her to have changed her true nature and had a personality transplant in Jane's hour of need, 'as to this reversionary Property's amending that part of her Character, expect it not my dear Anne;- too late, too late in the day,' she ranted at her friend.[29] Jane left 'yielding to the persuasion of friends hoping against hope.'[30] The family unit and the women at Chawton believed that this would help find the cure for what was ailing her. She felt their love follow her there; writing to James Edward, the nephew she shared with Martha, she reassured him of the affection and care, the 'blessed alleviations of anxious, sympathizing friends' that she was receiving, although she felt grossly unworthy of their love.[31] Martha was not there in person but was as attentive as she could be from a distance – she was in constant contact with Jane and the letter to their joint relative was almost jointly penned, 'Had I not engaged to write you, you would have heard again from your Aunt Martha, as she has charged me to tell you with her best Love.'[32] Martha was actively working behind the scenes, using her time to keep up communications with family and helping to spread the latest news and updates on Jane's condition. Jane was aware of the 'anxious affection of all my beloved family' in whom she included Martha.[33] She felt so moved by all that they were doing for her and in such a tender manner, 'I can only cry over it, and pray to God to bless them more and more.'[34]

Mary's strengths sprang most suddenly to the fore and in early June, she travelled to care for Jane whilst Cassandra went out to church. She became immediately involved and concerned, and her diary entries go further in their comments than any other remark, record or memorandum included before or after. In a complete contrast to her common style of entry, she mentions more than just the date and time of her attendance on Jane and comments oh, so poignantly, if still succinctly, on how 'Jane Austen was worse,' that she 'sat up with her' or as on 10 June – 'Jane in great danger.'[35] She notes by 13 June that 'Jane began to get better' and she was able to return home as Jane was 'much the same'.[36] However, by the middle of July, she had returned to Winchester and Jane's bedside, and only four days later on 17 July, she gives the account that things have taken a serious turn for the worse and that 'Jane was taken for death about half past 5 this evening.'[37] The news was passed on the next day to other family members by Jane's brother Frank; 'my dear sister was seized at five yesterday evening with extreme faintness and on Mr Lyford's arriving soon after he pronounced her to be dying.'[38] Mary added to her diary simply that 'Jane breathed her last half after four in the morning. Only Cass and I were with her. Henry came.'[39]

Martha was holding the fort back at Chawton, taking care of Mrs Austen throughout the whole ordeal. Jane noted that it was a strain for the older woman who 'suffered much for me when I was at my worst' and it would have been a pacifier to her that Martha was home taking care of her.[40] She could completely entrust her mother to Martha. In a letter to her family in the days just after Jane's death, Mrs Austen wrote, 'I was not prepared for the blow for though it in a manner hung over us, I had reason to think it at a distance, and was not quite without hope that she might in part recover.'[41] One can imagine the melancholy cloud that had been hovering over Chawton, the sad atmosphere that must have pervaded their little cottage and the 'us' that was her and Martha. Martha would not have been immune or impassive to this and she too must have felt the burden and the heaviness of her anxious feelings. The sudden nature of Jane's death was a shocking blow to them both back at home. Six days later on 24 July, Mary records with few words that 'Jane was buried in the cathedral. We all returned home.'[42] Mrs Austen stated simply that, 'Miss Lloyd does not go.'[43] Swept up in and included in Mrs Austen's recounting of funeral arrangements and plans, Martha is mentioned in the same breath as all the other siblings, important enough and newsworthy enough within the family for information on her status to be passed on. The women now returned to each other at Chawton, as was the practice for families in those times. Just as there was not a huge gathering and celebration of a marriage, so now a small group of the men of the family would take care of the burial arrangements.

Mrs Austen was quick to pass on praise of Cassandra who 'bears it like a Christian' and Mary, who she was so pleased could be there 'all kindness and affection,'[44] to her granddaughter Anna. In the midst of a terrible situation, her thoughts on paper were surprisingly calm and focused on all that was praiseworthy and good. She herself was seeking to play down the shock and to minimise the drama. One cannot help but think that Martha, who escaped direct praise in those moments after the event, did so well by Mrs Austen. Quietly and humbly in the deepest attitude of love and service to her friend, Martha had worked a minor miracle back at the cottage in Chawton. Because of Martha's excellent 'physicking', as Jane was wont to put it, all the chaos of the events, the toing and froing of her family and the flying off of letters and communications, Mrs Austen was left with feelings of sadness but also an overwhelming sense of reassurance; she was able to be filled with the hope and the belief that proper dignity was being shown to Jane. Mrs Austen's senses were able to rally to a surprising degree and her health remained firmly balanced, even in those painful hours. Martha had indeed pulled off the greatest gift to her departed friend. She had protected Mrs Austen and cared for her so well that her nerves and her emotions had not spiralled down into a deeper depression or shock.

Martha herself must have been in deep grief and suffering from the same 'great affliction' as Cassandra; the same great 'loss never to be repaired' had also befallen her.[45] She had her Christian faith and would have sought solace there, perhaps clutching Jane's topaz cross, that Cassandra had given to her, for comfort. The imparting of this gift to Martha in itself speaks volumes, of both the measure of the friendship and the faith that she and Jane shared. Others have remarked on the personal significance of Charles's choice of 'crosses, rather than lockets' all those years ago and the nod to Jane's penchant for fashionable trends that the selection of topaz denoted.[46] Martha would have appreciated the valuable and most precious connection to Jane that this cross represented. To wear it next to her heart would have been meaningful – but to have lost her dearest friend, whom she had held so close for twenty-eight years, when her friend was still of such a young age and just when they were at their happiest stage in life so far, would have been a monumental blow.

Chapter Fifteen

Life After Death

It is a testament to the strength of Jane and Martha's friendship that Martha was not now left abandoned and alone; she had a place in the family that Jane had welcomed her into. 'In the crisis of Jane's death', Mrs Austen had been 'watched at Chawton by the attentive Martha' who had been able to do her Christian duty in the midst of all the pain, just as Cassandra had done for her mother back at Ibthorpe all those years ago.[1]

Life, although forever altered, now settled back into a familiar and similar routine. One can imagine that in those early days, dressed in her mourning wear, Martha spent a lot of time reading Jane's books and walking out in their fields, organising the household and running errands, focusing on her care for others as a way of filling her time and distracting herself from the pain of the loss of Jane. She must also have spent a lot of time in prayer and in reading her bible, 'bearing it like a Christian' as Mrs Austen would say, as she processed her grief.

In coming to terms with the new order, Martha stayed in the safest place for her, the place where she could be close to her memories of Jane. She continued to live with Mrs Austen and Cassandra in the home that they had all co-created together. The Austen and Lloyd women gathered regularly to dine together, and life returned to the same patterns, with them continuing in their roles of caring for the children and welcoming and hosting visiting family members.

Sadness did not wander far from the family during this time. In the autumn following Jane's death, James, who had been ill on and off for some time since her funeral, became unwell and took to his bed; he attempted a revival of sorts and even planned and began a speculative tour with his family, but had to turn back as he was too sick. Only two short years after Jane's death, Mrs Austen was once more grieving for a child. James died on 13 December 1819 and was buried at Steventon. Martha's sister Mary was scattered to her friends' houses lodging in different locations, some as far away as Bath, before she settled eighteen months later at Speen near Newbury. Just a few years later, Mrs Francis-William Austen alas also died aged just 39 at the birth of their eleventh child. Four years after that, just under a decade since they all lost Jane, on 18 January 1827 Mrs Cassandra Leigh Austen herself died aged 87. She had overcome the shock of her children's deaths and, for some time, withstood the storm that this threw at her health and constitution, proving her strength and resilience of spirit. As the end of her life approached, Martha and Cassandra spent their time at the cottage, 'tending Mrs Austen, who endured continual pain from her rheumatic ailments not only patiently but with characteristic cheerfulness', no doubt helped to a large degree by Martha's application of her medicinal powers and knowledge of herbal cures.[2] In her hour of need, Martha's companionship and compassionate, intelligent nurturing must have brought significant relief to the elderly matriarch.

Cassandra and Martha were able to tend and visit Mrs Austen's grave at the nearby church in the environs of the Great House at Chawton. They stayed on 'living quietly' at Chawton Cottage, maintaining those now comforting routines that their household enjoyed and caring for those in need in their family and neighbourhood.[3] Maybe this would be a lovely place to leave Martha and to end our conversation with her. Jane had gone and with her perhaps the influence and reach of her love had left Martha's life forever, but this is not where our story ends.

For the previous five years, Frank's eldest daughter Mary-Jane had been his consort and companion, and chiefly in charge of caring for her younger siblings. Now, in the summer following the death of her grandmother, she was about to be married herself. There was at last the chance to fully enjoy such a happy occasion as Henry's and Charles's second marriages had both been shrouded in a time of grief and family loss.

Now Frank found himself at a cross-roads in his own life, and in need of someone to care for his children, seven of whom were still under the age of 16. However, rather than just choose to pay someone to move in and care for his young family, or even just to invite a friend to come and take on that role as part of his household, he fell in love – with Martha. They were married a month after Mary-Jane, on the same date as his marriage to Mary Gibson some twenty-two years earlier, 24 July, at St Maurice's Church, Winchester. Martha was 63 years old. Some thirty years earlier, Jane had been near obsessed with this match and had tried hard to coax this marriage into being. Finally, her wishes had come true. The event took place some eleven years after her death, yet she could not have been closer on their wedding day, buried as she was in the cathedral nearby.

Martha had been chosen from the 'safe circle of the family group.'[4] The serious-minded Frank trusted her, and he had done now for many years, previously sharing important family financial news with her and entrusting her with communications and messages to his brother James on his behalf. He knew her character and she was considered by him a 'lifelong friend of his sisters.'[5] Now, with the change of guard in his own home, he owned himself to be 'finding his situation very lonely.'[6] Cassandra was delighted that he had chosen for his second wife 'a very old friend of mine, who makes an excellent mother to his younger children.'[7] Perhaps it was a memory of their schemes that now all these years on encouraged Frank in his plans, but Martha had most definitely won his heart too, not simply his head. He considered her an intimate of the family, someone that he had 'long known and considered almost a sister.'[8] Yet Martha was 'womanly enough to suit Frank's notion of a wife' too.[9] He was mightily relieved that as she was 'several years older than himself', it 'made it improbable that there should be any child from such a union.'[10] It is clear here that Frank was looking for a complete and intimate marriage, full of expressions of love – his sigh of relief about the limited chances of children is audible, but he still desires to be close to Martha. He chose to marry her. Martha was a certain salve to practical needs, but he also made a choice of the heart. Frank had a desire to take a wife, as well as a mother to his current brood. He was not one to make decisions lightly and as a deeply religious man, the office of matrimony would have been particularly sacred to him.

The two were well-suited and had much in common, most notably their zeal for their Christian faith. Years earlier, he had been labelled as 'the officer who knelt in church,' and his grandchildren later remembered that he had a particular regard for how the bible should be read, preferring the old traditional way of pronunciation and that even into his old age, he had still regularly attended church, making it a priority of his life.[11] His faith was considered the 'mainspring' of all of Frank's purpose in life and the catalyst for all his actions; he found in Martha a devout woman in her own right, his perfect match.[12] Their religious life would become central to their place in their community. Taking after his father, Frank was commonly described as religious, self-disciplined, keen on details, unemotional, cool and modest. Martha, with her love of science and order and her skill at leading household events, her pleasant and agreeable temperament added with her fine sense of humour would have complimented his character and personality. Character was everything to Frank and he was particularly observant of it in others. It was Martha's personal qualities once again that endeared her to her husband as they had endeared her to Jane, who herself had matched them together as a perfect fit all those years earlier.

Martha's cooking and housekeeping 'did much to keep everyone content' at Frank's table and in time, the children would bear witness to her wonderful provision of a home for them although rumour has it that at the time of their nuptials, the older siblings were surprised and displeased.[13] With what must have seemed like a whirlwind of change for them all with their big sister leaving and with her, the routines that some of them remembered more than those from the days of their own mother, it must have been a shock and Frank was not known for his sensitivity to others' feelings. Yet the added bonus was that Martha had once lived with their mother herself and had known her and liked her – so she was actually a blessing for them, someone who would have been more than able to keep the memory of their mother alive in their hearts.

Frank's children, however, were not the only ones who had a negative reaction to his new marriage. He had not controversially married his dead wife's sister, as Charles did, but that did not stop the wrath of one influential female in the family. Mrs Leigh–Perrot, sister-in-law to Mrs George Austen and Frank's aunt and godmother, 'had been contemplating bequeathing Scarlets to Frank,' her beloved estate near Reading in Berkshire, but she could not tolerate his choice of marrying Martha.[14] Some say that she was 'incensed' and 'could not bear the idea of Martha succeeding her as mistress there.'[15] So instead of leaving Frank her large fortune and her country seat, she decided to give him a one-off payment, a lump sum of £10,000 and, in effect, cut him off with it. Mary must have been hopping from one foot to the other, ultimately delighted at this twist of fate – so her sister did not get the expected inheritance, but her son, James Edward, who had just married 'wealthy Emma Smith' the niece of Mary and James's great friends at the Vyne estate, did.[16] 'Do you know that Mrs LP has again quarrelled with Captain Austen,' James wrote to his sister Anna, hinting at the character of Frank's aunt and perhaps her wish to control her unemotional and unyielding nephew. 'But in the most agreeable way possible, as she has paid him off with nearly £10,000 and told him she will have nothing to do with him.' James sounds almost envious of the freedom attached to this gift and sees no real harm done to Frank. 'She will find plenty of people ready to offend her, if she pays them so liberally for it,'[17] he quips.

Frank was no 'Mr Collins' bowing and scraping, denying himself and his desires in order to pacify his benefactress. He showed the spirit of Lizzy Bennet, standing up for his love and his choice to his very own 'Lady Catherine de Bourgh' in real life. The injustice done to his own mother by this very same woman, in withholding many benefits to her at the time of her brother and Frank's uncle's death, may well have been in his heart as he took his decision. He was a man of principle and could not be bought, and he felt no honour-bound duty to his godmother. Frank fought for his love with all the integrity, self-control and calm self-assurance of one of Jane's heroes. How Martha must have wanted to gossip with Jane about this. Frank 'makes no mention of any regrets' at this decision; he was delighted and extolled his aunt's judgement, heaping praise and gratitude upon her decision in his own journal.[18] 'Thanks to the liberality of his aunt and godmother', with this money Frank was able to purchase

Portsdown Lodge, a home set atop a hill looking out over the River Solent and not far at all from the naval dockyard at Portsmouth that he was assigned to.[19] He was finally able to buy his own home and make it just perfect for the life of a gentleman and his large family, extending and improving it to house his children and his wife to his own satisfaction. He added shrubberies, which Martha would have loved to walk in, especially as she may have glimpsed views of the downs, the sea or of 'the island', perhaps chuckling to herself at Jane's prophecy that 'she will like it better in the end.'[20] She would have smelt the sea air whilst out walking in their thirty-five acres. Frank had a dell created, with gardens and paddocks for the children to play cricket and archery in, scenes that would have called to mind Martha's own recollections of her childhood days spent with her Fowle cousins in Kintbury. Martha's brilliance for creating a culinary storm, coupled with her reliable household book, helped her to provide picnics for idyllic childhood scenes of fun and laughter. Martha was known as a very 'self-effacing' friend, who did not seek the centre stage, but was happiest when creating the perfect atmosphere of hospitality for others.[21] She would have been the most perfect mother, loving and nurturing, practical and wise, and happiest herself when looking out for the happiness of others. She 'took little interest in any phase of life in which she could not serve or be useful', although she herself, through her friendship with Jane, knew what it was to kick back and have fun just for the sake of it too.[22] She was no martyr to her biblical namesake.

The childhood that she nurtured for Frank's offspring was natural by design, full of goodwill on her part and healthy activity outdoors; and playtime spent with their father and all together as children. The whim of his aunt worked to all their advantage and when he was offered other roles, Martha chose to stay back at their home and care for his children there. The everyday idyllic utopian life that Martha set the tone for at Portsdown Lodge was 'lively, cheerful and packed with entertainment.'[23] Frank's daughter Catherine had Cassandra's talent for sketching and drew pictures depicting the scenes that she observed on the sunny banks of their Portsmouth home. 'Dancing, music, charades and outdoor sports' are featured, and all sorts of family fun is laid out.[24] It is not so very hard at all to picture Martha and Jane strolling through the throng, joining in happily with the merriment together; they are scenes so reminiscent of the fun that Jane and Martha once enjoyed together. How often Martha must have thought that she caught a glimpse of Jane in her mind's eye amongst the family scattered on the lawns gazing out at the views over Portsmouth and the Spithead. In fact, it's so poignant that Jane is missing from these scenes and did not get to see Martha in her element or enjoy it all with her. We can tell from these heart-warming memories that Martha was happy here; her generous love is evidenced in the peaceful yet light-hearted atmosphere that she created. Here she championed childhood, fun and the best type of education – well-fed and well-cared for, Martha ensured that the children also had plenty of time outdoors amongst the power and charm of the best teacher of all: Mother Nature. This frisson of happiness at Portsdown Lodge that reflects Martha's character and personality helps us to picture more clearly the day-to-day rhythms and pulse of her happiest times with Jane.

The reputation left behind in people's memories of this era was of a 'well-regulated,' not 'luxurious' but active 'household'.[25] Creative cook and household managing supremo, we see in these accounts Martha's undisputed ability to run a home and family in ship-shape and royally reliable fashion. Knowing as we do of her sense of value for money and her respect for financial security, perhaps born from all those years of uncertainty in Ibthorpe, Southampton and Chawton – this description of her home rings true for us. This is the Martha we have come to know, and we love her for it; she rose to the challenge, adding to and amending the recipes in her household book, increasing the proportions of the ingredients to suit her larger family gatherings, yet unlike the highly efficient yet less warm style of her younger sister Mary, Martha and Frank's home was still sociable and active, as well as sensibly run. There seems to have been a compelling sense of fun and freedom alongside their frugality. Martha may not have been hanging out of a post-chaise nowadays, but the children and even her husband reportedly were zipping up and down the local countryside hills, wildly enjoying their exuberance and vitality.

Cassandra's blessing must have meant such a lot to Martha, and saying goodbye to her and to all the memories and comforts of their little Chawton Cottage would have been a wrench to her very soul. That she did leave is testament to the new lease of life that had now gripped her, and that love had most definitely bloomed in her heart. Nothing delighted her more than to invite and host Cassandra at their home, which she visited often. The fact that she made such frequent visits to both Frank and Martha reinforces the kindred links that had been sown between them in all the years they both lived together. The two must surely have found comfort together in talking about their beloved Jane whilst sitting by the fire or walking in the shrubbery, sharing memories of her with one another, the two people closest to Jane's heart. They could have talked and talked about Jane for as long as they wanted, confident that neither one of them would grow tired of talking of her and assured in the mutual mourning that the two still felt. They would have read her novels aloud again just as they always had, including the unpublished and unfinished fragments, such as *The Watsons* and early copies made just for family, proving once again the deep bonds set in the little upstairs room all those years ago at Steventon. In recreating those moments, they give us a picture of two women grieving yet commemorating, including and reconjuring their missing sister and best friend. In this beautiful act of homage and memorial, there is no finer portrait of Martha's meaning to Jane, and vice versa. For Jane's beloved Cassandra to engage in such an intimate and private pastime, when she was the most emotionally controlled and protective of both her own feelings and Jane's memory, confirms Martha's place as an acknowledged special friend of Jane's and is the most poignant of reminders to our hearts and minds. There must have been happy reminiscences that filled them both with laughter, and, of course, tears too.

Life threw Frank and Martha the usual curve balls – the lowest of lows when Elizabeth, Frank's 13-year-old daughter, died just two short years into their marriage and Mary-Jane died six years later at the age of 29. Yet also the highest of highs as Frank's naval career continued to thrive and he was promoted to Rear-Admiral in the same year, and then in the months surrounding their tenth wedding anniversary when he was knighted. 'Admiral Austen a KCB; we saw it in the newspaper,' Mary recorded in her pocketbook.[26] He became Sir and Martha was now Lady Austen. As a marker of this milestone Cassandra made Martha a present of Jane's copy of *Camilla*: a gift truly valued by the giver and the receiver. One of Jane's favourite books, it must have been one that she had read aloud with them often. No doubt Jane and Cassandra also read it together by the fire that day if only to 'hear' Jane's voice in the room. This was a very special way of invoking Jane and including her in the celebration. Martha would have treasured this as a precious gift for she knew and understood the significance, the personal sentimental value of the book to Jane and therefore to herself and Cassandra. The very act of Cassandra giving it to her was one of pure love towards Martha. In a magical moment in Martha's life, Cassandra wanted to put something of Jane into her hands; she wanted to include her, for her to be at the heart of it all, for Martha's sake. Tender and touching in her act of kindness to Martha, Cassandra knew how much the moment would have meant to Jane too; they both knew that Jane would have rejoiced at the good fortune and happiness of her brother and beloved friend – fortune that had been earned by their good grace, character and hard work. Cassandra was also aware of how strong their friendship had been and offered a moment of pause with her gift, a remembrance of those early days and of the unique moments in time that they had all experienced, that years later still evoked a sentiment and sensibility understood and shared between the three of them. Now, even twenty years after Jane's death, Cassandra acknowledged how much Martha still missed her friend. Martha and Cassandra would both have felt the poignancy in the parcel. At a time when almost any gift could have been bestowed, this generous giving of a unique, rare and precious treasure was a deeply personal exchange, that added a certain gravitas to the giving. It was a personal gift that serves even now as a public acknowledgement of a private bond. In this, a finite gift, infinite feelings, emotions, unspoken words and thoughts could be conveyed. This gift is perhaps the greatest testament and witness to just how special a friend Martha was to Jane. How the two of them must have wept bitter-sweet tears that Jane was not there to share personally in the moment that day.

The following year, Frank was promoted to Vice-Admiral of the British naval fleet and Mary was riding high on the happy news coming from Martha and her family. 'May the coming year be as happy and prosperous to us as the last has been & may we every year be more worthy of the blessings we enjoy,' she wrote at the front of her diary for 1838.[27] Mary had the distances from Speen to Portsdown Lodge noted in the front of her diary for this year; it was a larger one than she had ever used before – her sister's prosperity had sent ripples of joy across the family network.

Martha and Frank lived life to the fullest. Frank, a 'kindly presence' in his later years, with 'clear bright eyes'; together, their modest and measured manners made them a polite and principled partnership.[28] They were drawn to become involved in the parish church at Wymering just south of their home. It was of a doctrine that appealed to both Martha and Frank. In time, Frank became a church warden and Martha participated in the life of the church community. Frank's children continued their education, grew up and left home to follow their careers, his sons going their separate ways into the church, the navy and even taking to the bar. His unmarried daughters remained at their family home.

In the summer of 1842, Frank's daughter Catherine-Anne married, a happy occasion for all the family to celebrate and Cassandra came down to stay with them all. With the turn of the year, however, and the onset of winter, on 5 January 1843 Mary 'got a very bad account of Lady Austen.'[29] Distant as she was, she was reliant on news from Frank and his family, yet she did not make any move to go to her sister, intimating that perhaps they were used to aches and pains at their time of life; Martha was now well into her seventh decade. But Cassandra did go, arriving at Martha's side on the evening of Monday, 23 January. On Tuesday 24th Mary added sombre notes to her diary. 'I had a very bad account of my sister,' she wrote and then added: 'My sister Lady Austen died this morning. 20 past 10. At age 82.'[30] In her grief or clouded memory, she mistook Martha's age –

she was in fact 77 years old. Two days later, Mary remarked that she heard of her sister's death from Sir Frank Austen himself. Her fuller entries and lengthier remarks were reminiscent of the period of grief she experienced upon Jane's death. Cassandra, though, was fully present on the scene and had been with Martha until the end. How relieved and gratified Martha must have been to be in the loving hands of Jane's best nurse and beloved sister. She was going to join her friend, and there could be no better hand to pass her to Jane's than Cassandra's.

Mary's additions to her diary over the following days are stark and typical of her clear and precise unemotional entries. They feel cold in their formality yet the length of the entry, untypical of Mary's style, alerts us to her underlying grief. 'I heard from the two Mr Cravens the remains of my departed sister Martha, Lady Austen, were interred at the south side of Wymering Churchyard Hants, attended only by her husband Sir Francis and his two eldest sons Frank and Henry.'[31]

A week after her funeral, Mary received an account of it from Sir Frank himself and of 'the legacies she has desired may be made to myself and others on her husband's death.'[32] A stark reminder that gifts were not able to be passed by a dying woman to her family if she were married, particularly financial ones. This fact would not have been lost on Jane. Mary made an entry here – an extremely rare, emotional comment – 'a very sad day as can be called,'[33] she recorded. Just six months later, Mrs James Austen died too.

Frank, in his old age, had a very clear image of Martha in his heart, filtered through his lens of love and admiration – it is the most wonderful portrait of Jane's best friend. He admired her 'passive virtues' but he too saw deeper into her soul, to the active and altruistic motivation that dwelt within her.[34] Planted in a happy and secure home, with the love of her husband surrounding her, Martha no longer needed to give in to 'a slavish running off to those in need' – she could serve in the community where she was safely rooted and provided for.[35] Frank's words in her honour, those of a man who was normally serious and cool in his manner, show him 'considerate and kind, all gentleness to those around and eager only not to wound', just as Jane described him in her poem on the birth of his firstborn son.[36] His admiring words describe Martha with a heart full of love and in the light of this love, we see her come to life, the friend that became so beloved to Jane is reflected back at us; her common sense, her kind and gentle nature and her own deep and sincerely held Christian faith.

'Joined to the possession of much good sense, she possessed the blessings of a sweet temper, amiable disposition and what is of far greater importance, a mind deeply impressed with the truth of Christianity.'[37]

The pair were well-matched, proving Jane right in her observations of her friend and brother. That Martha's strong Christian faith found an echo in Frank's soul is undoubtedly true, yet the phenomenally sensible and serious Sir Francis William Austen was also known to ice-skate in the meadows by the 'beach' at Southampton and ride his horse and carriage recklessly, nay even riskily, along the roads to the docks at Portsmouth. Frank was creative and could make any manner of useful and beautiful things, including keepsake boxes, exquisitely carved containers for letters and toys for his children from pieces of wood. Their characters were 'equally true' of one another and together they loved and lost, laboured and laughed for fifteen happy years as husband and wife.[38]

Frank continued an active life after Martha's death; he was involved with the Portsmouth and Gosport Floating Bridge Company and was called back into service by the navy to become Commander in Chief of the North America and West India Station. Cassandra continued to visit with him and his family, and it was on one such occasion as he prepared to leave to take up a commission that she herself was taken dreadfully ill and died. Tragically, Frank, on the cusp of departure, was unable to stay and Cassandra was returned to Chawton where she was buried next to her mother, whilst Frank set sail with his two unmarried daughters; for him, a new chapter had begun.

A decade later, now in his mid-eighties, with three more of his children now passed away too, Frank himself grew less active and returned to Portsdown Lodge. Living his life there, now Admiral of the Fleet, he enjoyed spending time with his young grandchildren, even if he did need periods of quiet just that little bit more than he had back in those glory days of life at the Lodge. His grandchildren accompanied him to church where he was active in the leadership and later, in his nineties, when he was too frail to go, he would ask his grandsons to read him passages from the bible. Perhaps he heard Martha's voice echoed back to him in these moments.

Sir Francis Austen was offered a grand funeral with full naval honours, but in line with his modest character, he refused it, insisting instead on a simple and private affair when he died in 1865. Frank had made it known to everyone that if he died near his home, rather than away on a posting or at sea, he wanted to be buried 'in an unleaded coffin with Martha.'[39] Wanting to fulfil his wishes and also honour him with his own resting place, a special plaque was laid upon their shared tomb, with both his and Martha's dates and initials. This simple yet moving tablet has since been moved to lie in the ground between them and the church altar. Frank truly loved Martha and her faith joined with his gave him great comfort and inspiration. He wanted to be with her when resurrected into his eternal glory, as per the tenets of their shared Christian faith. It would seem that they were indeed soulmates.

Perhaps Cassandra had seen this too when she reflected later on the last of Jane's fully finished novels, *Persuasion*. Most unusually, we find revealed to us a glimpse of Cassandra's personal feelings and an example of her own emotional response. Normally the most conscientious keeper of her soul's secrets, she made a rare comment in her own personal copy of the novel, described as Jane's most romantic. In the story, Anne Elliot finds romantic love later in life after following the perceived 'greater wisdom' of her mentors in her youth. Their advice is revealed to have been full of folly and to have served her badly, however, most wonderfully, despite the many odds against her, love triumphs at last for our heroine. Cassandra highlighted the following: 'she had been forced into prudence in her youth, she learned romance as she grew older.'[40] Many believe that Cassandra may have been commenting on Jane's own life or perhaps mulling over her own, but what if we hold these words up as a candle to Martha's life? We would see once again how beautiful the last chapter for Martha really was.

Had this truly been the case with Martha? Perhaps she had been forced to bury her feelings and stand back from acting upon her own heart with her own Captain – or A. N. Other? Could her marriage to Frank in her later life really be 'the natural sequel of an unnatural beginning?'[41] Jane would have stood agape at her prophetic skills. 'Dear dear Jane!' inscribed Cassandra into her copy, 'this deserves to be written in letters of gold.'[42] The hope of the glory of love still burned in Cassandra's heart as it had in Jane's pen. How poetic an ending for her sister's best friend – life *can* be stranger than fiction and art *can* imitate life. Sadly, for Jane and Martha their timelines here did not coincide. How Cassandra and Martha might have wondered at Jane's reaction to her friend's life's events, of how Jane would have cheered and playfully swooned in delight, how she would have teased her old friend remorselessly, whilst at the same time crying and clapping her hands in glee at the final outcome of her schemes. Martha must indeed have had her dear friend smiling down on her. What a conversation, what a hoot they would have had on the other side of life's curtain as they rambled over heaven's hills.

Chapter Sixteen

Friendship Never Ends

'As to Martha, she had not the least chance in the World of hearing from me again, & I wonder at her impudence in proposing it. I assure you I am as tired of writing long letters as you can be. What a pity that one should still be so fond of receiving them!'[1] Jane wrote these words in a letter to Cassandra in the summer of 1808. I include it here as a measure of the meaningfulness of their particular friendship as it summarises so many feelings in just a few short words. There is joy in Jane's heart at the thought of Martha desperately desiring communication with her, and delight in the opportunity to tease her and withhold the satisfying of that need. There is a tacit understanding between her and Cassandra that, of course, Martha wants to hear from her, and that Jane wants to be in touch with her too in quite equal measure. Jane is enjoying the moment, the chance for light-hearted complaining, the rolling of the eyes and the grinning to herself at Martha's need for her. In this little cheeky comment hangs the further hope of friendship for them both.

Martha and Jane kept up close correspondence wherever they were, even if it was through Cassandra or another third party; they could not bear to be apart and not have news of each other. Even the dogs missed Martha when she was not at home and Jane had to 'hunt away the rogues every night from under her bed' as 'they feel the difference of her being gone.'[2] They were possessive of each other in a charming way and yet equally happy to set each other free. Theirs was an intense friendship and also a slow-burning one, one based on the mundane manufacture of everyday life and the stardust of their hopes and dreams. They were friends for nearly thirty years and lived together for over a decade; together they experienced many of the milestones of life and they were there for each other with equal enthusiasm through both the good times and the bad. Difficult and disastrous situations can build strong friendships just as well as happy times can, and their bond fused them together with equal measure at both extremes.

Both their lives involved the normal pattern of experience of the good, the bad and the ugly in life, but they were also each surrounded by other influences and friendships. The distinctions between them, such as Jane's love of drama and Martha's love of the Debary sisters, meant that they often drifted off in other directions and to other people for friendship too. Jane loved to talk to Anne Sharp about the theatre, and despite all the upset over her very brief and broken engagement to their brother, she retained and continued to enjoy the company of the Bigg sisters at Manydown. Jane drew such a strength from her relationship with her younger nieces, Anna and particularly Fanny, with whom she could share her interest in the craft of writing and also offer warmth and advice on their young love lives. She enjoyed fabulous holidays at Lyme and other resorts around the south coast of England, and loved feeling reinvigorated by the power of the sea. Martha had family friends that she stayed with to lend a hand, and she also loved visiting London with them or travelling around with her Kintbury relatives and her friends at Clifton and Harrogate.

Yet the colours of the mosaic of these relationships are thrown into relief by the black and white tiling of their own distinctive and particular friendship. The specific link to those friendships was of a different thread to the one that Jane and Martha enjoyed. The fact that these other friendships flourished showed that they loved and valued and felt secure enough with one another to send each other out into their own world, but that they did so knowing that they would be coming back to one another. It was the experience of these friendships that venerated their own and showed it up as something stronger, as different to the others – as best. Whenever they were back together it all just felt right. They didn't need to explain anything or justify anything, put on a brave face, or fight shyness – they knew each other's histories and they had a shared perspective on one another. In each other's company they felt comfortable and safe, stimulated and excited, all at the same time. It felt good and it felt right and joy of joys when they were together, they were always able to eliminate any niggling negative feelings. Trust, kindness and gratitude were the hallmarks of their lasting friendship.

Martha was always there to take care of business; she was reliable and steady and also great fun. She was easy-going yet she always took a high level of interest in everything that mattered to Jane. She had always been the most avid of Jane's readers, the most enthusiastic cheerleader of all her achievements. She would take Jane's cues and share in her sense of humour, but she was also quietly spoken and modest in her manner. Jane disliked constant garrulous and loud-mouthed behaviour – it put her off. The unhappy Miss Murden had this unfortunate trait: 'she talks so loud that one is quite ashamed.'[3] Jane and Martha complemented one another, and their personalities moulded together to fit within the perfect Venn diagram of friendship with one another. There were similarities that drew them to each other, yet at the same time allowed enough space for their differences to be expressed. Jane was sensitive to the values and manner of being of others, at times even wishing members of her own family had more of her and Martha's leanings and 'were not so very Palmery.'[4]

The essence of each woman combined to spark a vibrant flame of friendship and the life they built around each other kindled the flame, allowing it to burn perhaps even eternally, for their friendship still speaks to us today. Once upon a time Frank himself drew the conclusion that he saw reflected in Captain Harville of *Persuasion* aspects and details of his own personality and characteristics. Paula Byrne, author of *The Real Jane Austen: A Life in Small Things* asserts that this grants us permission to also draw lines from Jane's life experiences to her creative masterpieces. Could it be that Martha was more of an influence still, even upon the very fabric of Jane's works and characters? Certainly it was Martha's friendship with Jane that created not only the conditions for Jane's motivation and writing gift to thrive, but also a blueprint, a template, a model for the type of relationship that Jane could create with her audience, her as-yet-unknown reader. Jane wrote for that other friend, if not for Martha herself – then the one that Martha led and showed her the way to – to you and to me.

In learning about the things that Jane and Martha enjoyed doing together and how they shaped their days and years, we feel that we have been most properly introduced to Jane. The Jane as Martha knew her, not as her brothers or male relatives perceived her. Perhaps this is the greatest influence of Martha's life and times with her friend – in her light, we see light. In seeing how she related to Jane and what qualities Jane valued in her, we feel that we can step forward into Jane's friendship circle. We can witness a different side of Jane. We can get to know her even better than before. We learn what she valued, and we see it reflected in Martha, 'her fancy, her temper and her affections' come across more clearly to us.[5] Fostered via her friendship with Martha, we can see clear examples spring to life of Jane's 'cheerfulness, sensibility and benevolence.'[6] Through their relationship, we see practical demonstrations and examples of what Martha as chief amongst her friends 'deemed more important' in Jane, why she loved her and why she was worth so much more defined as a friend, than through her work or writing alone.[7] We get a clear view of what her brother Henry called the real 'endowments which sweetened every hour of their lives', exactly because we have borne witness to Martha as a frequently present part of those everyday hours.[8] We move from having a theory about our beloved authoress to a relatable experience of her.

Here in Martha, we find a friend who sticks as close as a sister and in entering into their escapades, we feel that we truly can draw up a chair to their table and relate to Jane in an entirely new way. We can feel the effect of Jane's company on Martha, and vice versa. We see just what Martha and Jane got up to when they spent time in each other's company and as we spend time with them both together, we too have that 'desire of obtaining her friendship and cherishing a hope of having obtained it' as Martha clearly had.[9] As we listen to Jane talking freely to Martha, we realise just how much Jane had welcomed her into what her brother called 'the bosom of her family'.[10] We too can feel taken there. This is the account that we have been waiting to explore, the one that Henry himself wished he had and expressed his 'deep regret' over, the 'materials for a more detailed account of so talented a woman' that according to his experience of Jane 'cannot be obtained' but through an exploration of her friendship with Martha, can be.[11] Through retracing the steps of Jane and Martha's friendship, we have that something 'more truly descriptive of her temper, taste and feeling, than anything which the pen of a biographer can produce.'[12] Now we can re-read her novels in a new light and perhaps find a different narrative and subtext. What other interpretations might we find in her stories, what aspects might we see depicted in her characters and what other messages might she have to share with us now that we have been able to get to know her better?

Jane apparently 'seldom changed her mind about books or men.'[13] Her opinion of Martha was made early on and never shaken off; it only deepened. Jane witnessed Martha's character and personality and saw first-hand how it was 'acted upon by education and circumstance and how, when once formed, it shows itself through every hour of every day, and in every speech to every person.'[14] She knew her friend inside and out, smallpox scars and all, and she found her full of grace and elegance in body, mind and spirit. For an authoress so invested in seeking the truth and striving to know the full measure of someone's character, Jane most definitely had made up her mind about Martha. She was the best of women in her mind, encapsulating the best of universal human nature. Martha was a faithful friend in many senses of the word, someone modest and humble enough to keep learning and growing as a person, and yet confident enough in her own judgement and motivation to garner a self-worth based upon her sense of calling and purpose here on earth. She was her best friend, as close as a sister and someone after Jane's own heart. If Jane Austen's 'highest word of praise' was reserved for those defined as 'rational creatures' whose 'good sense' she prized over everything else – then Martha Lloyd truly was Jane's 'ideal woman'.[15]

I've heard it said that 'Jane Austen can never be out of date, because she was never in any particular date' and I know exactly what the writer means.[16] Jane's novels are timeless because at their heart, they are all about relating as human beings and doing so honestly with one another, taking off our many masks, accepting and acknowledging in our self-awareness our good bits and our bad bits, our successes and our flaws, and then aiming to live out life as our best selves. The quality of friendship that Jane and Martha enjoyed – a special harmony and affection, and an unshakeable goodwill towards one another – reflects the essence of this key message contained in the heart of Jane's novels. The personalities of the settings, the people, the times, the places were all included in order to help the reader deconstruct, regard and enquire after the truth. In each story a quest for sincerity between one another unfolds so that the greater good might be prioritised, so that a way could be made for creativity, life and a higher love to flow equally to one and all. That particular quality of life is what Jane sought and it was the feeling she found with Martha. Perhaps that is why Jane Austen went 'from a moderately successful provincial novelist to a global celebrity' because we can all relate to that quest.[17] Even today, in a world of virtual 'friends' and 'likes', we are still fundamentally all looking for the same thing – hoping to find a mutual soul with whom we can let down our guard and just be ourselves, with whom 'we can share and share alike' as Mrs Lloyd once said, all that life has to offer us.[18] I'm so pleased and grateful that Jane enjoyed such a special 'Love and Freindship' [sic] with Martha. Martha gave her the best gift ever and Jane in her novels passed it on to us. Isn't that just what best friends are for?

Postscript

Philip Pullman once said that, 'Writing is a dictatorship,' but that 'once a book is written' he could not 'control what the words would mean.' The 'experience between the same book and each different reader' was 'an individual and a private experience.' It is in his view quite simply 'where the magic happens.' Different meanings and conclusions are drawn by each reader and this is what he says 'turns the whole process into a democratic one.'[1] Jane Austen too knew that 'the whole point of reading lies in eager cooperation with a sympathetic writer.'[2] She knew this when she wrote her letters to Martha and Cassandra, and when she wrote her stories for us, her audience. My hope is that after learning about Martha and Jane's friendship, each reader's relationship, their 'co-operation' with Jane Austen and with her work will deepen and that all will become more valuable, more meaningful and feel more personal with each subsequent re-reading. May our lives be richer for the time we have spent in the company of these two friends.

Notes

Introduction

1. Letter 58, Jane Austen to Cassandra Austen, Castle Square (13 October 1808) in Le Faye, D., *Jane Austen's Letters*, Fourth Edition. Oxford: Oxford University Press, p.152 (2011).
2. Rev. George Austen letter to Mrs Walter, Steventon (17 December 1775) in Worsley, L., *Jane Austen at Home*, London: Hodder & Stoughton, p.21 (2017).
3. Letter 107, Jane Austen to Anna Austen, Chawton (9 September 1814) in Le Faye, D., (2011), p.287.
4. Friedman, Soshana, 'The Eight Defining Characteristics of a Best Friend', 30 July 2015 "http://www.goodnet.org" www.goodnet.org accessed on 27.1.2019.
5. Fergus, J., "Biography" in edited by Todd, J., *Jane Austen in Context*, Cambridge: Cambridge University Press, p.4 (2005).
6. Sutherland, K., "Jane Austen's Life and Letters" in edited by Johnson, C.L., and Tuite, C., *A Companion to Jane Austen*, Oxford: Wiley Blackwell, p.25 (2012).
7. Ibid. p.27.
8. Ibid. p.29.

Chapter One: In the Beginning

1. Austen, C., *Reminiscences of Caroline Austen*, Guildford: Biddles Ltd. for The Jane Austen Society, p.11 (1986).
2. Ibid.
3. Ibid. p.12.
4. Ibid. p.16.
5. Ibid.
6. Le Faye, D., *Jane Austen A Family Record*, 2nd Edition. Cambridge: Cambridge University Press, p.69 (2004).
7. Honan, P., *Jane Austen Her Life,* London: Max Press, Little Books Ltd, p.40 (2007).
8. *Reading Mercury* (18 Aug 1788) in Vick, R., "Deane Parsonage" in *The Jane Austen Society Report*. Winchester: Sarsen Press for The Jane Austen Society, p.14 (1994).
9. Vick, R., "Deane Parsonage" in *The Jane Austen Society Report*, Winchester: Sarsen Press for The Jane Austen Society, p.13 (1994).
10. Farrer, R., "Farrer on Jane Austen" (1917) in edited by Southam, B., *Jane Austen the Critical Heritage Volume 2 1870–1940*, London: Routledge and Kegan Paul Ltd, p.246 (1987).
11. Ibid. p.247.
12. Honan, P., (2007), p.18.
13. Ibid. p.54.
14. Ibid. pp. 34 and 63.
15. Letter 50, Jane Austen to Cassandra Austen, Southampton (8 February 1807) in Le Faye, D., (2011), pp.124/125.

16. Honan, P., (2007), p.78.
17. Ibid. p.79.

Chapter Two: Early Writings
1. Alexander, C., *Love and Friendship and Other Youthful Writings by Jane Austen*, London: Penguin Books, p. xiii (2014).
2. Honan, P., (2007), pp.37/38.
3. Alexander, C., (2014), p.xiv.
4. Rev. George Austen's inscription in Jane Austen's third notebook in edited by Alexander, C., (2014), p.xvii.
5. Farrer, R., (1917) in edited by Southam, B., (1987), p.262.
6. Southam, B.C., *Jane Austen's Literary Manuscripts*, Oxford: Oxford University Press, p.2 (1964).
7. Brownstein, R.M., "Endless Imitation: Austen's and Byron's Juvenilia" in edited by Alexander, C. and McMaster, J., *The Child Writer from Austen to Woolf.* Cambridge: Cambridge University Press, p126 (2005).
8. Southam, B.C., (1964), p.vi.
9. Ibid. p4.
10. Ibid. p.14.
11. Austen-Leigh, W., and Austen-Leigh, R.A., *Jane Austen: Her Life and Letters, A Family Record*, London: Smith Elder, p.15 (1913).
12. Brownstein, R.M., (2005), p.131.
13. Ibid. p.130.
14. Chesterton, G.K., in Doody, M.A., "Jane Austen, That Disconcerting 'Child'" in edited by Alexander, C. and McMaster, J., *The Child Writer from Austen to Woolf*, Cambridge: Cambridge University Press, p.103 (2005).
15. Ibid. p.101.
16. Ibid. p.103.
17. Doody, M.A., "The Early Short Fiction" in edited by Copeland, E., and McMaster, J., *The Cambridge Companion to Jane Austen*, 2nd Edition. Cambridge: Cambridge University Press, p.80 (2011)
18. McMaster, J., "Young Jane Austen Author" in edited by Johnson, L., and Tuite, C., (2012). *A Companion to Jane Austen*, Oxford: Wiley Blackwell, p.90 (2012).
19. Ibid. p.81.
20. Letter 79, Jane Austen to Cassandra Austen, Chawton (29 January 1813) in Le Faye, D., (2011), p.210.
21. Southam, B.C., (1964), p.2.
22. Dedication by Jane Austen in edited by Alexander, C., *Love and Friendship and Other Youthful Writings Jane Austen,* London: Penguin Books, p.6 (2014).
23. Brownstein, R.M., (2005), p.132.
24. Juliet McMaster quoted in Alexander, C., (2014), p.19.
25. Southam, B.C., (1964), p.6.
26. Edited by Sabor, P., Hunt, S., and Kortes-Papp, V., *Frederic and Elfrida*, Edmonton, Canada: Juvenilia Press, p.xi (2002).
27. McMaster, J., (2012). "Young Jane Austen Author", p.83.
28. Southam, B.C., (1964), p.7.
29. Honan, P., (2007), p.77.
30. Edited by Sabor, P., Hunt, S., and Kortes-Papp, V., (2002), p.vii.
31. Ibid. p. xi.

32. Le Faye, D., (2004), p.69.
33. Edited by Alexander, C., (2014), p. xxxix.

Chapter Three: Moving Away
 1. Sawtell, G., "Neither Rich nor Handsome" in *Collected Reports of the Jane Austen Society 1976–1985*, Wiltshire: Antony Rowe Ltd. for The Jane Austen Society, p.307 (1984).
 2. Austen-Leigh, J.E., edited by Sutherland, K., *A Memoir of Jane Austen and Other Family Recollections*, 2nd Edition. Oxford: Oxford University Press, p.79 (2008).
 3. Edited by Sabor, P., Hunt, S., and Kortes-Papp, V., (2002), p. xi.
 4. Austen, J., *The History of England by a Partial, Prejudiced and Ignorant Historian* (1791) published by Carr, J.L., Bury St Edmunds: Quince Tree Press, p.8 (2016).
 5. Ibid. p.9.
 6. Tomalin, C., *Jane Austen: A Life*, London: Viking, p.78 (1997).
 7. Austen-Leigh, W., and Austen-Leigh, R.A., in Le Faye, D., (1989), p.65.
 8. Honan, P., (2007), p.78.
 9. Ibid.
10. From Volume the 2nd in edited by Alexander, C., *Love and Friendship and Other Youthful Writings by Jane Austen*, London: Penguin Books, p.125 (2014).
11. Ibid. p.143.

Chapter Four: Love Lives
 1. Letter 1, Jane Austen to Cassandra Austen, Steventon (9 January 1796) in Le Faye, D., (2011), p.1.
 2. Austen-Leigh, J.E., edited by Sutherland, K., (2008), p.133.
 3. Austen-Leigh, W., and Austen-Leigh, R.A., in Le Faye, D., (1989), p.92.
 4. Ibid.
 5. Austen, J., *The History of England by a Partial, Prejudiced and Ignorant Historian (1791)*, p.9.
 6. Austen-Leigh, W., and Austen-Leigh, R.A., in Le Faye, D., (1989), p.92.
 7. Tomalin, C., (1997), p.127.
 8. Le Faye, D., (2004), p.100.
 9. Honan, P., (2007), p.77.
10. Ibid, p.113.
11. Austen, C., (1986), p.5.
12. Letter 10, Jane Austen to Cassandra Austen, Steventon (27–28 October 1798) in Le Faye, D., (2011), p.17.
13. Ibid.
14. Letter 14, Jane Austen to Cassandra Austen, Steventon (18–19 December 1798) in Le Faye, D., (2011), p.28.
15. Letter 15, Jane Austen to Cassandra Austen, Steventon (24–26 December 1798) in Le Faye, D., (2011), p.30.
16. Ibid.
17. Letter 28, Jane Austen to Cassandra Austen, Steventon (30 November-1 December 1800) and Letter 145, Jane Austen to Cassandra Austen, Chawton (8–9 September 1816) in Le Faye, D., (2011), pp.67 and 336.
18. Letter 50, Jane Austen to Cassandra Austen, Southampton (8–9 February 1807) in Le Faye, D., (2011), p.123.
19. Letter 51, Jane Austen to Cassandra Austen, Southampton (20–22 February 1807) in Le Faye, D., (2011), p.129.

20. Letter 66, Jane Austen to Cassandra Austen, Castle Square (24 January 1809) in Le Faye, D., (2011), p.178.
21. Letter 65, Jane Austen to Cassandra Austen, Castle Square (17–18 January 1809) in Le Faye, D., (2011), p.173.
22. Letter 66, Jane Austen to Cassandra Austen, Castle Square (24 January 1809) in Le Faye, D., (2011), p.178.
23. Letter 26, Jane Austen to Martha Lloyd, Steventon (12–13 November 1800) in Le Faye, D., (2011), p.62.
24. Letter 63, Jane Austen to Cassandra Austen, Castle Square (27–28 December 1808) in Le Faye, D., (2011), p.166.
25. Letter 17, Jane Austen to Cassandra Austen, Steventon (8–9 January 1799) in Le Faye, D., (2011), p.34.
26. Letter from Caroline Austen to JEAL, (1869) in Austen-Leigh, J.E., edited by Sutherland, K., (2008), p.187.
27. Letter from Catherine Hubback to JEAL, (1870) in Ibid, p.191.
28. Ibid.
29. Letter from Caroline Austen to JEAL, (1869) in Ibid, p.188.
30. Extract from 'Family History by Fanny C. Lefroy' in Ibid, p.198.

Chapter Five: Fashion Fun

1. Letter 15, Jane Austen to Cassandra Austen, Steventon (24–26 December 1798) in Le Faye, D., (2011), p.31.
2. Ibid.
3. Ibid.
4. Hickman, P., *A Jane Austen Household Book with Martha Lloyd's Recipes*, 2nd Edition. Exeter, Devon: A. Wheaton & Co. Ltd for Readers Union, p34 (1978).
5. Letter 39, Jane Austen to Cassandra Austen, Lyme (14 September 1804) in Le Faye, D., (2011), p.99.
6. Letter 35, Jane Austen to Cassandra Austen, Paragon (5–6 May 1801) in Le Faye, D., (2011), p.85.
7. Letter 31, Jane Austen to Cassandra Austen, Steventon (14–16 January 1801) in Le Faye, D., (2011), p.75.
8. Letter 77, Jane Austen to Martha Lloyd, Chawton (29–30 November 1812) in Le Faye, D., (2011), p.204.
9. Letter 22, Jane Austen to Cassandra Austen, Queen Square (19 June 1799) in Le Faye, D., (2011), p.48.
10. Letter 20, Jane Austen to Cassandra Austen, Queen Square (2 June 1799) in Le Faye, D., (2011), p.43.
11. Ibid.
12. Ibid p.44.
13. Letter 88, Jane Austen to Cassandra Austen, Henrietta Street (16 September 1813) in Le Faye, D., (2011), p.233, Note 11 to letter 88, p.427.
14. Ibid, p.233.
15. Letter 84, Jane Austen to Cassandra Austen, Sloane Street (20 May 1813) in Le Faye, D., (2011), p.218.
16. Letter 88, Jane Austen to Cassandra Austen, Henrietta Street (16 September 1813) in Le Faye, D., (2011), p.233.
17. Ibid and Letter 21, Jane Austen to Cassandra Austen, Queen Square (11 June 1799) in Le Faye, D., (2011, p.47.

18. Letter 106, Jane Austen to Martha Lloyd, Hans Place (2 September 1814) in Le Faye, D., (2011), p.285.
19. Ibid.
20. Letter 30, Jane Austen to Cassandra Austen, Steventon (8–9 January 1801) in Le Faye, D., (2011), p.73.
21. Letter 26, Jane Austen to Martha Lloyd, Steventon (12–13 November 1800) in Le Faye, D., (2011), p.60.
22. Letter 20, Jane Austen to Cassandra Austen, Queen Square (2 June 1799) in Le Faye, D., (2011), p.45.
23. Letter 89, Jane Austen to Cassandra Austen, Godmersham Park (23–24 September 1813) in Le Faye, D., (2011), p.238.
24. Letter 21, Jane Austen to Cassandra Austen, Queen Square (11 June 1799) in Le Faye, D., (2011), p.46.
25. Letter 28, Jane Austen to Cassandra Austen, Ibthorpe (30 November–1 December 1800) in Le Faye, D., (2011), p.68.
26. Le Faye, D., "Memoirs and Biographies" in edited by Todd, J., *Jane Austen in Context*, Cambridge: Cambridge University Press, p.53 (2005).

Chapter Six: Fun and Frolics – Out and About
1. Letter 17, Jane Austen to Cassandra Austen, Steventon (8–9 January 1799) in Le Faye, D., (2011), p.35.
2. Ibid.
3. Ibid.
4. Austen-Leigh, J.E., edited by Sutherland, K., (2008)., p.54.
5. Letter 25, Jane Austen to Cassandra Austen, Steventon (8–9 November 1800) in Le Faye, D., (2011), p.59.
6. Letter 26, Jane Austen to Martha Lloyd, Steventon (12–13 November 1800) in Le Faye, D., (2011), p.61.
7. Letter 25, Jane Austen to Cassandra Austen, Steventon (8–9 November 1800) in Le Faye, D., (2011), p.59.
8. Letter 33, Jane Austen to Cassandra Austen, Steventon (25 January 1801) in Le Faye, D., (2011), p.82.
9. Letter 28, Jane Austen to Cassandra Austen, Ibthorpe (30 November-1 December 1800) in Le Faye, D., (2011), p.68.
10. Letter 31, Jane Austen to Cassandra Austen, Steventon (14–16 January 1801) in Le Faye, D., (2011), p.75.
11. Letter 62, Jane Austen to Cassandra Austen, Castle Square (9 December 1808) in Le Faye, D., (2011), p.163.
12. Ibid.
13. Ibid.
14. Ibid.
15. Ibid.
16. Ibid.
17. Letter 61, Jane Austen to Cassandra Austen, Castle Square (20 November 1808) in Le Faye, D., (2011), p.159.
18. Letter 28, Jane Austen to Cassandra Austen, Ibthorpe (30 November-1 December 1800) in Le Faye, D., (2011), p.66.
19. Ibid, p.67.
20. Letter 61, Jane Austen to Cassandra Austen, Castle Square (20 November 1808) in Le Faye, D., (2011), p.161.
21. Letter 62, Jane Austen to Cassandra Austen, Castle Square (9 December 1808) in Le Faye, D., (2011), p.164.

22. Ibid.
23. Austen, J., *Mansfield Park*, London: Penguin Books Ltd, p90 (2014).
24. Letter 28, Jane Austen to Cassandra Austen, Ibthorpe (30 November–1 December 1800) in Le Faye, D., (2011), p.68.
25. Ibid.
26. Honan, P., (2007), p.155.
27. Ibid.

Chapter Seven: Home Sweet Home
 1. Letter 106, Jane Austen to Martha Lloyd, Hans Place (2 September 1814) in Le Faye, D., (2011), pp.284/285.
 2. Letter 21, Jane Austen to Cassandra Austen, Queen Square (11 June 1799) in Le Faye, D., (2011), p.45.
 3. Letter 74, Jane Austen to Cassandra Austen, Chawton (31 May 1811) in Le Faye, D., (2011), p.198.
 4. Letter 7, Jane Austen to Cassandra Austen, Rowling (18 September 1796) in Le Faye, D., (2011), p.13.
 5. Ibid.
 6. Letter 53, Jane Austen to Cassandra Austen, Godmersham (20–22 June 1808) in Le Faye, D., (2011), p.135.
 7. Letter 18, Jane Austen to Cassandra Austen, Steventon (21–23 January 1799) in Le Faye, D., (2011), p.40.
 8. Ibid.
 9. Letter 29, Jane Austen to Cassandra Austen, Steventon (3–5 January 1801) in Le Faye, D., (2011), pp.71/72.
10. Letter 51, Jane Austen to Cassandra Austen, Southampton (20–22 February 1807) in Le Faye, D., (2011), p.129.
11. Letter 26, Jane Austen to Martha Lloyd, Steventon (12–13 November 1800) in Le Faye, D., (2011), pp.60/61.
12. Ibid. p.61.
13. Ibid.
14. Ibid.
15. Letter 28, Jane Austen to Cassandra Austen, Ibthorpe (30 November–1 December 1800) in Le Faye, D., (2011), p.66.
16. Ibid.
17. Kelly, H., *Jane Austen the Secret Radical*, London: Icon Books, (2016), p.113.
18. Letter 106, Jane Austen to Martha Lloyd, Hans Place (2 September 1814) in Le Faye, D., (2011), p.285.
19. Ibid.
20. Ibid.
21. Ibid.
22. Ibid.
23. Letter 21, Jane Austen to Cassandra Austen, Queen Square (11 June 1799) in Le Faye, D., (2011), p.46.
24. Tomalin, C., (1997), p.167.
25. Letter 26, Jane Austen to Martha Lloyd, Steventon (12–13 November 1800) in Le Faye, D., (2011), p.61.
26. Ibid.
27. Ibid. p.62.
28. Ibid.

Chapter Eight: In Sickness and In Health

1. Austen-Leigh, W., and Austen-Leigh, R.A., in Le Faye, D., (1989), p.113.
2. Ibid.
3. Ibid.
4. Ibid.
5. Letter 29, Jane Austen to Cassandra Austen, Steventon (3–5 January 1801) in Le Faye, D., (2011), p.71.
6. Letter 28, Jane Austen to Cassandra Austen, Ibthorpe (30 November-1 December 1800) in Le Faye, D., (2011), p.66.
7. Ibid.
8. Letter 89, Jane Austen to Cassandra Austen, Godmersham Park (23–24 September 1813) in Le Faye, D., (2011), p.238.
9. Ibid.
10. Letter 99, Jane Austen to Cassandra Austen, Henrietta Street (9 March 1814) in Le Faye, D., (2011), p.272.
11. Letter 39, Jane Austen to Cassandra Austen, Lyme (14 September 1804) in Le Faye, D., (2011), p.99.
12. Ibid.
13. Letter 43, Jane Austen to Cassandra Austen, Gay Street (8–11 April 1805) in Le Faye, D., (2011), p.104.
14. Austen, C., (1986), p.7.
15. Letter 44, Jane Austen to Cassandra Austen, Gay Street (21–23 April 1805) in Le Faye, D., (2011), p.107.
16. Letter 43, Jane Austen to Cassandra Austen, Gay Street (8–11 April 1805) in Le Faye, D., (2011), p.104.
17. Ibid.
18. Letter 44, Jane Austen to Cassandra Austen, Gay Street (21–23 April 1805) in Le Faye, D., (2011), p.107.
19. Ibid.
20. Ibid, p.109.
21. Letter 43, Jane Austen to Cassandra Austen, Gay Street (8–11 April 1805) in Le Faye, D., (2011), p.104.
22. Selwyn, D., *Collected Poems and Verse of The Austen Family*, Manchester: Fyfield Books, Carcanet Press Ltd and The Jane Austen Society, (1996), p.xv.
23. Ibid.
24. Ibid, p.xiv.
25. Ibid, p.20

Chapter Nine: Home is Where the Heart is

1. Letter 44, Jane Austen to Cassandra Austen, Gay Street (21–23 April 1805) in Le Faye, D., (2011), p.109.
2. Austen-Leigh, W., and Austen-Leigh, R.A., in Le Faye, D., (1989), p.133.
3. Letter 44, Jane Austen to Cassandra Austen, Gay Street (21–23 April 1805) in Le Faye, D., (2011), p.109.
4. Letter 47, Jane Austen to Cassandra Austen, Goodnestone Farm (30 August 1805) in Le Faye, D., (2011), p.117.
5. Lloyd, M., Last Will and Testament, PROB 11/1435/45, London: National Archives.
6. Ibid.
7. Selwyn, D., (1996), pp.5/6.

8. Ibid, p.79.
9. Ibid.
10. Letter 49, Jane Austen to Cassandra Austen, Southampton (7–8 January 1807) in Le Faye, D., (2011), p.120.
11. Ibid.
12. Ibid, p.122.
13. Letter 50, Jane Austen to Cassandra Austen, Southampton (8–9 February 1807) in Le Faye, D., (2011), p.123.
14. Letter 57, Jane Austen to Cassandra Austen, Castle Square (7–9 October 1808) in Le Faye, D., (2011), p.151.

Chapter Ten: Charity Begins at Home
1. Letter 107, Jane Austen to Anna Austen, Chawton (9 September 1814) in Le Faye, D., (2011), p.287.
2. Austen, C., (1986), p.7.
3. Lloyd, M., Last Will and Testament, PROB 11/1435/45, London: National Archives.
4. Austen, C., (1986), p.7.
5. Letter 77, Jane Austen to Martha Lloyd, Chawton (29–30 November 1812) in Le Faye, D., (2011), p.206.
6. Letter 63, Jane Austen to Cassandra Austen, Castle Square (27–28 December 1808) in Le Faye, D., (2011), p.166.
7. Letter 82, Jane Austen to Martha Lloyd, Chawton (16 February 1813) in Le Faye, D., (2011), p.216.
8. Letter 63, Jane Austen to Cassandra Austen, Castle Square (27–28 December 1808) in Le Faye, D., (2011), p.167.
9. Letter 67, Jane Austen to Cassandra Austen, Castle Square (30 January 1809) in Le Faye, D., (2011), p.180.
10. Ibid.
11. Letter 57, Jane Austen to Cassandra Austen, Castle Square (7–9 October 1808) in Le Faye, D., (2011), p.150.
12. Ibid. p.151.
13. Letter 77, Jane Austen to Martha Lloyd, Chawton (29–30 November 1812) in Le Faye, D., (2011), p.204.
14. Ibid.
15. Ibid.
16. Ibid.
17. Ibid.
18. Ibid. p. 206.
19. Letter 80, Jane Austen to Cassandra Austen, Chawton (4 February 1813) in Le Faye, D., (2011), p.212.
20. Ibid.
21. Letter 79, Jane Austen to Cassandra Austen, Chawton (29 January 1813) in Le Faye, D., (2011), p.211.
22. Ibid.
23. Letter 77, Jane Austen to Martha Lloyd, Chawton (29–30 November 1812) in Le Faye, D., (2011), p.205.
24. Letter 82, Jane Austen to Martha Lloyd, Chawton (16 February 1813) in Le Faye, D., (2011), p.217.
25. Letter 77, Jane Austen to Martha Lloyd, Chawton (29–30 November 1812) in Le Faye, D., (2011), p.205.

26. Letter 78, Jane Austen to Cassandra Austen, Chawton (24 January 1813) in Le Faye, D., (2011), p.209.
27. Letter 18, Jane Austen to Cassandra Austen, Steventon (21–23 January 1799) in Le Faye, D., (2011), pp.38/39.
28. Ibid, p.38.
29. Ibid.
30. Letter 77, Jane Austen to Martha Lloyd, Chawton (29–30 November 1812) in Le Faye, D., (2011), pp.205/206.
31. Letter 82, Jane Austen to Martha Lloyd, Chawton (16 February 1813) in Le Faye, D., (2011), p.216.
32. Letter 57, Jane Austen to Cassandra Austen, Castle Square (7–9 October 1808) in Le Faye, D., (2011), p.150.
33. Letter 93, Elizabeth Knight to her Aunt Cassandra Austen, Godmersham (18–21 October 1813) in Le Faye, D., (2011), p.253.
34. Letter 57, Jane Austen to Cassandra Austen, Castle Square (7–9 October 1808) in Le Faye, D., (2011), p.150.
35. Letter 71, Jane Austen to Cassandra Austen, Sloane Street (25 April 1811) in Le Faye, D., (2011), p.192.
36. Letter 59, Jane Austen to Cassandra Austen, Castle Square (15–16 October 1808) in Le Faye, D., (2011), pp.154/5.
37. Letter 58, Jane Austen to Cassandra Austen, Castle Square (13 October 1808) in Le Faye, D., (2011), p.152.
38. Ibid, p.153.
39. Ibid, p152.
40. Letter 58, Jane Austen to Cassandra Austen, Castle Square (13 October 1808) in Le Faye, D., (2011), p.152.
41. Letter 59, Jane Austen to Cassandra Austen, Castle Square (15–16 October 1808) in Le Faye, D., (2011), pp.153/154.
42. Letter 60, Jane Austen to Cassandra Austen, Castle Square (24–25 October 1808) in Le Faye, D., (2011), p.156.
43. Ibid, p.157.
44. Ibid.
45. Letter 77, Jane Austen to Martha Lloyd, Chawton (29–30 November 1812) in Le Faye, D., (2011), p.204.
46. Ibid.
47. Ibid, p.205.
48. Ibid.
49. Letter 82, Jane Austen to Martha Lloyd, Chawton (16 February 1813) in Le Faye, D., (2011), p.216.
50. Ibid.
51. Letter 119, Jane Austen to Caroline Austen, ? (2 March 1815) in Le Faye, D., (2011), p.302.

Chapter Eleven: Our Chawton Home
1. Letter 60, Jane Austen to Cassandra Austen, (24–25 October 1808) in Le Faye, D., (2011), p.157.
2. Ibid.
3. Ibid, p.158.
4. Austen, C., (1986), p20.

5. Letter 69, Jane Austen to Francis Austen, Chawton (26 July 1809) in Le Faye, D., (2011), p.185.
6. Austen-Leigh, J.E., edited by Sutherland, K., (2008), p.67. (Definition from Online Etymology Dictionary. August 2019.)
7. Ibid, p.166.
8. Ibid, p.69.
9. Ibid, p.67.
10. Letter 77, Jane Austen to Martha Lloyd, Chawton (29–30 November 1812) in Le Faye, D., (2011), p.205.
11. Letter 57, Jane Austen to Cassandra Austen, Castle Square (7–9 October 1808) in Le Faye, D., (2011), p.151.
12. Austen-Leigh, J.E., edited by Sutherland, K., (2008), p.69.
13. Ibid.
14. Letter 63, Jane Austen to Cassandra Austen, Castle Square (27–28 December 1808) in Le Faye, D., (2011), p.168.
15. Austen-Leigh, W., and Austen-Leigh, R.A., in Le Faye, D., (1989), p.158.
16. Honan, P., (2007), p.175.
17. Ibid, p.184.
18. Rubin, G., www.gretchenrubin.com/2011/11/theeightsplendidtruthsofhappiness. Accessed August 2019.
19. Honan, P., (2007), p.184.
20. Ibid, p.205.
21. Ibid.
22. Doody, M.A., "The Early Short Fiction" in edited by Copeland, E., and McMaster, J., *The Cambridge Companion to Jane Austen*, 2nd Edition. Cambridge: Cambridge University Press, (2011), p.75.
23. Letter 68(D), Jane Austen to B.Crosby &Co. Southampton (5 April 1809) in in Le Faye, D., (2011), p.182.
24. Doody, M.A., (2011)., p.73.
25. Sutherland, K., "Chronology of Composition and Publication" in edited by Todd, J., *Jane Austen in Context*. Cambridge: Cambridge University Press, (2005), p.13.
26. Southam, B.C., (1964), p.4.
27. Lindbergh, A.M., *Gift from the Sea*, Anniversary Edition. London: Chatto & WIndus, (2015), p.48.
28. Honan, P., (2007), p.351.
29. Austen-Leigh, J.E., edited by Sutherland, K., (2008), p.67.
30. Sutherland, K., (2005), p.17.
31. Ibid, p.14.
32. Doody, M.A., (2011), p.74.
33. Ibid, p.75.
34. Lindbergh, A.M., (2015), p.54.
35. Ibid, p.56.
36. Ibid, p.58.
37. Ibid, p.65.
38. Quote attributed to Maya Angelou, 'I've learned that people will forget what you said, people will forget what you did, but people will never forget how you made them feel.'
39. Lindbergh, A.M., (2015), p.61.
40. Farrer, R., (1917). "Farrer on Jane Austen" in edited by Southam, B., (1987), p.262.

41. Ibid.
42. Ibid, p.247.
43. Ibid, p.262.
44. Lindbergh, A.M., (2015), p.74.
45. Letter 71, Jane Austen to Cassandra Austen, Sloane Street (25 April 1811) in Le Faye, D., (2011), p.190.
46. Letter 77, Jane Austen to Martha Lloyd, Chawton (29–30 November 1812) in Le Faye, D., (2011), p.205.
47. Ibid.
48. Ibid.
49. Ibid.
50. Ibid.
51. Letter 106, Jane Austen to Martha Lloyd, Hans Place (2 September 1814) in Le Faye, D., (2011), p.285.
52. Letter 82, Jane Austen to Martha Lloyd, Chawton (16 February 1813) in Le Faye, D., (2011), p.216.
53. Ibid.
54. Letter 79, Jane Austen to Cassandra Austen, Chawton (29 January 1813) in Le Faye, D., (2011), p.210.
55. Letter 80, Jane Austen to Cassandra Austen, Chawton (4 February 1813) in Le Faye, D., (2011), p.212.
56. Southam, B.C., (1964), p.V.
57. Sutherland, K., (2005), p.15.
58. Ibid.

Chapter Twelve: The Character of Friendship

1. Letter 106, Jane Austen to Martha Lloyd, Hans Place (2 September 1814) in Le Faye, D., (2011), p.286.
2. Farrer, R., (1917). "Farrer on Jane Austen" in edited by Southam, B., (1987), p.248.
3. Letter 82, Jane Austen to Martha Lloyd, Chawton (16 February 1813) in Le Faye, D., (2011), pp.216/217.
4. Letter 128, Jane Austen to Cassandra Austen, Hans Place (26 November 1815) in Le Faye, D., (2011), p.313.
5. Doody, M.A., (2011), p.75.
6. Letter 128, Jane Austen to Cassandra Austen, Hans Place (26 November 1815) in Le Faye, D., (2011), p.313.
7. Doody, M.A., (2011), p.86.
8. Southam, B.C., (1968), p.49.
9. Ibid.
10. Ibid
11. Ibid, p.55.
12. Letter 79, Jane Austen to Cassandra Austen, Chawton (29 January 1813) in Le Faye, D., (2011), p.210.
13. Southam, B.C., (1968), p.56.
14. Honan, P., (2007), p.251.
15. Farrer, R., (1917). "Farrer on Jane Austen" in edited by Southam, B., (1987), p.252.
16. Ibid.

17. Ibid, pp.254/5.
18. Ibid, p.255.
19. Ibid, p.257.
20. Ibid, p.255.
21. Lindbergh, A.M., (2015), p.62.
22. Farrer, R., (1917). "Farrer on Jane Austen" in edited by Southam, B., (1987), p.256.
23. Definition from Online Etymology Dictionary. Accessed August 2019.
24. Farrer, R., (1917). "Farrer on Jane Austen" in edited by Southam, B., (1987), p.256.
25. Ibid, p.257.
26. Ibid, p.268.
27. Ibid, p.259.
28. Austen, C., (1986), p.10.
29. Letter 61, Jane Austen to Cassandra Austen, Castle Square (20 November 1808) in Le Faye, D., (2011), p.160.
30. Honan, P., (2007), p.184.
31. Doody, M.A., (2005), p.118.
32. Honan, P., (2007), p.251.
33. Ibid, p.264.
34. Ibid, pp.351/352.
35. Ibid, p.352.

Chapter Thirteen: Anything You Can Do...

1. Austen-Leigh, J.E., edited by Sutherland, K., (2008), p.69.
2. Letter 75, Jane Austen to Cassandra Austen, Chawton (6 June 1811) in Le Faye, D., (2011), p.202.
3. Letter 63, Jane Austen to Cassandra Austen, Castle Square (27–28 December 1808) in Le Faye, D., (2011), p.168.
4. Le Faye, D., (2011), Biographical Index, p.505.
5. Letter 102, Jane Austen to Cassandra Austen (23 June 1814) in Le Faye, D., (2011), p.277.
6. Letter 106, Jane Austen to Martha Lloyd, Hans Place (2 September 1814) in Le Faye, D., (2011), p.284.
7. Letter 87, Jane Austen to Cassandra Austen, Henrietta Street (15–16 September 1813) in Le Faye, D., (2011), p.230.
8. Letter 84, Jane Austen to Cassandra Austen, Sloane Street (20 May 1813) in Le Faye, D., (2011), p.219.
9. Ibid, Note 4 to Letter 84, p.423.
10. Letter 77, Jane Austen to Martha Lloyd, Chawton (29–30 November 1812) in Le Faye, D., (2011), p.205.
11. Letter 11, Jane Austen to Cassandra Austen, (17–18 November 1798) in Le Faye, D., (2011), pp.20/21.
12. Letter 57, Jane Austen to Cassandra Austen, Castle Square (7–9 October 1808) in Le Faye, D., (2011), pp.20/21.
13. Letter 55, Jane Austen to Cassandra Austen, Godmersham (30 June-1 July 1808) in Le Faye, D., (2011), p.144.
14. Ibid, p.145.
15. Black, M., and Le Faye, D., *The Jane Austen Cookbook*, Sixth paperback Edition. London: The British Museum Press, (2011), p.34.

16. Hickman, P., *A Jane Austen Household Book with Martha Lloyd's Recipes*, 2nd Edition. Exeter, Devon: A. Wheaton & Co. Ltd for Readers Union, (1978), p.7.
17. Tomalin, C., (1997), p.212.
18. Black, M., and Le Faye, D., (2011), p.35.
19. Hickman, P., (1978), p.10.
20. Black, M., and Le Faye, D., (2011), pp. 34/35.
21. Austen-Leigh, W., and Austen-Leigh, R.A., in Le Faye, D., (1989), p.158.
22. Hickman, P., (1978), p.38.
23. Ibid, p.32.
24. Ibid, p.119.
25. Ibid.
26. Letter 11, Jane Austen to Cassandra Austen (17–18 November 1798) in Le Faye, D., (2011), p.20.
27. Lloyd, M., Household Book held by the Jane Austen House Museum, Chawton.
28. Hickman, P., (1978), p.24.
29. Ibid, p.35.

Chapter Fourteen: The Spirit of Friendship
1. Honan, P., (2007), p.231.
2. Ibid, p.156.
3. Austen, C., (1986), p.26.
4. Ibid, p.46.
5. Ibid.
6. Letter 11, Jane Austen to Cassandra Austen (17–18 November 1798) in Le Faye, D., (2011), p.21.
7. Letter 89, Jane Austen to Cassandra Austen, Godmersham Park (23–24 September 1813) in Le Faye, D., (2011), p.234.
8. Ibid.
9. Austen, C., (1986), p.46.
10. Letter 58, Jane Austen to Cassandra Austen, Castle Square (13 October 1808) in Le Faye, D., (2011), p.152.
11. Letter 50, Jane Austen to Cassandra Austen, Southampton (8–9 February 1807) in Le Faye, D., (2011), p.126.
12. Letter 13, Jane Austen to Cassandra Austen, Steventon (1–2 December 1798) in Le Faye, D., (2011), pp.24/25.
13. Letter 11, Jane Austen to Cassandra Austen (17–18 November 1798) in Le Faye, D., (2011), p.20.
14. Letter 13, Jane Austen to Cassandra Austen, Steventon (1–2 December 1798) in Le Faye, D., (2011), p.24.
15. Letter 65, Jane Austen to Cassandra Austen, Castle Square (17–18 January 1809) in Le Faye, D., (2011), p.173.
16. Austen, M., Personal Pocket Books and Diaries, 23M93/62/1. Winchester: Hampshire Record Office.
17. Letter 65, Jane Austen to Cassandra Austen, Castle Square (17–18 January 1809) in Le Faye, D., (2011), p.173.
18. Letter 78, Jane Austen to Cassandra Austen, Chawton (24 January 1813) in Le Faye, D., (2011), p.209.
19. Austen-Leigh, W., and Austen-Leigh, R.A., in Le Faye, D., (1989), p.177.
20. Pendleton, V., (5 August 2019) in conversation with Everard, S., and Cotton, F., *Happy Place Podcast*.

21. Ibid, Everard, S., and Pendleton, V.
22. Ibid, Everard, S.
23. Ibid, Everard, S.
24. Letter 153, Jane Austen to Fanny Knight, Chawton (13 March 1817) in Le Faye, D., (2011), p.348.
25. Letter 159, Jane Austen to Anne Sharp, Chawton (22 May 1817) in Le Faye, D., (2011), p.355/356.
26. Ibid, p.355.
27. Ibid, p.357.
28. Ibid.
29. Ibid, p.356.
30. Austen-Leigh, J.E., edited by Sutherland, K., (2008), p.67.
31. Letter 160, Jane Austen to James Edward Austen, College Street, Winchester (27 May 1817) in Le Faye, D., (2011), p.358.
32. Ibid.
33. Letter 161, Jane Austen to Frances Tilson, College Street, Winchester (28–29 May 1817) in Le Faye, D., (2011), p.358.
34. Ibid.
35. Austen, M., Personal Pocket Books and Diaries, 23M93/62/1. Winchester: Hampshire Record Office.
36. Ibid.
37. Ibid.
38. Extract from 'Family History by Fanny C. Lefroy' in Austen-Leigh, J.E., edited by Sutherland, K., (2008), p.197.
39. Austen, M., Personal Pocket Books and Diaries, 23M93/62/1. Winchester: Hampshire Record Office.
40. Letter 159, Jane Austen to Anne Sharp, Chawton (22 May 1817) in Le Faye, D., (2011, p.357.
41. Extract from 'Family History by Fanny C. Lefroy' in Austen-Leigh, J.E., edited by Sutherland, K., (2008), p.197.
42. Austen, M., Personal Pocket Books and Diaries, 23M93/62/1. Winchester: Hampshire Record Office.
43. Extract from 'Family History by Fanny C. Lefroy' in Austen-Leigh, J.E., edited by Sutherland, K., (2008), p.198.
44. Ibid.
45. Ibid, pp.197/198.
46. Byrne, P., *The Real Jane Austen: A Life in Small Things*, London: Harper Press/ Harper Collins (2013), p239.

Chapter Fifteen: Life After Death

1. Honan, P., (2007), p.405.
2. Austen-Leigh, W., and Austen-Leigh, R.A., in Le Faye, D., (1989), p.240.
3. Ibid.
4. Ibid.
5. Ibid.
6. Hopkinson, D., "Admiral of The Fleet Sir Francis Austen KCB" in *Collected Reports of the Jane Austen Society 1976–1985*,Wiltshire: Antony Rowe Ltd. for The Jane Austen Society, (1983) p.255.
7. Honan, P., (2007), p.399.
8. Hopkinson, D., (1983), p.255.
9. Honan, P., (2007), p.231.

10. Hopkinson, D., (1983), p.255.
11. Hubback, J.H., and Hubback, E., *Jane Austen's Sailor Brothers*, Cambridge: Cambridge University Press, (2012), p.114.
12. Ibid.
13. Honan, P., (2007), p.251.
14. Austen-Leigh, W., and Austen-Leigh, R.A., in Le Faye, D., (1989), p.240.
15. Hopkinson, D., (1983), p.255 and Austen-Leigh, W., and Austen-Leigh, R.A., in Le Faye, D., (1989), p.240.
16. Hopkinson, D., (1983), p.255.
17. Ibid.
18. Ibid.
19. Ibid.
20. Letter 55, Jane Austen to Cassandra Austen, Godmersham (30 June -1 July 1808) in Le Faye, D., (2011), p.144.
21. Honan, P., (2007), p.250.
22. Ibid.
23. Hopkinson, D., (1983), p.256.
24. Ibid.
25. Ibid.
26. Austen, C., (1986), p.63.
27. Austen, M., Personal Pocket Books and Diaries, 23M93/62/1. Winchester: Hampshire Record Office.
28. Hopkinson, D., (1983), p.258.
29. Austen, M., Personal Pocket Books and Diaries, 23M93/62/1. Winchester: Hampshire Record Office.
30. Ibid.
31. Ibid.
32. Ibid.
33. Ibid.
34. Honan, P., (2007), p.250.
35. Ibid, p.231.
36. Letter 69, Jane Austen to Francis Austen, Chawton (26 July 1809) in Le Faye, D., (2011), p.185.
37. Hopkinson, D., (1983), p.256.
38. Ibid.
39. In conversation with Coles, G., Wymering Church, April 2019.
40. Austen, J., *Persuasion*, London: Penguin Books Ltd, (2011), p.29.
41. Ibid.
42. Worsley, L., *Jane Austen at Home*, London: Hodder & Stoughton, (2017), p.305.

Chapter Sixteen: Friendship Never Ends

1. Letter 55, Jane Austen to Cassandra Austen, Godmersham (30 June-1 July 1808) in Le Faye, D., (2011), p.143.
2. Letter 78, Jane Austen to Cassandra Austen, Chawton (24 January 1813) in Le Faye, D., (2011), p.209.
3. Letter 65, Jane Austen to Cassandra Austen, Castle Square (17–18 January 1809) in Le Faye, D., (2011), p.175.
4. Letter 92, Jane Austen to Cassandra Austen, Godmersham Park (14–15 October 1813) in Le Faye, D., (2011, p.250.
5. Austen, H., (1833) "Memoir of Miss Austen" in Austen-Leigh, J.E., edited by Sutherland, K., (2008), p.147.

6. Ibid, p.148.
7. Ibid.
8. Ibid.
9. Ibid, p.149.
10. Ibid.
11. Ibid, p.151.
12. Ibid, p.150.
13. Ibid, p.141.
14. Ibid, p.152.
15. Farrer, R., (1917). "Farrer on Jane Austen" in edited by Southam, B., (1987), p.256.
16. Ibid, p.250.
17. Dow, G.E, and Simpson, K., Online Course *Jane Austen: Myth, Reality and Global Celebrity*. Southampton: University of Southampton with Futurelearn.com/certificates/7p24p67.
18. Lloyd, M., Last Will and Testament, PROB 11/1435/45, London: National Archives.

Postscript
1. Pullman, P., in interview with Beard, M. (8.2.2019). *Front Row Late*. BBC Two, Series 4, Episode 5. (Used with permission of United Agents on behalf of Philip Pullman)
2. Farrer, R., (1917). "Farrer on Jane Austen" in edited by Southam, B., (1987), p.251.

Bibliography

Austen, C., *Reminiscences of Caroline Austen*, Guildford: Biddles Ltd. for The Jane Austen Society (1986).

Austen, J., edited by Sabor, P., Hunt, S., and Kortes-Papp, V., *Frederic and Elfrida*, Edmonton, Canada: Juvenilia Press (2002).

Austen, J., edited by Alexander, C., *Love and Friendship and Other Youthful Writings*, London: Penguin Books Ltd. (2014).

Austen, J., *The History of England By a Partial, Prejudiced and Ignorant Historian*, (1791) published by Carr, J.L., Bury St. Edmunds: Quince Tree Press (2016).

Austen-Leigh, J.E., edited by Sutherland, K., *A Memoir of Jane Austen and Other Family Recollections*, 2nd Edition. Oxford: Oxford University Press (2008).

Austen, M., Personal Pocketbooks and Diaries, 23M93/62/1, Winchester: Hampshire Record Office.

Austen-Leigh, W., Austen-Leigh, R.A., and Le Faye, D., *Jane Austen: A Family Record*, London: British Library (1989).

Austen-Leigh, W., Austen-Leigh, R.A., and Le Faye, D., *Jane Austen: A Family Record*, 2nd Edition. Cambridge: Cambridge University Press (2004).

Black, M., and Le Faye, D., *The Jane Austen Cookbook,* 5th edition. London: British Museum (2011).

Brownstein, R.M., "Endless Imitation: Austen's and Byron's Juvenilia" in edited by Alexander, C., and McMaster, J., *The Child Writer from Austen to Woolf.* Cambridge: Cambridge University Press, pp.122–137 (2005).

Byrne, P., *The Real Jane Austen: A Life in Small Things*, London: HarperPress (2014).

Devlin, D.D., "The Background" in Devlin, D.D., *Jane Austen and Education.* London: Macmillan, pp.1–28 (1975).

Doody, M.A., "Jane Austen, That Disconcerting 'Child'" in edited by Alexander, C., and McMaster, J., *The Child Writer from Austen to Woolf*, Cambridge: Cambridge University Press, pp.101–121 (2005).

Doody, M.A., "The Early Short Fiction" in edited Copeland, E., and McMaster, J., *The Cambridge Companion to Jane Austen.* 2nd Edition. Cambridge: Cambridge University Press, pp. 72–86, (2011).

Farrer, R., "Farrer on Jane Austen" (1917) in edited Southam, B., *Jane Austen The Critical Heritage Volume 2 1870–1940*, London: Routledge and Kegan Paul Ltd., pp.245–272 (1987).

Fergus, J., "Biography" in edited Todd, J., *Jane Austen in Context*, Cambridge: Cambridge University Press, pp.3–11 (2005).

Fergus, J., "The Literary Marketplace" in edited Johnson, C.L., and Tuite, C., *A Companion to Jane Austen*, Oxford: Wiley Blackwell, pp.41–50 (2012).

Hickman, P., *A Jane Austen Household Book, with Martha Lloyd's Recipes*, 2nd Edition. Newton Abbot: Readers Union (1978).

Honan, P., *Jane Austen: Her Life*, 2nd Edition. London: Max Press, Little Books Ltd. (2007).

Hopkinson, D., "Admiral of The Fleet Sir Francis Austen KCB" in *Collected Reports of The Jane Austen Society 1976–1985*, Wiltshire: Antony Rowe Ltd. for The Jane Austen Society, pp. 253–259 (1983).

Hubback, J.H, and E.C., *Jane Austen's Sailor Brothers*, Cambridge: Cambridge University Press (2012).

Kelly, H., *Jane Austen, the Secret Radical*, London: Icon Books (2016).

Le Faye, D., "Letters" in edited Todd, J., *Jane Austen in Context*, Cambridge: Cambridge University Press, pp.33–40 (2005).

Le Faye, D., "Memoirs and Biographies" in edited Todd, J., *Jane Austen in Context*, Cambridge: Cambridge University Press, pp. 51–58 (2005).

Le Faye, D., "Catherine Hubback's Memoir of Francis Austen" in edited by Selwyn, D., *Report*, Bristol: The Jane Austen Society (2009).

Le Faye, D., *Jane Austen's Letters*, 4th Edition. Oxford: Oxford University Press (2011).

Lloyd, M. (Senior)., (1805), Last Will and Testament. Probate: 11/1435/45. Kew: The National Archives.

Lloyd, M., (unknown). Household Book. Held in trust by The Jane Austen House Museum.

Mack, R.L., "The Austen Family Writing: Gossip, Parody and Corporate Personality" in edited Johnson, C.L, and Tuite, C., *A Companion to Jane Austen*, Oxford: Wiley Blackwell, pp.31–40 (2012).

McMaster, J., "Young Jane Austen Author" in edited Johnson, C.L, and Tuite, C., *A Companion to Jane Austen*, Oxford: Wiley Blackwell, pp.81–90 (2012).

Morrow Lindbergh, A., *Gift From The Sea*, 60th Anniversary Edition, London: Chatto & Windus (2015).

Sawtell, G., "Neither Rich Nor Handsome…" in *Collected Reports of The Jane Austen Society 1976–1985*, Wiltshire: Antony Rowe Ltd. for The Jane Austen Society, pp.304–311 (1984).

Selwyn, D., *Collected Poems and Verse of the Austen Family*, Manchester: Fyfield Books, Carcanet Press Ltd and The Jane Austen Society (1996).

Southam, B.C., *Jane Austen's Literary Manuscripts: A Study of The Novelist's Development Through the Surviving Papers*, Oxford: Oxford University Press (1964).

Southam, B.C., *Jane Austen: The Critical Heritage*, London: Routledge and Kegan Paul Ltd. (1968).

Southam, B.C., *Jane Austen: The Critical Heritage Volume 2*, London: Routledge and Kegan Paul Ltd. (1987).

Sutherland, K., "Chronology of Composition and Publication" in edited Todd, J., *Jane Austen in Context*, Cambridge: Cambridge University Press, pp.12–22 (2005).

Sutherland, K., "Jane Austen's Life and Letters" in edited Johnson, C.L, and Tuite, C., *A Companion to Jane Austen*, Oxford: Wiley Blackwell, pp.13–30 (2012).

Todd, J., *Jane Austen: Her Life, Her Times, Her Novels*, London: Andre Deutsch (2013).

Tomalin, C., *Jane Austen: A Life*, London: Viking (1997).

Vick, R., *The Jane Austen Society Report*, Winchester: Sarsen Press (1994).

Worsley, L., *Jane Austen at Home*, London: Hodder and Stoughton Ltd. (2017).

Index